ics

Shakespeare In America

OXFORD SHAKESPEARE TOPICS
Published and Forthcoming Titles Include:

David Bevington, *Shakespeare and Biography*
Lawrence Danson, *Shakespeare's Dramatic Genres*
Janette Dillon, *Shakespeare and the Staging of English History*
Paul Edmondson and Stanley Wells, *Shakespeare's Sonnets*
Gabriel Egan, *Shakespeare and Marx*
Andrew Gurr and Mariko Ichikawa, *Staging in Shakespeare's Theatres*
Jonathan Gil Harris, *Shakespeare and Literary Theory*
John Jowett, *Shakespeare and Text*
Douglas Lanier, *Shakespeare and Modern Popular Culture*
Ania Loomba, *Shakespeare, Race, and Colonialism*
Raphael Lyne, *Shakespeare's Late Work*
Russ McDonald, *Shakespeare and the Arts of Language*
Steven Marx, *Shakespeare and the Bible*
Robert S. Miola, *Shakespeare's Reading*
Phyllis Rackin, *Shakespeare and Women*
Catherine Richardson, *Shakespeare and Material Culture*
Bruce R. Smith, *Shakespeare and Masculinity*
Zdeněk Stříbrný, *Shakespeare and Eastern Europe*
Michael Taylor, *Shakespeare Criticism in the Twentieth Century*
Alden T. Vaughan and Virginia Mason Vaughan, *Shakespeare in America*
Stanley Wells, ed., *Shakespeare in the Theatre: An Anthology of Criticism*
Martin Wiggins, *Shakespeare and the Drama of his Time*

Oxford Shakespeare Topics

Shakespeare In America

ALDEN T. VAUGHAN

AND

VIRGINIA MASON VAUGHAN

OXFORD
UNIVERSITY PRESS

Great Clarendon Street, Oxford OX2 6DP

Oxford University Press is a department of the University of Oxford.
It furthers the University's objective of excellence in research, scholarship,
and education by publishing worldwide in

Oxford New York

Auckland Cape Town Dar es Salaam Hong Kong Karachi
Kuala Lumpur Madrid Melbourne Mexico City Nairobi
New Delhi Shanghai Taipei Toronto

With offices in

Argentina Austria Brazil Chile Czech Republic France Greece
Guatemala Hungary Italy Japan Poland Portugal Singapore
South Korea Switzerland Thailand Turkey Ukraine Vietnam

Published in the United States
by Oxford University Press Inc., New York

First published 2012

British Library Cataloguing in Publication Data
Data available

Library of Congress Cataloging in Publication Data
Library of Congress Control Number: 2011945229

Typeset by SPI Publisher Services, Pondicherry, India
Printed in Great Britain
on acid-free paper by
MPG Books Group, Bodmin and King's Lynn

ISBN 978–0–19–956638–9 (Hbk.)
978–0–19–956637–2 (Pbk.)

1 3 5 7 9 10 8 6 4 2

To Emery Battis
1915–2011
Actor, Scholar, Friend

Acknowledgements

For first enticing us to gather materials on Shakespeare's American career, we thank Gail Kern Paster, then director of the Folger Shakespeare Library, and Rachel Doggett, curator of rare books at the Folger, who invited us to curate the library's 75th anniversary exhibition, "Shakespeare in American Life" (2007), and edit the exhibition catalogue. That experience taught us more about Shakespeare and America than we had time or place to tell. This book is in one sense an expansion of the Folger exhibit and catalogue. As the present venture—made possible by the kind invitation of Shakespeare Topics series editors Stanley Wells and Peter Holland—has taken shape, we have benefited from the help of many friends and professional colleagues.

For providing citations to works we might otherwise have missed or for answering queries on a wide variety of issues, we are grateful to Iska Alter, Georgia Barnhill, George and Margaret Billias, Jonathan Burton, José Esquea, James N. Green, Betsy Huang, YuJin Ko, Russ McDonald, Barbara Mowat, Lena Cowen Orlin, Katherine Scheil, James Shapiro, Frances Teague, Lucilia Valerio, Helen Whall, David Whitesell, Douglas L. Wilson, Hobson Woodward, and Georgianna Ziegler. Irene Dash and Harry Keyishian gave us books essential to our project. For providing superb library services, we are indebted (once again) to the staffs of the American Antiquarian Society, the Folger Shakespeare Library, Goddard Library of Clark University, and the Library of Congress. For helping us gather illustrations and permission to reproduce them, we thank Jesse Aaron Cohen of the Yivo Institute for Jewish Research, Pamela Madsen of the Harvard Theatre Collection, Marianne Martin of Colonial Williamsburg, Rebecca Oviedo of the Folger Shakespeare Library, Jaclyn Penny of the American Antiquarian Society, Amy Richard of the Oregon Shakespeare Festival, and Ben Simons of the Nantucket Historical Association.

We owe special thanks to Douglas Lanier for a perceptive critique of the manuscript at an advanced stage and to Stanley Wells and Peter

Holland for speedy and constructive criticism of the penultimate version. We also thank each other for patience and good humour.

Our book is dedicated to Emery Battis, whose life parallels many of this book's themes. During his undergraduate years at Harvard, Emery studied Shakespeare with George Lyman Kittredge and American Puritanism with Perry Miller. Bitten early by the acting bug, he was "First Gentleman of Cyprus" and assistant stage manager when Margaret Webster's Theatre Guild production of *Othello* opened in Cambridge, Massachusetts, in 1943. Military service kept Emery from joining the production's move to Broadway, and after the war, he pursued his other passion through doctoral studies in American history at Columbia University. He became a professor at Douglass College of Rutgers University, where he electrified students with his lively portrayals of America's past. After a twenty-five-year teaching career, the acting bug struck again, and Emery returned to the professional stage, first at Minneapolis's Guthrie Theatre, later at New Haven's Long Wharf Theatre, and finally at Washington, DC's Shakespeare Theatre. During this second, illustrious career, Emery Battis performed in all of Shakespeare's plays except *Cymbeline*.

Contents

Illustrations

A Note on Texts

All quotations from Shakespeare are taken from *The Complete Works of William Shakespeare*, ed. Stanley Wells and Gary Taylor (Oxford, 1986). Spelling and punctuation in all quotations from older texts have been modernized throughout.

Introduction

Shakespeare in America in many ways parallels the larger narrative of American history: tentative beginnings in the seventeenth century, strong but uneven expansion in the second half of the eighteenth century, geographic diversification and heightened sophistication in the nineteenth century, bifurcation in the twentieth century—at least on the surface—into competing scholarly (mainly academic) and lighthearted (mainly mass market) cultural trends. Although prospects for the remainder of the twenty-first century are unclear, Shakespeare's vitality persists.

Our purpose in this book is to narrate Shakespeare's American history from its colonial origins, through America's break with the empire in the late eighteenth century, through America's nineteenth-century growth as a transcontinental nation and its shift from an agrarian to an industrialized society, through the twentieth century's rapid changes in technology, to the twenty-first century's uncertain future. Given the extensive terrain of this project, our narrative cannot linger on any one era or topic, but underlying throughout is an attempt to explain, explicitly or implicitly, how Shakespeare in America differs from Shakespeare in Britain or in any of the other countries that have adopted him as a significant component of their cultural property.

Beneath the narrative's particulars lie several themes that we believe are characteristic of Shakespeare in America. First, the demands of colonial settlement meant that from the beginning Americans took a utilitarian approach to literature in general, Shakespeare in particular. The early colonists had little time to attend or read the era's dramas, and once they gained a modicum of leisure they sought a rationale for their choice of pastimes. Many found it in Shakespeare's moral teaching, a theme that continues, however muted, to the present day. In puritanical New England and sometimes elsewhere, plays were initially presented as "moral lessons." Later, passages from Shakespeare (sometimes "improved") were incorporated into

William H. McGuffey's *Readers* and other school books in hopes of educating American youths in moral wisdom, even as they were exposed to his rhetorical excellence. Widespread recognition of Shakespeare's universality encouraged local Shakespeare Clubs and regional forums to improve American minds, hearts, and moral characters by providing lectures, discussions, and readings of the plays. No wonder that as settlers moved west in the nineteenth century, they often carried with them two cherished volumes: the Bible and Shakespeare.

Nowadays Shakespeare remains a mainstay in the curricula of America's schools and colleges, and the value of reading his work is still assumed—but often with a twist. Rather than expecting Shakespearian drama to reveal the answers to moral questions, teachers are generally more interested in the social questions he implicitly poses. When, for example, Lady Macbeth tells her husband that "to be a man" he should murder the king, what does this tell us about the way society constructs gender expectations? Can Othello ever be assimilated into Venetian society? What is the effect of Christian anti-Semitism on Shylock? How does Richard III gain power? The close consideration of Shakespeare's texts may not yield definitive answers, but the process of reading and debating his words forces us to consider modern society's social and ethical questions. In school, if nowhere else, Americans still believe that reading Shakespeare is good for you.

From the nineteenth century to the present, America's emphasis on individual improvement has gone hand in hand with another American trait: entrepreneurship. The history of Shakespeare in America is replete with enterprising individuals who brought their ingenuity and energy to Shakespeare in ways that revolutionized his cultural impact. In mid-nineteenth-century Philadelphia, for example, when Horace Howard Furness couldn't find an edition of Shakespeare that incorporated all the important textual variants, he created his own variorum, producing eighteen volumes over a forty-year career. Henry Clay Folger, a Standard Oil executive, believed that American scholars should have access to the rare books they needed to study Shakespeare's texts—so he bought them and built a library, opened in 1932, for the scholars' convenience. Professor Angus Bowmer insisted that high quality Shakespeare performances be available to people living outside the urban East, so in 1935 he founded the Oregon Shakespeare Festival. Joseph Papp, son of Jewish immigrants, was convinced that Shakespeare's lines were just as effective if delivered by Americans of all backgrounds in their own accents, so he established New York's Shakespeare Festival in the 1950s and made the plays widely available at summer productions in Central Park. Throughout the twentieth century, American inventiveness also brought Shakespeare in a variety of transmutations to a mass audience through silent and then talking movies, as well as through Broadway musical spectaculars like *Kiss Me Kate* and *West Side Story*.

Papp's belief that all Americans, rich or poor, should have access to Shakespeare is also characteristically American. The growth of Shakespeare festivals across the country, many of them offering cheap (or even free) performances, is but one manifestation of a commitment to equal ethnic and economic opportunity, both on the stage and in the audience. From the early nineteenth century, African Americans have read and studied Shakespeare even when they were prohibited from performing his work. To nineteenth-century immigrants from Europe, knowledge of Shakespeare's plays was a sign and a means of assimilation into American culture. In the years since World War II, ethnic minorities sometimes resent Shakespeare's ascendancy, but they continue to appropriate Shakespeare in new and exciting ways.

Still another American motif has been its lack of a formal guiding authority on cultural matters. American theater is largely decentralized, with no equivalent to the Royal Shakespeare Company or a dominant school of acting. Theater companies have been relatively autonomous and often short-lived. With little support from the federal government, regional theaters are dependent on grants and fund-raising to remain operational, and each responds to the manifold needs of its own community. Similarly, American education has no reigning universities like Oxford and Cambridge (Harvard pales in comparison) and no uniform system of secondary education. Public school districts are largely independent, and private schools almost entirely so, with each school board or board of trustees determining through its hired officials how much exposure the pupils will have to Shakespeare or anything else. Shakespeare is taught in secondary schools across the nation, but despite occasional widespread preferences for certain plays, the number and choice of texts has customarily varied from community to community.

As a corollary to that decentralization of American theatres and education, Americans have developed an enthusiasm for Shakespeare that is widespread and genuine but seldom reverential or hidebound. Some Americans love their Shakespeare as "pure" as it can be—as much as possible like the RSC and in matching leather-bound volumes—but most approach the Bard more playfully. Having fun with Shakespeare is a traditional American pastime. It is surely no accident that burlesques of Shakespeare—although originally from England and well-attended there—were wildly popular in the third quarter of nineteenth-century America, and musical comedy Shakespeare is almost exclusively an American-made phenomenon.

It becomes more difficult to identify American Shakespeare in the second decade of the twenty-first century when all media have become global, but our final chapter returns to these themes as they persist in the twenty-first century, and suggests likely outcomes. Like many other elements of American culture, America's democratic, multicultural Shakespeare has been appropriated around the world. How he got to that point is the story outlined in these pages.

* * *

In telling that story we have attempted to give proportionate attention to Shakespeare on the stage (legitimate and burlesque) and on the page (editions, criticism, school books, handbooks, and appropriations) in the context of an expanding nation. We have tried also to mention, occasionally at some length, the major participants in bringing Shakespeare to America and helping to make him feel at home. On the stage, that includes the Hallam family of the colonial era; early English visitors who helped to shape American enthusiasm for Shakespeare like George Frederick Cooke and Edmund Kean; American actors like Edwin Forrest, Charlotte Cushman, and the Booths who emerged in the early to mid-nineteenth century to largely supplant the itinerant stars; educators like William Holmes McGuffey who introduced Shakespeare to countless American youths, or who, like George Lyman Kittredge, promoted serious study of his plays among older students; African Americans like James Wells Brown, Ira Aldridge (though mostly abroad), and Paul

Robeson who fostered an appreciation of Shakespeare despite white hostility; pioneer American Shakespeare scholars like Henry Norman Hudson and Richard Grant White; non-specialist heralds like Ralph Waldo Emerson and Walt Whitman; collectors of books and builders of libraries like Horace Howard Furness and Henry Clay Folger; challengers of the orthodox view of Shakespeare's authorship like Delia Bacon and Charlton Ogburn, Jr.; impresarios like Augustin Daly and Joseph Papp; and many more Americans from many walks of life who did their share, or more, to enhance Shakespeare in America.

* * *

At the risk of appearing parochial, we have confined the "America" in our title to the parts of North America that were colonized under English auspices, eventually became the United States of America, and have been augmented since by many territorial additions. In short, we use the label as most of the world uses it today, as synonymous with the evolving United States. But we are well aware that other places on the continent are also "American" if the term is used more expansively. In some of those places, especially Mexico City and Quebec, dramas were staged before the first recorded theatrical performances in the English colonies (though none that we know of by Shakespeare), and many parts of the present United States had indigenous performances and even European dramas before they were absorbed by the expanding nation. Again, we exclude such traditions and events, however important they are in their own right, because they played little part, if any, in Shakespeare's westerly transmission and development in the current United States.

Harder to justify to some readers may be our decision to almost wholly omit Canada's important contributions to Shakespeare in the New World. There have been many Shakespeare performances "north of the border," of course, especially in its eastern urban centers and at London, Ontario's venerable Shakespeare festival. The Canadian scholarly community from coast to coast, moreover, has contributed richly to the advance of Shakespeare studies. Equally hard to justify might be our almost total disregard of Shakespeare in the British West Indies, where the colonial era's itinerant acting companies escaped the mainland colonies' inhospitable winter weather and where most professional actors took refuge during the American Revolution. Especially in Jamaica but also in Barbados, the Leeward Island, the Bahamas, and several other insular venues, Shakespeare prospered for many years in primarily British communities. We eschew inclusion of them here because of our limited space—like Shakespeare in Canada, the topic deserves a separate study—and because the islands, again like Canada, remain outside the United States' geopolitical boundaries.

Such limitations on our territorial target still leave a big story to tell. We have divided that story into seven chapters. Chapters 1–3 relate chronologically (with occasional digressions) the history of Shakespearian performance, reading, and criticism from the early seventeenth century to the late nineteenth. Chapters 4–6 focus on topics that have been especially vital in the twentieth century and beyond. Again, our approach is largely chronological but each chapter is limited by its topic's unique evolution. Chapter 7 gazes both backward and forward to assess the state of Shakespeare in America today and to guess where it may go in the future.

1

American Beginnings

On the afternoon of July 14, 1787, George Washington escaped the political wrangling of the Constitutional Convention to attend a performance of *The Tempest* at the Opera House in Philadelphia's Southwark suburb.[1] General Washington's presence that day typified the emerging nation's enjoyment of stage plays despite the colonial era's ambivalent theatrical legacy and Congress's wartime edicts against performances, while his choice of plays signaled the former colonists' appreciation of the works of William Shakespeare. Whereas British America's founders—Captain John Smith, John Winthrop, and William Penn, for example—either implicitly or explicitly opposed actors and acting and wrote disparagingly, if at all, about Shakespeare, the Revolutionary Era's founding fathers and at least one founding mother—Washington, Jefferson, and the Adamses (John and Abigail), and many others—attended plays by English itinerant actors and frequently and approvingly cited Shakespeare in their diaries, correspondence, and sometimes in their public documents. Although the transformation from disapproval or indifference toward Shakespeare to enthusiasm for his works had taken a century and a half, it was firmly established by the time thirteen of Britain's American colonies became a separate nation.

* * *

Unlike many of his contemporaries, Shakespeare wrote sparsely about the New World. While George Chapman, Ben Jonson, and John Marston were spoofing the lost Roanoke Colony in *Eastward Ho!*, Michael Drayton was penning an "Ode to the Virginia Voyage," and Ben Jonson was weaving Powhatan visitors to England into his plays,

Shakespeare focused almost exclusively on Europe. His occasional allusions to America or the Indies were brief, and the latter were sometimes unclear whether he meant the Indies of the East or West. He was similarly ambiguous about individual Indians. An exception is *King Henry VIII*'s "strange Indian with the great tool come to court, the women so besiege us" (5.3.32–3), which alludes, almost certainly, to the Algonquian captive Epenow, whose impressive physique caused him to be "showed up and down London . . . as a wonder" while Shakespeare and John Fletcher were writing the play.[2] That specific reference of 1613 suggests that Shakespeare was growing more alert to England's incipient empire.

And there is *The Tempest*. Shakespeare's final solo play has been hailed since the early nineteenth century (with some dissent) as partly the poet's imaginative response to the wreck of the *Sea Venture* off the coast of Bermuda in 1609 while en route to Virginia. Had William Strachey's eye-witness narrative been published immediately after its arrival in England in September 1610, the connection between the event and Shakespeare's play would have been obvious from the outset, but the epistle to an anonymous "Excellent Lady" remained in manuscript until 1625. It nonetheless circulated widely, as Strachey surely intended. The "large discourse" that came from Strachey's "fluent and copious pen" (in the words of a reader of the manuscript in 1616) would join two shorter accounts published in 1610 and countless oral reports by Sir Thomas Gates and other survivors of the hurricane to form a copious source book on the Bermuda episode. After a year of national anguish about *Sea Venture*'s probable fate, the sudden good news merited a timely and poignant drama.[3]

Shakespeare seized the opportunity. Especially in *The Tempest*'s opening scene, he drew words and images from Strachey's vivid description of the storm that blew *Sea Venture* far off course and nearly drowned its 150 passengers and crew, including Gates, the new governor of Virginia, and Sir George Somers, admiral of the fleet of nine vessels of which *Sea Venture* was the flagship. In subsequent scenes, the playwright interspersed events (loosely disguised) from the castaways' nine and a half months on Bermuda and borrowed, obliquely, some of its plot and characters. To take two brief examples: the multiple conspiracies against Prospero and King Alonzo appear to be figurative retellings of the mutinies, rebellions, and "bloody issues" that Strachey revealed about the sojourn on the islands. In the words of a subsequent Bermuda settler: "[L]est the island should lose that former name of Devil's . . . some [survivors] entered into devilish conspiracy three several time[s]" against the community's legitimate leaders, Gates and Somers. Gates, moreover, recounted that two Powhatan Indians were among *Sea Venture*'s passengers and that on Bermuda one had murdered the other (coincidentally, the very Indian that Ben Jonson had invoked in *Epicoene*); another report accused the murderer of hacking off his victim's legs and burying them beside the corpse—a partial model, perhaps, for Caliban's bloody schemes against Prospero.[4] In short, early Bermuda, like Prospero's/Caliban's island, was naturally idyllic (except for periodic storms) but profoundly corrupted by its transient occupants. Although Shakespeare set his play in the Mediterranean and plucked most of his characters from Italy and Africa, critics have long detected an American undertone. On the eve of the Revolution, *The Tempest* would be, fittingly, one of the most popular plays in British America, even before any links to the Bermuda episode had been publicized.

* * *

Shakespeare was in his prime when England established its first American colonies. Some of the English folk who settled the Virginia Colony in 1607 and subsequent outposts along the Atlantic Coast must have seen a Shakespeare performance or, in a few instances, read a Shakespeare quarto text. A very few early westward travellers may have brought a printed play or poem for solace in the wilderness.

Although plays were regularly performed in seventeenth-century England except during the Puritan regime of 1642–60, the early colonies shunned the theater. Colonizing companies sought hard-working craftsmen, farmers, and laborers; actors and playwrights were deemed undesirable distractions to struggling communities. Dramas by Shakespeare and other playwrights would have to wait until survival and a modicum of prosperity had been achieved and objections to the theater in ecclesiastical and government circles had been overcome. Not until the eighteenth century was well under way did the most liberal colonies welcome actors of any stripe, and no Shakespeare play, apparently, was staged until the third decade.

No public plays were performed in puritanical New England until the final quarter of the eighteenth century.

Virginia would eventually be the first colony to respond favorably to actors and to the construction of a theater, but it was initially as disapproving as its northern neighbors. Less than three years after the founding of Jamestown, the Reverend William Crashaw noted in a sermon to the Virginia Company of London that players, being "idle persons," were unwelcome in a colony that struggled to survive the unfamiliar environment, the opposition of indigenous Indians, and the lethargy of many of its settlers. The company's advertisements for migrants to America solicited "carpenters, smiths, coopers, fishermen, brickmen, and such like," rather than the "vagrant and unnecessary persons as do commonly profer themselves;" entertainers of all sorts were implicitly rejected. That attitude lingered for more than a century, despite the ascendancy of Governor William Berkeley—a writer of plays himself—during much of the seventeenth century. The three men who performed an amateur play at a Virginia tavern in 1665 were arrested for violating prohibitions against acting but eventually exonerated.[5] The Restoration's more liberal laws and attitudes were beginning to reach America.

Quaker Pennsylvania resisted that trend. Before William Penn founded the colony, he complained about "the infamous plays of those comical wits, Sylvester, Shakespeare, Johnson [presumably Ben Jonson], etc.... wherein the preciseness and singularity of Puritans and others are abusively represented... for the entertainment of vain and irreligious persons." Not surprisingly, the proprietor's first laws, issued in 1682, authorized severe punishment for "stage plays, cards, dice,... masques, revels, bull-baitings, cock-fightings, bear-baitings, and the like." Between the founding of the colony and the middle of the eighteenth century, an uneasy coalition of Quakers, Presbyterians, and Lutherans upheld Penn's strictures. Performances near Philadelphia began in 1723, but opposition from the mayor caused them to stop, with a brief exception, until the 1760s. By then Pennsylvania's growing diversity of settlers combined with Philadelphia's emergence as British America's largest community to undermine opposition to the stage. In the final decades of the century, Philadelphia's 40,000 inhabitants could readily support a theater, though, as in London, for many years the playhouses were constructed in the suburbs to avoid the city's moral objections. As late as 1766, a Quaker spokesman lamented that an acting company had arrived in Philadelphia "with intention to exhibit plays, which we conceive if permitted will tend to subvert... good order, morals and prosperity." The colony's Anglican governor dismissed the protest as "very ridiculous,"[6] and the ensuing season at the suburban Southwark Theatre was notably successful. From then on, Philadelphia (including Southwark, a separate jurisdiction until 1820) was a leading center of colonial theater, with Shakespeare among its favorite dramatists.

New England was even more resistant than Pennsylvania. Many of its early immigrants were so accustomed to anti-theatrical harangues in their English conventicles that proscriptive legislation was unnecessary, especially after Parliament closed England's theaters in 1642. Predictably, clergymen and magistrates in the puritan colonies became more vocal after English theaters reopened in 1660. In 1687, for example, the Reverend Increase Mather of Massachusetts complained that "persons who have been corrupted by stage-plays are seldom, and with much difficulty reclaimed"; Judge Samuel Sewall in 1714 opposed plays at Boston's Town House lest "Christian Boston go beyond Heathen Rome in the practice of shameful vanities"; and in 1750 the Massachusetts General Court authorized fines of £20 for the proprietor and £5 for every actor and spectator at "public stage-plays."[7] Thespian-minded New Englanders must have wondered if performances of Shakespeare or any other playwright would ever appear in their hidebound region.

* * *

Long before America's moral climate welcomed Shakespeare on the stage, colonists in New England and elsewhere were enjoying Shakespeare in print. The earliest evidence comes from Virginia, where the prosperous planter William Byrd II apparently brought a copy of the Fourth Folio of Shakespeare's works, published in 1685, when he returned in 1696 from schooling in England. Early eighteenth-century Virginia gentlemen's wills bequeathed a few individual plays and complete sets; the latter were almost certainly of Nicholas Rowe's multi-volume editions (1709, 1714). In Pennsylvania, colonial secretary James Logan owned Rowe's later edition, and the Library Company of Philadelphia, at Benjamin Franklin's urging, purchased

Thomas Hanmer's edition of 1743–4. In New England, the newspaper published by Franklin's elder brother James acquired a full set by 1722, as did Harvard and Yale colleges by about 1723 and 1743 respectively.[8] Reading Shakespeare, rather than watching a performance, avoided the theatrical world's corruptions: immoral venues, frivolous participants, wasted expense, and portrayals of lascivious or mean-spirited behavior. Accordingly, New England and for a while Pennsylvania resisted theatrical productions but embraced books, while ethnically and religiously diverse New York, Virginia, and South Carolina (with many wealthy and cosmopolitan immigrants from overcrowded Barbados) were by the second quarter of the eighteenth century—with occasional regressions—fertile territory for actors as well as readers of Shakespeare.

Among the students who presumably first encountered Shakespeare in a college library was the future second President of the United States, John Adams (Harvard 1755), whose diaries abound with praise for "that great master of every affection of the heart and every sentiment of the mind as well as of all the powers of expression." Adams's wife, Abigail, kept a pocket edition of the works on her nursery table, with the result that their son John Quincy Adams (another future president) would later recall having been "man and boy, a reader of Shakespeare.... [A]t ten years of age I was as familiarly acquainted with his lovers and his clowns, as with Robinson Crusoe, the Pilgrim's Progress, and the Bible." Thomas Jefferson, the future third President, may not have encountered Shakespeare's works at quite so early an age, but he was only 28 when he declared that "a lively and lasting sense of filial duty is more effectually impressed on the mind of a son or daughter by reading *King Lear* than by all the dry volumes of ethics and divinity that ever were written." Jefferson advised a friend to purchase Edward Capell's new edition of Shakespeare's works, published in 1768.[9]

The volumes of Shakespeare's works that impressed John Adams and his contemporaries were all British imports. Besides the multivolume editions by Rowe, Hanmer, and Capell, already mentioned, the poet Alexander Pope published a major compilation in 1725, as did, among many other scholars, the great lexicographer Samuel Johnson in 1765 and 1768 and, in collaboration with another textual editor, George Steevens, in 1773. The collected editions varied appreciably in the number of plays they attributed to Shakespeare (even the Third and Fourth Folios disagree with the First) as well as in the sources on which the editors relied; Pope, for instance, drew heavily from original quarto editions. The early English editions differed also on the inclusion of stage directions and on adherence to First Folio precedents. Colonial buyers thus had a wide range of English editions from which to choose if they wanted to add Shakespeare's writings to their private libraries. And increasingly they did, ordering cheap quarto editions of individual plays or expensive multi-volume editions of the collected works directly from London or through local booksellers in Boston, New York, Philadelphia, and many smaller towns.

Some colonial booksellers emphasized their close link to English publications by naming their shops The London Bookstore. One such establishment in New York City, owned by a recent immigrant from Ireland, the printer and editor Hugh Gaine, advertised in 1760—along with a great many other books—"Shakespeare's Plays, 9 Vols." (probably Hanmer's sixth edition, 1760); in 1772 Gaine advertised "Shakespear[e]'s Plays, 10 Vols." (perhaps Capell's of 1768).[10] By then, copies of the dramas were numerous in the hinterland as well as along the eastern seaboard. On British America's northwestern frontier (in the 1760s it was in Illinois territory), a Shakespeare volume saved the life of a British officer, according to his oft-told tale. The book, taken by an Indian from a victim of the massacre of General Edward Braddock's army in western Pennsylvania in 1755, was given nine years later by a minor chief to Captain Thomas Morris during Pontiac's Rebellion. Morris lingered over *Antony and Cleopatra* in a drifting canoe while his companions confronted angry Miami villagers intent on killing him.[11]

By the 1760s, American booksellers sometimes "published" (a word with multiple meanings in the eighteenth century) copies of British books that had been typeset and printed abroad but now carried the colonial merchant's title page. By importing unbound copies of recent English, Irish, or Scottish printings, the American bookman could quickly and cheaply produce ostensibly new editions. That may have been the backdrop for Hugh Gaine's advertisements of July 1761 in the *New-York Mercury* for about a dozen British and Continental comedies that he had "This Day...published," including *The*

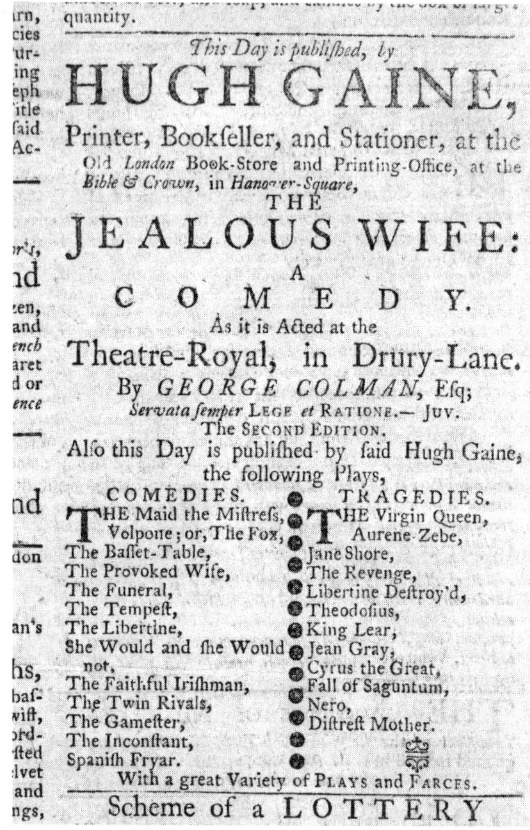
quantity.

This Day is publiſhed, by

HUGH GAINE,

Printer, Bookſeller, and Stationer, at the Old London Book-Store and Printing-Office, at the Bible & Crown, in Hanover-Square,

THE

JEALOUS WIFE:

A

COMEDY.

As it is Acted at the

Theatre-Royal, in Drury-Lane.

By GEORGE COLMAN, Eſq;

Servata ſemper LEGE et RATIONE.— JUV.

The SECOND EDITION.

Alſo this Day is publiſhed by ſaid Hugh Gaine, the following Plays,

COMEDIES.	TRAGEDIES.
THE Maid the Miſtreſs,	THE Virgin Queen,
Volpone; or, The Fox,	Aurene-Zebe,
The Baſſet-Table,	Jane Shore,
The Provoked Wife,	The Revenge,
The Funeral,	Libertine Deſtroy'd,
The Tempeſt,	Theodoſius,
The Libertine,	King Lear,
She Would and ſhe Would not,	Jean Gray,
The Faithful Iriſhman,	Cyrus the Great,
The Twin Rivals,	Fall of Saguntum,
The Gameſter,	Nero,
The Inconſtant,	Diſtreſt Mother.
Spaniſh Fryar.	

With a great Variety of PLAYS and FARCES.

Scheme of a LOTTERY

Figure 1.1. Hugh Gaine's newspaper advertisement in the *New-York Mercury* (1761) announces new editions of *The Tempest* and *King Lear*. Courtesy of the American Antiquarian Society.

Tempest, and nearly as many tragedies, including *King Lear* (Fig. 1.1). If Gaine was reissuing books printed abroad, he violated no colonial copyright law (there was none), and Britain's licensing and copyright act of 1710 was ambiguous about overseas republication.[12]

But Gaine may have meant "published" in a different sense—that he was the sales agent for a collection of recently received English books. The plays in his advertisements were among the most popular in London, and the inclusion of two by Shakespeare would have strengthened his list's appeal. Although the records suggest that *King Lear* had been performed only twice in the colonies before 1761 and *The Tempest*'s first documented performance was still nine years in the future, Shakespeare's star was rising, in both print and performance. (Whether these were Shakespeare's texts or, more likely, adaptations of *The Tempest* by the English playwrights John Dryden and Sir William Davenant and of *King Lear* by the Irish-born dramatist Nahum Tate is unknown. No copy has been found of either book.) From a colonial perspective, what mattered was that quartos of some Shakespeare plays could now be identified, however tenuously, with a colonial rather than an English bookseller-printer. It was an early, hopeful step toward giving Shakespeare's works an American affinity.

* * *

The interval between the first appearance of a Shakespeare text in America (*c.*1696) and the first stage performance was more than three decades. Unless evidence of a prior instance emerges, the initial staging was of *Romeo and Juliet* in March 1730. Dr. Joachimus Bertrand advertised in the *New York Gazette* that he would act the apothecary in Shakespeare's play at the city's Revenge Meeting House, "which is fitting up for that purpose." Lost issues of the newspaper presumably assessed this amateur production's success and revealed the length of its run, though both may have been minimal, for a twenty-year lapse ensued before the next documented performance of a play by Shakespeare. In 1750–51 the adaptation of *Richard III* by the early eighteenth-century English playwright and theater manager Colley Cibber merited four performances by an itinerant acting company at the Nassau Street Theatre in New York and one in Williamsburg, Virginia; late in 1751 a different company acted *Othello* in New York. Shakespeare at last had a toehold on the colonial stage.[13]

British America's prolonged paucity of stage performances of any kind can largely be explained by its shortage of acting companies and adequate theaters. That, in turn, can be attributed to the lingering official hostility to actors and acting and to the slow growth of population centers that could sustain even a small entertainment company and a dedicated building. The first documented theater—a plain rectangular structure about 86 by 30 feet that doubled as a dancing school—opened in 1718 in Williamsburg, Virginia's capital, a small town that expanded seasonally from an influx of legislators and other colonial officials, visiting tradesmen and dignitaries, and students at the College of William and Mary. Little information survives about Williamsburg's early performances before a local newspaper began publication nearly two decades after the theater opened, but presumably the actors were mostly from England—some of them probably indentured servants "owned" temporarily by producers of colonial entertainment—and college students. The few extant clues suggest that the plays were from the standard London fare: John Gay's *The Beggar's Opera*, George Farquhar's *The Beaux' Stratagem* and *The Recruiting Officer*, Joseph Addison's *Cato* and *The Drummer*, and the like. Except for *Richard III* in 1751, there is no mention of Shakespeare at Williamsburg either before or after the *Virginia Gazette* began to provide news of the playhouse in 1736 until the theater's fitful career ended a decade later.[14] By the 1750s New York, Philadelphia, and Charleston also had intermittent quasi-professional performances. South of New England, taverns, churches, and warehouses provided temporary venues for itinerant companies in communities such as Lancaster, Pennsylvania, Annapolis and Chester, Maryland, Fredericksburg and Suffolk, Virginia. Shakespeare's plays may have been performed occasionally at these venues, with the evidence unintentionally masked by the cryptic "went to the play"—a common entry in colonial diaries, including George Washington's.[15]

Shortly before mid-century, professional English touring companies broadened the number and quality of theatrical performances and introduced the current versions of Shakespeare's most popular plays. The first such company was probably the group assembled by actor-manager Walter Murray and actor-playwright Thomas Kean that came from the West Indies in 1749 and performed for a season near Philadelphia. Except for Addison's *Cato*, their early repertoire in Pennsylvania is unknown, but when government opposition forced Murray and Kean to move to New York the following year, they opened a new theater on Nassau Street with Cibber's rendition of *Richard III* in repertoire with several other standard London shows. The offerings were similar when Murray and Kean moved again, this time to Williamsburg and vicinity, where they played at a new theater in the Virginia capital and at impromptu venues in small towns throughout Virginia and Maryland. In the summer of 1752 they called themselves the Annapolis Company but continued playing the same repertoire in Fredericksburg and Williamsburg as well as the Maryland capital. Meanwhile, a short-lived company in New York under another English visitor, Robert Upton, performed *Othello* in December 1751 and added *Richard III* in January and February 1752.[16] Shakespeare was gaining momentum in British America.

The likelihood of colonial Americans seeing well-performed plays increased substantially when the London Company of Comedians arrived in early 1752. Most of its actors belonged to the Hallam family or were their professional colleagues; most had performed at provincial venues and at Bartholomew Fair and elsewhere in London. The principal organizer, William Hallam, remained in England, while his brother Lewis went to the colonies as the resident manager and acted in comedy roles; Lewis's wife, Sarah Smythies Hallam, played the female leads, and several of their sons and daughters took supporting roles. The Hallam troupe began its American career in Williamsburg with the purchase and improvement of the Murray–Kean building, where its first production was a musical adaptation of *The Merchant of Venice* (Fig. 1.2); later that season the Hallams performed *Othello*. Because the audiences for these and other productions were smaller than expected, the company moved to New York after only one season in Virginia and later to Philadelphia, where the Hallams fared only slightly better. They persevered for the next few years in several cities and towns in the mid-Atlantic and southern colonies, but except for one performance of *Richard III* in 1753, one performance of Tate's adaptation of *King Lear*, and two of *Romeo and Juliet* (probably the adaptation by David Garrick) in 1754, they seem to have eschewed Shakespeare.[17]

* * *

From their winter retreat in Jamaica, the Hallams often played in Barbados and other West Indian islands, as did a company headed by another English actor-manager, David Douglass. The companies merged after Lewis Hallam's death in 1756 and his widow's marriage to Douglass two years later. The blended entourage, now usually called the Douglass Company, continued to tour the mainland colonies almost every year, from spring through autumn, but with a new

By PERMISSION of the Honble *ROBERT DINWIDDIE*, Esq; His Majesty's Lieutenant-Governor, and Commander in Chief of the Colony and Dominion of *Virginia*.

By a Company of COMEDIANS, *from* LONDON,
At the THEATRE *in* WILLIAMSBURG,
On *Friday* next, being the 15th of *September*, will be presented,
A PLAY, Call'd,
THE
MERCHANT of *VENICE*.
(Written by *Shakespear*.)
The Part of *ANTONIO* (the MERCHANT) to be perform'd by
Mr. CLARKSON.
GRATIANO, by Mr. SINGLETON,
Lorenzo, (with Songs in Character) by Mr. ADCOCK.
The Part of *BASSANIO* to be perform'd by
Mr. RIGBY.
Duke, by Mr. Wynell.
Salanio, by Mr. Herbert.
The Part of *LAUNCELOT*, by Mr. HALLAM.
And the Part of *SHYLOCK*, (the JEW) to be perform'd by
Mr. MALONE.
The Part of *NERISSA*, by Mrs. ADCOCK,
Jessica, by Mrs. Rigby.
And the Part of *PORTIA*, to be perform'd by
Mrs. HALLAM.
With a new occasional PROLOGUE.
To which will be added, a FARCE, call'd,
The ANATOMIST:
OR,
SHAM DOCTOR.
The Part of *Monsieur le Medecin*, by
Mr. RIGBY.
And the Part of *BEATRICE*, by Mrs. ADCOCK.
*** No Person, whatsoever, to be admitted behind the Scenes.
BOXES, 7*s*. 6*d*. PIT and BALCONIES, 5*s*. 9*d*. GALLERY, 3*s*. 9*d*.
To begin at Six o'Clock.
Vivat Rex.

Figure 1.2. The *Virginia Gazette* (1752) advertises a production of *The Merchant of Venice*, the first performance in America by the Hallam troupe, calling itself "a Company of Comedians, from London." The Colonial Williamsburg Foundation, Williamsburg, VA.

attention to Shakespeare that reflected Douglass's influence and, presumably, the growing audience appreciation of Shakespeare in the colonies as in the mother country. In the latter, the proliferation of collected editions had helped to inform the public of Shakespeare's rich and varied texts; in London, the eminent actor and theatrical manager David Garrick produced, and often acted in, Shakespeare plays at Drury Lane; and in Stratford-upon-Avon, the author's reputation would reach a temporary apogee with the Jubilee of 1769 in which actors dressed as Shakespeare's characters celebrated the man Garrick called "the greatest dramatic poet in the world." Whatever the reasons, the year 1759—David Douglass's first in the combined troupe—witnessed a sharp upturn in British America's Shakespeare productions. To the old standbys *Richard III* (twice) and *Othello* were added *Hamlet* (three times), *Macbeth* (twice), *Romeo and Juliet* (twice), and *King Lear*—a total of eleven performances. The following year, 1760, the Douglass troupe offered slightly fewer Shakespeare performances but introduced the colonies to another adaptation of *The Merchant of Venice* and the next year added 1 *Henry IV*.[18]

By then the Douglass Company's personnel had changed appreciably, with new actors from England replacing many of the original Hallams. Most of the elder male leads were taken by an experienced actor, John Harman (Lear, Richard III), while Lewis Hallam, Jr. played younger leads (Hamlet, Romeo) and his mother took several female parts; they played husband and wife in *Macbeth*. In 1763 the troupe renamed itself the American Company of Comedians in tacit acknowledgment of British America's emerging identity and the company's extensive touring of the island and mainland colonies. And if for a few years Shakespeare seems to have been less popular, judging from the number of documented productions, in 1767 he enjoyed a revival. That year the American Company staged at least twenty-one performances of nine of Shakespeare's plays—counting Garrick's drastically shortened and revamped *Catherine and Petruchio* (1754, but not played in America until 1766)—mostly at Philadelphia's Southwark Theatre, with *Cymbeline* (three times) and an adaptation of *Coriolanus* supplementing the earlier offerings. The American Company expanded its Shakespeare repertoire with *King John* in 1768, and *The Tempest*, *The Merry Wives of Windsor*, and *Julius Caesar* in 1770. Shakespeare's high-water mark in colonial America came at Charleston's Court Street Theatre between December 24, 1773, and May 19, 1774, where in under five months the American Company performed twelve of his plays, some of them multiple times, plus the afterpiece *Catherine and Petruchio*, interspersed among the customary post-Restoration dramas. *The Tempest*, with three performances, led the Shakespeare list because, reported a New York newspaper's summary of recent events in Charleston, "a crowded and brilliant audience... expressed the highest satisfaction at their entertainment" after the play's first production. Especially appealing were "the deceptions, machinery, and decorations, [which] surpassed everybody's expectation; and the public appear impatient for a second representation of that excellent comedy."[19]

Continuity between the American Company and its predecessor organizations persisted in Lewis Hallam, Jr.'s continuing appearance in leading roles and the emergence to stardom of Nancy Hallam, a niece of Mrs Hallam-Douglass. Praise for Nancy Hallam was sometimes lavish. Her performance as *Cymbeline*'s Imogen "exceeded my utmost idea!" gushed a fan in 1770. "Such delicacy of manner! Such *classical* strictness of expression! The music of her tongue! The *vox liquida*, how melting!" In 1771 the great portraitist Charles Willson Peale painted Nancy Hallam as Imogen (based, presumably, on a performance of October 1771 in Annapolis), although she was renowned as well for her portrayals of Ophelia, Juliet, and Cordelia (Fig. 1.3). At about the same time, an important new actor and a new acting company refreshed the colonial scene. Beginning in 1767, many of the American Company's male leads were played in northeastern theaters by an imposing Irishman, John Henry, who excelled as Othello and Shylock, while a breakaway group under the English manager-actor William Verling, calling itself the Virginia Company and then the New American Company, played *Henry IV* (with, at least once, a transvestite Hal), *The Merchant of Venice*, *Romeo and Juliet*, and other dramas in Williamsburg and vicinity. Although Verling's company lasted only a few seasons, as did two other companies that performed in the Carolinas, all of them helped to spread the public's awareness and appreciation of Shakespeare.[20]

Shakespeare finally appeared in New England under the guise of "Moral Dialogues"—public readings of selected passages rather than performances of an entire play. A handbill in June 1761 from the King's Arms Tavern in Newport, Rhode Island, promised *Othello* "in Five Parts, Depicting the Evil Effects of Jealousy and other Bad Passions, and Proving that Happiness can only Spring from the Pursuit of Virtue." The handbill summarizes several of the play's episodes, with a moral lesson for each. Cassio's drunkenness, for example, demonstrates "The ill effect of drinking would ye see,/Be warned and keep from evil company," while Brabantio's vilification of the Moor "because his face is not white" warns, "Fathers beware what

Figure 1.3. Charles Willson Peale's portrait of Nancy Hallam as *Cymbeline*'s Imogen (1771). From Special Collections, John D. Rockefeller, Jr. Library, The Colonial Williamsburg Foundation.

sense and love ye lack./'Tis crime, not color, makes the being black." The dialogues would end by 10.30 p.m., the advertisement promised, "In order that every spectator may go home at a sober hour, and reflect upon what he has seen, before he retires to rest." So successful was this Shakespearian adaptation that a playhouse was soon constructed in Providence, but most of Rhode Island's early shows were performed for charity in a vain attempt to quell public opposition.[21] For the rest of the eighteenth century, theater in New England lagged woefully behind New York City, Philadelphia, Charleston, Annapolis,

Baltimore, and Williamsburg, which supported lively seasons almost annually, with frequent Shakespeare productions.

Although the colonial stage was, by definition, provincial, by the late eighteenth century its productions bore many similarities to the mother country's. Key exceptions were the quality of acting and the elaborateness of staging at the biggest venues, for the colonies had nothing comparable to London's Drury Lane or Covent Garden theaters, no truly great actors, and no producer of plays like David Garrick. (It is a truism, of course, that English actors and entrepreneurs often went to America in the early years because they had fallen short, or feared they would, in highly competitive London.) But while colonial venues outside the major towns, which were in most cases the capitals of the seaboard colonies, were usually makeshift and quite small, so too were most British theatrical venues outside of London and a few market towns. By the 1760s, American spaces were roughly on a par with those in Bristol, Brighton, Hull, Belfast, and Aberdeen, for example, and were served by similar itinerant companies. They played on impromptu stages at inns and taverns if the town did not have a dedicated theatrical building, and performed Shakespeare's plays and the rest of the usual English repertoire with comparable skill.

In 1770 a letter to the *Maryland Gazette* opined that the Douglass Company was widely believed to be "superior to that of any company in England, except those of the metropolis." The following year a recent English immigrant wrote home from Annapolis: "When I bade farewell to England, I little expected that my passion for the drama could have been gratified in any tolerable degree at a distance so remote from the great mart of genius," but he was pleasantly surprised to find "performers in this country equal at least to those ... in your most celebrated provincial theatres."[22] As residents of British provinces themselves, colonial Americans must have taken real pride in favorable comparisons of their productions to those in Britain's older and often larger venues.

Even the occasional presence of American Indians at colonial theaters did not make the American experience unique. At Williamsburg in 1752, "The Emperor of the Cherokee Nation with his empress and their son the young prince, attended by several of his warriors and great men and their ladies," saw *Othello*, to the great delight of the audience. What the Indians thought of Shakespeare's play is unrecorded, but a newspaper reported that they expressed "great surprise" at the Harlequin pantomime afterpiece, "as did the fighting with naked swords on the stage, which occasioned the empress to order some about her to go and prevent their killing one another." Fifteen years later, nine Cherokee dignitaries, including the celebrated Attakullakulla (a.k.a. Little Carpenter), stopped at New York en route to Albany for a conference with Superintendent of Indian Affairs Sir William Johnson; on December 14, 1767 before a packed house at the John Street Theatre they witnessed the American Company's "Command Performance" of *Richard III*. "The Indians regarded the play...with seriousness and attention," the *New-York Journal* reported, "but as it cannot be supposed that they were sufficiently acquainted with the language to understand the plot and design, and enter into the spirit of the author, their countenances and behaviour were rather expressive of surprise and curiosity, than any other passions." Several months later the same group, minus Attakullakulla, stopped at New York on their way home and attended two non-Shakespearian comedies; after the second show, Susanna Centlivre's popular comedy of 1718, *The Wonder, A Woman Keeps a Secret!*, the Cherokees performed a war dance on the stage.[23] The events of 1752 and 1767–8 drew the newspapers' attention because the guests were distinguished members of a powerful Indian nation, but presumably there were other, unreported instances of less prominent aborigines in American audiences.

In any case, the presence of Indians was not unusual in the Anglophone theatrical world. Delegations to London in 1710, 1730 (including Attakullakulla), 1734, 1762, and 1773 attended professional plays, many by Shakespeare, where, as in the colonies, overflow audiences came to ogle exotic strangers struggling to comprehend Shakespearian drama or the antics of silent comedians. These episodes reinforce a broad conclusion that by the second half of the eighteenth century the colonies and mother country shared a single theatrical culture in which the works of William Shakespeare were of prominent and expanding importance. A plausible estimate of the number of colonial performances of Shakespeare before the outbreak of the American Revolution is in the vicinity of 500, although fewer than 200 have so far been documented. In some years and some American communities, Shakespeare was arguably a more prominent part of the shared theatrical culture than he was in London. During Charleston's 1773–4 season, approximately 27 per cent of the productions were of Shakespeare's plays; at Drury Lane that year the figure was 15 per cent.[24]

Like their mother-country counterparts, colonial Americans did not see the whole canon. Judging from newspaper advertisements (the era's principal theatrical evidence), only fourteen of the dramas were staged in America before the Revolution. *Romeo and Juliet* and *Richard III* were especially popular, followed at some distance by *Hamlet* and—in imprecise order—by *Othello*, *Cymbeline*, *The Tempest*, *Macbeth*, *The Merchant of Venice*, *King Lear*, a drastically revised and retitled *Antony and Cleopatra*, and, with few performances, 1 *Henry IV*, *King John*, *Julius Caesar*, and *The Merry Wives of Windsor*. Near the top of this list, arguably, could be added *The Taming of the Shrew*, but it always appeared as a musical afterpiece in the form of Garrick's *Catherine and Petruchio*. Garrick's comic adaptation of *The Winter's Tale*, entitled *Florizel and Perdita*, seems not to have been performed in mainland America before the early 1790s although Garrick introduced it to English audiences in 1756, and it played at least once in Jamaica in about 1780.

With the exception of *Othello* and *Hamlet*, and perhaps *Cymbeline*, the versions of Shakespeare plays in colonial and Revolutionary America diverged widely from the original texts, with wholesale deletions and additions, and often with the insertion of music and dance. British audiences saw the same versions until late in the era, when some closer approximations to Shakespeare's texts appeared. Americans, however, continued to see *Macbeth* in the musical variant by Sir William Davenant and the composer Matthew Locke, and *Richard III* in Colley Cibber's adaptation, with an enlarged title role which Cibber usually played in London; in America it was usually performed by Lewis Hallam, Jr. *King Lear and His Three Daughters* owed almost as much to Nahum Tate as to Shakespeare, with drastic changes to the plot, language, and characters, and a happy ending. *Antony and Cleopatra* became, in John Dryden's adaptation, *All for Love, or, The World Well Lost*. George Granville, Lord Lansdowne, had turned *The Merchant of Venice* into *The Jew of Venice, or the Female Lawyer*. The version of *The Tempest* performed in the eighteenth century (as in the late seventeenth) added masques by Thomas

Shadwell and compositions by Locke and Henry Purcell to Dryden and Davenant's drastic rewriting of Shakespeare's play; its subtitle, *The Enchanted Island*, signaled the transformation. Although Garrick in 1757 crafted a shortened version of the original *Tempest* for London audiences, it seems not to have reached the colonies. In 1787 George Washington, who was partial to operatic productions, saw the Dryden–Davenant rendition, featuring, said a newspaper advertisement, "entire new scenery, machinery, etc. etc. The music composed by Doctor Purcell."[25]

* * *

The rift between the colonies and mother country after 1763 interrupted British America's mounting affection for all things Shakespearian. To some Americans, Shakespeare was uncomfortably British for people in search of home-grown symbols and traditions. For many loyalists and British officers in America, especially during the war years from 1775 to 1783, he offered too few opportunities to ridicule the American upstarts; it was easier to write their own lampoons of George Washington and his country bumpkin army. But because many of Shakespeare's plays were widely known, either side could borrow passages to convey political messages with minimal explanation. Disgruntled colonists asked in 1770:

> Be taxed or not be taxed, that is the question:
> Whether 'tis nobler in our minds to suffer
> The sleights and cunning of deceitful statesmen,
> Or to petition 'gainst illegal taxes,
> And by opposing end them?...

Four years later, an anonymous rhymester lamented the loyalists' dilemma over Congress's drive for signatures on "associations" against the importation of British goods.

> To sign, or not to sign?—That is the question,
> Whether 'twere better for an honest man
> To sign, and so be safe; or to resolve,
> Betide what will, against associations,
> And, by retreating, shun them....

And so forth for twenty-eight more lines. And in March 1776 a loyalist opened his column against Thomas Paine's recently published

Common Sense ("or common *Nonsense*," the critic suggested) with thirty lines of poetry that began "To write, or not to write: that is the question—." The author in this case invoked Shakespeare's name and even Hamlet's, but surely everyone, rebels and loyalists alike, already recognized the soliloquy's prototype.[26]

Although there is no hard evidence that the sales of Shakespeare's books suffered during the war, the need for frugality and the various non-importation resolutions of 1774 and 1775—some by individual colonies, others by the Continental Congress—must have seriously curtailed purchases in the colonies and fresh imports from England. More damaging to the enjoyment of Shakespeare throughout America for several years was the First Continental Congress's campaign in 1774 to "discountenance and discourage" theatrical performances as well as horse racing, cock-fighting, elaborate funerals, and other forms of "extravagance and dissipation"—all of them, in Congress's eyes, English vices inimical to American virtues and detrimental to the American economy. Although plays continued to be performed here and there in defiance of that proscription, the professional theater companies spent the war years in the West Indies.[27] If Congress's issuance of new restrictions in 1778 reveals the failure of the first ban to be wholly effective, it also shows the government's determination to keep performances to a minimum. With a few exceptions, professional Shakespeare had to wait for an armistice.

Amateur performances were a different matter. Some Americans mounted them in violation of the ban, such as the staging at Valley Forge in April 1778 of Addison's *Cato*—a paean to liberty and patriotism. Meanwhile, loyalists and British officers perforce denied Congress's jurisdiction over territories under the British army's control, most notably by occupying forces in Boston during the war's first year, in Philadelphia during the third year, and in New York during most of the war. Because many British officers missed the entertainment they were accustomed to back home, including Shakespeare's plays, and some also harbored acting or writing ambitions, the occupying armies in America's three largest towns recreated, or even expanded, the theatrical opportunities that had formerly depended on itinerant companies. Boston, for example, witnessed vibrant performances for the first time when, to the outrage of its pro-Revolutionary inhabitants, British soldiers turned Faneuil Hall into a busy playhouse.

Among other indignities, General John Burgoyne, a published playwright, mocked Yankee prudery. The town's puritanical policies resembled, said Burgoyne's prologue to the first play performed by troops in Boston (Aaron Hill's *Zara*), Oliver Cromwell's actions of more than a century earlier, which had "sunk the stage, quelled by the bigot roar,/Truth fled with sense and Shakespeare charmed no more."[28] Bostonians would get their revenge with Britain's forced evacuation of the town in March 1776 and Burgoyne's devastating defeat at Saratoga the following year.

The British occupation of Philadelphia from September 1777 to June 1778 gave that city a brief theatrical boost. Sir William Howe's "Strolling Players," who had performed in New York when Howe commanded there in 1776–7, reopened the Southwark Theatre, which had been shut since the American Company's departure in November 1773. The fourteen plays put on by British soldiers and loyalist amateurs—and at least one professional actress—included two performances of 1 *Henry IV*. Meanwhile, Washington's army, only twenty miles away at Valley Forge, had plans for two or more standard English dramas after the success of *Cato*, though none apparently by Shakespeare, before General Howe's withdrawal from Philadelphia in the summer of 1778 changed the military situation. With the return of Congress to the city, the efforts of some patriots to use the Southwark Theatre encountered old prejudices. Massachusetts delegate Samuel Adams denounced a proposed performance as "vice, idleness, dissipation, and a general depravity of principles and manners" that was "disagreeable to the sober inhabitants of this city," and Congress prohibited the involvement of military personnel as actors, producers, or audience, on pain of discharge from the armed forces. But Congress was deeply divided: Georgia, North Carolina, Virginia, Maryland, and New York voted against the bill. As a French observer opined, "northern rigidity" had been "mollified in contact with southern sensuousness." Pennsylvania remained rigid by outlawing the construction of new theaters, but elsewhere American officers staged *Cato* at a military encampment in New Brunswick, New Jersey, apparently without retribution, and other soldiers acted *Coriolanus* at Portsmouth, New Hampshire.[29]

Throughout the war, cosmopolitan New York maintained a lively theatrical culture that frequently included Shakespeare's plays. After the British seized the city in September 1776, the printer-editor-bookseller Hugh Gaine—a recent convert to loyalism—encouraged performances by citizens and soldiers in the theaters that had been dark since early 1775. Four months after General Howe arrived, the John Street Theatre launched a season of twenty shows, most of them featuring two plays each. Although the acting fell short of English standards, a commentator in Gaine's *New-York Mercury* thought the scenery, painted by a British officer, "has great merit, and would not disgrace a theater, though under the management of a Garrick." Later in the war, with Sir Henry Clinton commanding the city, the John Street Theatre was refurbished and renamed The Theatre Royal, where "Clinton's Thespians" included civilians and military officers and a few professional actors (some in each category had previously acted in New York or Philadelphia under General Howe), although many in the cast could be considered at least semi-professionals because the officers shared in the company's profits. A disproportionate part of those profits came from *Richard III*, *Macbeth*, *Othello*, and *King Lear*, for although the total number of performances favored other English dramatists, attendance figures for Shakespeare's plays were unusually high. The few actors who can be identified illustrate the eclectic nature of occupied New York's theaters. The title role in *Othello*, for example, on March 27, 1778 was played by Major James Moncrieff, formerly of the American Company; Desdemona was performed by the leading female actor of that season, now known only as "Major Williams's mistress," while Emilia was played by Anna Tomlinson, another former member of the American Company who had declined to take refuge in Jamaica.[30]

The decisive American victory at Yorktown in October 1781 did not appreciably alter Shakespeare's popularity in New York. During the remaining two years of British occupation, the city's theatrical life expanded when John Henry came back from Jamaica in 1782 as a one-man show featuring "Shadows of Shakespeare, or Shakespeare's Characters paying Homage to Garrick" (who had died in 1779), while British military forces performed *Macbeth* in January 1782 and *Othello* in September 1783, two months before the final evacuation of the city. More attentive to Shakespeare was a civilian troupe, drawn mostly from the American Company, that produced eight Shakespeare plays, most of them several times, at Baltimore and Annapolis in 1782 and early 1783 before moving to New York in the summer of 1783. Between August and October they performed *Richard III*, *Romeo and Juliet*, and *Macbeth* (twice), as well as *Catherine and Petruchio*. After a brief outburst of anti-theatrical prejudice in northern cities in 1783–5 forced Lewis Hallam, Jr., who returned from Jamaica and reopened New York's John Street Theatre in July 1785, to shape his shows as "lectures," by the end of the year he had merged the American Company with John Henry's small troupe and resumed regular performances. Subterfuges lingered longer in Quaker-dominated Philadelphia, where some productions were called "concerts," the "Opera-House" in Southwark was an intentional misnomer, while *Hamlet* and *Richard III* were disguised as *Filial Piety* and *The Fate of Tyranny*.[31] By 1789, however, America had almost wholly revived its pre-war enthusiasm for theatricals in general and Shakespeare's plays in particular. In the following decade, the re-Americanization of Shakespeare would proceed apace.

One reason for Shakespeare's speedy revival was his perceived neutrality during the Revolutionary era. Both sides recognized the theater's potential for propaganda: Some American-authored plays, both amateur and professional, and some plays by British occupying forces had partisan objectives, as did rebel performances of Addison's *Cato*. But rebels and loyalists alike rarely enlisted Shakespeare in their causes. The frequent borrowing of the quintessential Hamlet quotation during the build-up to the war was a rhetorical device to catch readers' attention, with no ideological implications. The first colonial performance of *Julius Caesar* in 1770 tried to make political points through its republican speeches, but contrary to long-standing assumptions, the drama was rarely staged. The surviving records suggest that *Julius Caesar* was not performed again until 1774 (once) and not after that until 1788 (again, once). The most popular Shakespearian text during the Revolutionary era, as earlier, was *Richard III*, played by both parties to the conflict despite the centrality of its malignant monarch. In war as in peace, Shakespeare was primarily an entertainer or moral guide, not an advocate.[32]

The nascent nation's continuing affection for the English language's premier dramatist was epitomized in 1786 during Thomas Jefferson and John Adams's diplomatic visit to England. On a side trip to Stratford-upon-Avon, these American founding fathers verged on bardolatry. Jefferson, Adams later claimed, got on his knees to kiss the ground, and at the run-down Shakespeare birthplace they cut a souvenir piece from a wooden chair, Adams recorded, "according to the custom." Although Adams was unimpressed by the bust of Shakespeare in Holy Trinity Church, he believed any sculpture or painting of Shakespeare must be inconsequential, because his "wit, and fancy, his taste and judgment, his knowledge of nature, of life and character, are immortal."[33] In retrospect, Jefferson and Adams's homage is not surprising. Both men were devoted readers of Shakespeare's works, and throughout the colonies Shakespeare's plays had been among the most frequently performed since 1752; between 1767 and 1789, he was the most popular playwright.

But Shakespeare's influence ran deeper than the pleasures of reading his books or watching his plays. Several of the nation's founders were so thoroughly immersed in Shakespearian drama that they incorporated lessons they discerned in the texts into the momentous political discussions and decisions of their day. That was especially true of John Adams, who appreciated Shakespeare's "knowledge of nature, of life and character" long before and long after his pilgrimage to Stratford. In letters to Abigail from his courting days onward, and later in letters to his sons and in his political writings as early as the 1760s and as late as his post-presidential years, John Adams derived inspiration and practical lessons from Shakespeare. He drew on *Macbeth* to criticize England's maltreatment of its colonial progeny, on *Henry VIII* to argue against unjust taxation, on *The Merry Wives of Windsor* to warn against dangerous temptations, on *Troilus and Cressida* to justify class distinctions, on *Coriolanus* and *Julius Caesar* as well as the English history plays to illustrate the perils of internecine politics. "I would like to think," writes a scholar who has closely and subtly examined Shakespeare's influence on the founding generation, that:

> Shakespeare is "in America" in more important ways than we usually realize. We already know that he is in America as an eminently quotable writer, a creator of characters we continue to love, and a crafter of plays we enjoy on the American stage.... I would like to suggest that he may also be woven into the very fabric of America, his insight, his perceptions a part of the very Constitution of our nation.[34]

Adams, Jefferson, and their peers, one suspects, would nod in agreement.

The story of Shakespeare's influence on America, and its glorification of him, did not end, of course, with national independence. Americans—at least the educated "better sort," in the parlance of the times—already appreciated the poet widely and enthusiastically. Rather, political autonomy spurred Americans over the next century to expand the social spectrum that read or watched Shakespeare's plays, to widen the range of institutional opportunities for reaping benefits from this literary goldmine, and to encourage many Americans to participate actively in the performance, publication, and criticism of Shakespeare's works.

Notes

1. *The Diaries of George Washington, 1748–1799*, ed. John C. Fitzpatrick (4 vols, New York: Houghton Mifflin, 1925), 3.227; *The Independent Gazetteer or, The Chronicle of Freedom* (Philadelphia), July 14, 1787.
2. John Smith, *The Generall Historie of Virginia, New-England, and the Summer Isles* (London: Michael Sparkes, 1624), 206.
3. J. H. Lefroy, *Memorials of the Discovery and Early Settlement of the Bermudas or Somers Islands, 1515–1685* (2 vols, London: Longmans, Green, 1877–79), 1.103; Alden T. Vaughan, "William Strachey's 'True Reportory' and Shakespeare: A Closer Look at the Evidence," *Shakespeare Quarterly* 59 (2008), 245–73.
4. Lefroy, *Memorials of the Bermudas*, 1.104; John Parker, *Van Meteren's Virginia, 1607–1612* (Minneapolis: University of Minnesota Press, 1961), 65–7; Smith, *Generall Historie*, 175.
5. William Crashaw in Alexander Brown, *The Genesis of the United States:... Historical Documents Now First Printed* (2 vols, Boston: Houghton, Mifflin, 1890), 1.367; Broadside by the [Virginia] Council, ibid. 1.439; Odai Johnson and William J. Burling, *The Colonial American Stage, 1665–1774: A Documentary Calendar* (Cranbury, NJ: Associated University Presses, 2001), 92–3.
6. William Penn, *The Christian-Quaker and His Divine Testimony Vindicated...* ([London]: [Andrew Sowle], 1674), 1.8; Jean R. Soderlund (ed.), *William Penn and the Founding of Pennsylvania, 1680–1684: A Documentary History* (Philadelphia: University of Pennsylvania Press, 1983), 132; Kenneth Silverman, *A Cultural History of the American Revolution: Painting, Music, Literature, and the Theatre...* (New York: Thomas Y. Crowell, 1976), 103–4.

7. Increase Mather, *A Testimony against Several Prophane and Superstitious Customs Now Practised by Some in New-England* (London: n.p., 1687), sig. A3; *Collections of the Massachusetts Historical Society* 6th ser. 2 (1888), 29–30; *Acts and Resolves, Public and Private, of the Province of the Massachusetts Bay*, 3 (Boston: Printed for the Commonwealth, 1878), 500–501.
8. Edwin Eliott Willoughby, "The Reading of Shakespeare in Colonial America," *Papers of the Bibliographical Society of America* 31 (1937), 48; *The Printed Catalogues of the Harvard College Library*, ed. W. H. Bond and Hugh Amory (Boston: Colonial Society of Massachusetts, 1996), 101.
9. *Diary and Autobiography of John Adams*, ed. L. H. Butterfield (4 vols, New York: Atheneum, 1964), 1.61, 2.53; John Quincy Adams to James Henry Hackett, n.d., in Hackett, *Notes, Criticisms, and Correspondence upon Shakespeare's Plays and Actors* (New York: Carleton, 1863), 229; Thomas Jefferson to Robert Skipwith, August 3, 1771, in *The Papers of Thomas Jefferson*, ed. Julian P. Boyd, 1 (Princeton, NJ: Princeton University Press, 1950), 77–8.
10. Andrew Murphy, *Shakespeare in Print: A History and Chronology of Shakespeare Publishing* (Cambridge: Cambridge University Press, 2003), 311–31; *New-York Mercury*, June 23, 1760, October 12, 1772.
11. "The Journal of Captain Thomas Morris," in Morris, *Miscellaneous Prose and Verse* (London: Printed for James Ridgway, 1791; repr. NY: Readex Microprint, 1966), 12, 16–17.
12. *New-York Mercury*, July 20, 1761, and repeated verbatim a week later; Hugh Amory and David D. Hall (eds.), *The Colonial Book in the Atlantic World* (Chapel Hill: University of North Carolina Press, 2000), 33–4 (in essay by Amory), 265–6, 279–83, 296 (in essay by James N. Green).
13. Hugh F. Rankin, *The Theater in Colonial America* (Chapel Hill: University of North Carolina Press, 1960), 12–25 (quotation on 23).
14. Johnson and Burling, *Colonial American Stage*, 106–7, 134, 136, 144, 148–50; *New York Gazette*, March 16–23, 1730.
15. Rankin, *Theater in Colonial America*, 25–9; Johnson and Burling, *Colonial American Stage*, 113–23.
16. Ibid. 128–32, 150–4, 158–62.
17. Ibid. 151–2, 159–60, 168, 173, 175; Charles H. Shattuck, *Shakespeare on the American Stage: From the Hallams to Edwin Booth* (Washington, DC: Folger Shakespeare Library, 1976), 3–5.
18. Johnson and Burling, *Colonial American Stage*, 184–5, 188–99, 207, 216. Garrick is quoted in Gary Taylor, *Reinventing Shakespeare: A Cultural History from the Restoration to the Present* (New York: Weidenfeld & Nicolson, 1989), 121.

19. Shattuck, *American Stage*, 13; Johnson and Burling, *Colonial American Stage*, 233, 243, 252, 255, 257–86 *passim*, 318, 359, 360, 365; *South Carolina Gazette*, May 30, 1774 (list of plays); *Rivington's New-York Gazette or Weekly Advertiser*, February 24, 1774 (quotation); Hennig Cohen, "Shakespeare in Charleston on the Eve of the Revolution," *Shakespeare Quarterly* 4 (1953), 329.
20. *Maryland Gazette*, September 6, 1770; Shattuck, *American Stage*, 13–15; Johnson and Burling, *Colonial American Stage*, 286–9, 299–354 *passim*.
21. The entire handbill is reproduced in Rankin, *Theater in Colonial America*, 94–5, and in Shattuck, *American Stage*, 12.
22. *Maryland Gazette*, September 6, 1770; William Eddis, *Letters from America*, ed. Aubrey C. Land (Cambridge, MA: Harvard University Press, 1969), 48, 55.
23. *Virginia Gazette*, November 10, 1752, November 17, 1752; *New-York Journal*, December 17, 1767, April 7, 1768.
24. Alden T. Vaughan, *Transatlantic Encounters: American Indians in Britain, 1500–1776* (New York: Cambridge University Press, 2006), 113, 126, 143, 158–9, 170–72, 174, 215–16; Rankin, *Theater in Colonial America*, 191; Cohen, "Shakespeare in Charleston," 329–30.
25. Johnson and Burling, *Colonial American Stage*, 66–8; *Independent Gazetteer, or Chronicle of Freedom*, July 14, 1787. For a succinct list of 17th- and 18th-century adaptations, see Michael Dobson, *The Making of the National Poet: Shakespeare, Adaptation and Authorship, 1660–1769* (Oxford: Clarendon Press, 1992), 262–4.
26. *Massachusetts Spy*, August 11–14, 1770; Frank Moore (ed.), *Diary of the American Revolution: From Newspapers and Original Documents* (2 vols, New York: Scribner, 1860), 1.169, quoting *Middlesex Journal* [London], January 30, 1776; *Pennsylvania Gazette*, March 27, 1776.
27. "The Association," in Henry Steele Commager (ed.), *Documents of American History*, 6th edn (New York: Appleton-Century-Crofts, 1958), 86; Ann Fairfax Withington, *Toward a More Perfect Union: Virtue and the Formation of American Republics* (New York: Oxford University Press, 1991), 20–91; Peter A. Davis, "Puritan Mercantilism and the Politics of Anti-theatrical Legislation in Colonial America," in Ron Engle and Tice L. Miller (eds.), *The American Stage: Social and Economic Issues from the Colonial Period to the Present* (Cambridge: Cambridge University Press, 1993), 18–32.
28. Silverman, *Cultural History*, 291–5; Jared Brown, *Theatre in America during the Revolution* (Cambridge: Cambridge University Press, 1995), 22–6 (quotation on 25).

29. Silverman, *Cultural History*, 333–7, 350, 364–5 (quotation from S. Adams); Brown, *Theatre during the Revolution*, 57–65 (quotation from French observer on 61), 174–5, 180–86.
30. *Virginia Gazette*, January 28, 1775; *New-York Gazette*, January 27, 1777; Brown, *Theatre during the Revolution*, 29–44, 90–91, 96–8, 173–8.
31. Ibid. 147–68, 179–87; Thomas Clark Pollock, *Philadelphia Theatre in the Eighteenth Century, Together with the Day Book of the Same Period* (Philadelphia: University of Pennsylvania Press, 1933), 137–43.
32. S. E. Wilmer, *Theatre, Society and the Nation: Staging American Identities* (Cambridge: Cambridge University Press, 2002), 18, repeats the *Julius Caesar* claim but is otherwise insightful. Performances of the plays are documented in John Ripley, *Julius Caesar on Stage in England and America, 1599–1973* (Cambridge: Cambridge University Press, 1980), and Brown, *Theatre during the Revolution*, 173–87.
33. Adams, *Diary and Autobiography*, 3:184–5 (quotation on 185); John Adams to John Quincy Adams, January 20, 1805, Abigail Adams to George Adams, August 7, 1815, Adams Papers, Massachusetts Historical Society; Esther Cloudman Dunn, *Shakespeare in America* (New York: Macmillan, 1939), 84–90.
34. Barbara A. Mowat, "The Founders and the Bard," *Yale Review* 97.4 (2009), 1–18 (quotation on 18).

2

Making Shakespeare American

New York City, May 7, 1849: Three performances of *Macbeth* vied for the public's attention. The Astor Place Opera House featured the great English actor William Charles Macready; the Broadway Theatre starred the dynamic American Edwin Forrest; and the Bowery, recently renamed the American Theatre, cast the popular English-bred performer and the theater's long-time manager, Thomas S. Hamblin, in the title role. These simultaneous stagings of one of Shakespeare's major dramas tell volumes about America's evolving theatrical culture. Most conspicuously, they demonstrate Shakespeare's importance to mid-nineteenth-century audiences, for surely no other author had ever had—or, most likely, has since had—such a tribute to his popularity. But the fact that two of the three lead actors were British-born and trained illustrates America's ongoing reliance on imported stars, even as Forrest's impressive list of Shakespearian and other roles and his unparalleled financial success signal the emergence of home-grown talent.

Seething below the surface of the rival performances was the animosity between Forrest and Macready and especially between their respective camps of supporters that was often—then and since—oversimplified as American egalitarians versus Anglophile snobs. But whatever the true causes of the animosity, it had frightful results. On the night in question, pro-Forrest ruffians so thoroughly disrupted Macready's performance that he fled for safety during the third act, while rioters ransacked the theater. That was only a foretaste. The Forrest–Macready rivalry exploded three nights later into one of the deadliest riots in theatrical history. Half a century earlier, the nascent American nation had displayed a genuine fondness for Shakespeare's plays without concern for who played the feature roles. No one, it's safe to assume, predicted that differences in an actor's nationality would by the 1840s foment such intensity and irrationality among many of Shakespeare's fans.

The theater, of course, was not the only place to measure Shakespeare's popularity or his admirers' zeal. His plays—and to a lesser extent his sonnets—had long been among Americans' favorite reading, and they would remain so. But as the young nation became increasingly self-conscious about its cultural accomplishments, an emerging scholarly community insisted on producing American editions of Shakespeare's works and eventually on making American contributions to Shakespeare criticism. Meanwhile, a great variety of American writers and speakers wove Shakespeare into their texts and hailed his genius in books, essays, and public lectures throughout the expanding nation. The "long nineteenth century" witnessed the embracing and remaking of Shakespeare into an American staple.

* * *

In the aftermath of national independence, expanding cosmopolitanism and commerce encouraged Americans to shed their puritanical impediments to the theater. A few pockets of hostility lingered, but by and large the new nation accepted the cultural standards of London—without, for the most part, acknowledging any indebtedness to the former mother country. With little fanfare, Philadelphia ended its prohibition on plays in 1789, and four years later Massachusetts suspended its law against plays and players; unofficial restraints also faded until Boston and Philadelphia matched New York and Charleston as America's foremost theatrical centers. Enlarged audiences everywhere caused old theaters to be refurbished and new ones to be built. Although the biggest and best equipped playhouses were still along the eastern seaboard, and the leading actors were still English itinerants, additional acting companies emerged to serve new cities to the west: Pittsburgh, Mobile, Cincinnati, St Louis, and dozens more. As new repertoires were established and old ones expanded, more American actors filled the supporting roles and a few experienced brief glory as regional stars, especially in the hinterland. Federalist America enjoyed a theatrical boom in which Shakespeare's plays were more vital than ever.

Some continuities with the colonial era lingered. The American Company had returned to the mainland from the Caribbean in 1784, playing mostly in New York, and lasted into the new century. When its leader since 1756, David Douglass, died in 1786, the company persisted under Lewis Hallam, Jr. and John Henry until 1806. But as Hallam aged, his roles gradually changed from Ferdinand, Petruchio, and Shylock, to Dogberry and similarly unglamorous parts, and his "Old School" style no longer drew critical acclaim. The other members of the once-dominant Hallam family also exited the stage, as new, younger actors assumed the major roles in Shakespearian and modern plays. Even the popular Nancy Hallam disappears from the theatrical records after the Revolution.

There was continuity too in the presence of American Indians in Federalist era audiences. At Philadelphia—the national capital during the 1790s—Indian delegations from far and wide observed the latest theatrical offerings, even if the English dialogue was barely comprehensible. Newspapers spurred public curiosity and increased profits by announcing that certain performances were "For the Entertainment of the Seneca Chiefs," or "By Request of the FARMER'S BROTHER, Head Chief of the Five Nations," or that "The Indian Chiefs will attend the Theatre This Evening, dressed in their Robes." In at least one instance, the delegation may have asked for Shakespeare: "By particular desire, and for the entertainment of the Chiefs of the Wyandot Indians," *Romeo and Juliet* was performed on January 22, 1798 at the handsome New Theatre at Chestnut and Sixth Streets where, six years earlier, Henry Jones's *Earl of Essex* had been performed "By Desire of the Indian Chiefs," with Garrick's *Florizel and Perdita* as the afterpiece.[1]

What American theaters needed near the end of the eighteenth century besides the slowly emerging generation of new performers were imaginatively run theatrical companies, especially at several large, new venues. Most notable were Philadelphia's Chestnut Street Theatre (1793), designed by John Inigo Richards of Covent Garden and improved by Benjamin Latrobe; Boston's Federal Street Theatre, designed by the eminent American architect Charles Bullfinch (1794); and New York's Park Street Theatre (1798), designed by the American

Joseph Mangin, though it is sometimes attributed to the notable French engineer Marc Isambard Brunel. All of the buildings were impressive in their day, and each was rebuilt and improved when fires, as frequently happened, destroyed the original structures. Boston's first major theater burned barely four years after it opened.[2] With new and better venues at hand, Americans could host a higher level of performance than they had witnessed in the colonial and Revolutionary eras.

In response to enlarged opportunities for profitable American tours, English actors steeped in Shakespeare began to cross the Atlantic for one or more seasons; some never went home. James Fennell, for example, arrived at Philadelphia in 1793. To avoid the city's yellow fever epidemic, he opened at Annapolis the next year, but soon played at the Chestnut Street Theatre and other prominent houses throughout the eastern states. Fennell's 6 ft. 6 in. height and strong voice were admirably suited to vigorous roles, especially Othello, which he had played at Covent Garden and repeated with considerable success in New York in 1799 and in various cities and towns for the next decade. His popularity earned unprecedented box office receipts. He also gave readings from Shakespeare and began a concordance to Shakespeare's works. By the time Fennell died in Philadelphia in 1816 at age 50, he had contributed significantly to the expansion of Shakespeare's primacy on the American stage.[3]

By then, two other actors of British birth and with considerable acting experience, mostly in the English provinces, vied with Fennell for top billing. In 1796 Anne Brunton Merry and Thomas Abthorpe Cooper arrived in Philadelphia on the same ship. Although Merry usually performed at the Chestnut Street Theatre, she also appeared in New York, Baltimore, and in September 1800 in the brand new federal capital, Washington, DC. Her leading roles, including Portia, Gertrude, Juliet, and Desdemona, earned high praise. Her voice "was all music," a contemporary recalled, her "face all emotion"; around the turn of the century, according to a leading theater historian, Merry was "America's leading actress, so excellent in her art as frequently to rob the critics of all but superlatives."[4] Merry was also—like several other leading British actors—adept at theatrical management. After the death in 1803 of her second husband, the transplanted British actor/manager Thomas Wignell, Anne Brunton Merry Wignell shared the control of the Chestnut Street Theatre until her own death in 1808. Thomas Cooper, in the meantime, initially appeared in Philadelphia but toured as far west as New Orleans before settling at New York's Park Theatre, where he was the manager for several years. Cooper remained on the stage until the 1830s, when he swapped the theatrical life for a political sinecure and a glamorous role in New York society. Yet Cooper, like Fennell and Merry before him, had boosted Shakespeare's reputation in eastern America by performing thirty roles in seventeen Shakespeare plays, including Hamlet, Macbeth, Iago, Romeo, Coriolanus, King John, and most notably Othello, which he first acted in 1805 in Providence, Rhode Island, "in Moorish costume," to the vehement disapproval of the critics. With slavery still legal in most of the United States and Rhode Island heavily involved in the slave trade, audiences expected Othello to wear the customary Venetian gentleman's or military officer's garb.[5]

By the early nineteenth century, even major British stars trekked to the new nation. Despite a sterling career in provincial and London theaters, George Frederick Cooke's addiction to alcohol sometimes marred his performances or forced their cancellation. The actor-impresario Thomas Cooper, on a trip to England in 1810, signed the 55-year old Cooke to a three-year tour of eastern America, where his fame would almost guarantee handsome profits. With Cooke's health revived by forty-three days at sea (the ship ran out of liquor), he opened in New York in *King Richard III* before an audience of 2200—reputed, according to Cooke, "to be the greatest house ever known in America." Although Cooke was occasionally befuddled by drink in subsequent performances, he was usually sober and thoroughly rehearsed. In every city on the tour—New York, Philadelphia, Baltimore, Boston, and Providence—he attracted long ticket lines.

Americans had never witnessed such impressive acting. "After the tedious, monotonous syllabizing, dead march speechifying, to which this country has hitherto been so much accustomed," one critic enthused, Cooke's "natural acting and familiar colloquial speech" set a new standard. The *Boston Gazette* hailed Cooke as "the finest actor England can produce." Not every play in his repertoire was by Shakespeare, of course, but ten were. Cooke dazzled audiences as

Shylock, Iago, Macbeth, King Lear, Falstaff (in *Henry IV* and *The Merry Wives of Windsor*), as well as America's favorite villain, Richard III. (Fig. 2.1) The celebrated novelist Washington Irving watched Cooke's Macbeth "with admiration and delight" and thought it "among the highest pieces of acting I have ever witnessed."[6]

Cooke's tour began in 1810 and lasted, with a summer break in 1811, through July 1812. His final nine performances, which included Shylock, Richard III, Macbeth, Lear, and Falstaff, were in Providence, where the actor seemed to be in good health and regularly walked the

Figure 2.1. George Frederick Cooke as Richard III, based on a painting by Thomas Sully. By permission of the Folger Shakespeare Library.

three-quarters of a mile between the theater and his lodging. He was, in fact, very ill, cut short his tour, and died that September of cirrhosis of the liver at his New York apartment over Mechanics Hall tavern. The city's flags were lowered to half staff; his funeral was attended by many of New York's political and cultural dignitaries, including the governor and the mayor. His body was interred in the Strangers' Vault at St Paul's Church, but in 1821 the eminent British actor Edmund Kean, who had arrived in New York the year before, caused Cooke's casket to be moved to a more respectful location and an impressive monument to be erected at the site. The tribute was well deserved. Cooke's popularity had encouraged the enlargement of theaters in Boston and Philadelphia, and he had almost single-handedly added Providence to America's theatrical circuit. He had performed 160 times in less than two full seasons, of which a remarkable 98 were in Shakespearian roles—a huge stimulus to American appreciation of the theater in general and Shakespeare in particular. Cooke, moreover, had demonstrated that Americans need not settle for "dead . . . speechifying."

Edmund Kean was brilliant but controversial. By 1820 he was the leading actor of his day, but he equaled Cooke in addiction to alcohol and exceeded him in wenching, reckless habits, and boorish behavior. Although the American press initially disliked Kean's arrogance and histrionic style, he mesmerized audiences in America as he had in Britain. Despite his short stature (5 ft. 4 in.), Kean filled the stage with dynamic energy, agility of movement, and fluctuations of voice. The English-American actress Fanny Kemble, whose father played many of the same Shakespeare roles, pronounced Kean to be "a man of genius . . . [who] with a word, a look, a gesture, tears away the veil from the heart of our common humanity. . . . Kean speaks with his whole living frame to us, and every fiber of ours answers his appeal."[7]

Kean opened his American career, as did so many touring Britons, in *Richard III*, and quickly silenced the newspaper critics. For the next year, he played great Shakespearian roles—Othello, Shylock, Hamlet, Macbeth, King Lear, and Richard III—at the best playhouses in New York, Philadelphia, Baltimore, and Boston. But in the last, in May 1821, Kean notoriously insulted the unusually small audience that turned out for his Richard III by refusing to perform and refusing to apologize, thus igniting a firestorm of criticism throughout the eastern United States. A fortnight later he sailed to England, only to return again to America when his private life turned so openly to public scandal that he was shunned in London and the provinces. In November 1825 he again opened in New York in *Richard III*, and after weathering an initially rocky reception, regained much of his popularity.

But not in Boston, where Kean's insult still festered. Although he apologized in a newspaper essay for his refusal to perform in 1821 and attempted to apologize to the first-night audience, much of that audience arrived with its mind made up. He was yelled at and pelted mercilessly. Kean fled the theater while pro-Kean and anti-Kean factions battled each other and almost demolished the building. After Kean enjoyed some success in New York, Philadelphia, and Charleston, Baltimore rioters ended his United States tour. By 1827 he was back in London, where he encountered sympathetic audiences. A transatlantic rivalry, sometimes violent, had been launched. American audiences appreciated fine Shakespearian performances, but visiting actors must conform to American notions of theatrical propriety or endure incredibly crude abuse, both verbal and physical.

The rivalry would come to a head in New York nearly a quarter century later. Kean was long since dead, and many of the Boston and Baltimore rioters must have been also. Filling their places were new leading actors from both sides of the Atlantic and a more fractious theater-going population. Goading them on were more vociferous newspapers, eager to exploit national and international tensions, and more openly partisan crowds, especially in New York.

Kean had had no American rival. His competition for theatrical stardom in the United States came from other English itinerants such as Thomas Cooper, James William Wallack, and Mary Ann Duff, who were not nearly his equal. By contrast, William Charles Macready, whose first American tour began in 1826, had to contend with Edwin Forrest, a Philadelphia-born actor who honed his style in the American hinterland (Vincennes, New Orleans, Albany) until 1826, when, at age 21, he had his New York debut at the Park Street Theatre in *Othello*. Eight years later Forrest sailed to Europe. By then, he was probably the wealthiest actor in the world and immensely popular throughout the eastern United States, where, it was said, his name graced "fire companies and militia units, . . . steamboats, racehorses, and locomotives." In London, when his initial performance was received ambivalently—the audience admired his vigor but disliked his choice of *The Gladiator*'s Spartacus rather than one of Shakespeare's great characters—Forrest responded with a blockbuster Othello. That performance pleased many critics but not a caustic journalist and friend of William Charles Macready, John Forster. While Macready in fact admired Forrest's performances and genuinely befriended the American, Forrest suspected that Macready was behind Forster's strident slurs. "Not a single ray of the genius of Shakespeare's wonderful Macbeth," read a representative Forster review, "flickered upon Mr Forrest from the commencement to the close." To Forster, Edwin Forrest looked at times like "a savage newly caught from out of the American backwoods."[8]

Such sentiments reflected a growing tension between Britain and America. In the two decades after the last Anglo-American war (1812–15), a general rapprochement had prevailed, but by the 1830s it was in tatters. Contentions over the boundary between Canada and the United States in the northeast, and between those nations and Spain in the northwest, revived calls for military action, egged on by recent waves of ardently anti-British Irish immigrants. On the cultural front, virulent public criticism of Americans by British visitors such as Frances Trollope (*Domestic Manners of the Americans*, 1832), Frederick Marryat (*Diary in America*, 1840), and Charles Dickens (*American Notes*, 1842; *Martin Chuzzlewit*, 1843), heightened a widespread British belief that Americans were incredibly boorish. "I do not like them," Mrs. Trollope concluded. "I do not like their principles, I do not like their manners, I do not like their opinions." Americans who resented such judgments decided that Britons were effete snobs.[9] Competing performances of Shakespearian roles became a microcosm of the Anglo-American feud.

In 1843 Macready arrived in America for the second time. Forrest greeted him warmly and entertained him often, but their fans preferred to see the actors as rivals. And professional rivals they became—England's "Eminent Tragedian" versus America's "National Tragedian"—traveling from city to city, often playing the same roles, sometimes on the same nights, with Forrest purposely following a step behind but offering more robust—more American—performances. American audiences (but not, generally, British audiences) loved Forrest's vehement speeches, his roaring interjections, his "hideous looks and furious gestures"; they neither noticed nor cared that Forrest's lacked the "refined sensibility" that distinguished most British acting. By the time Macready returned to England in 1844, audiences were taking sides, especially when Forrest launched his second tour of Britain in early 1845, seemingly an extension of the stalking policy he had adopted the previous year in America. And once again, Forrest blamed the tepid critical reception he received in England on Macready and especially Forster, whereas the fundamental reasons were antagonistic national loyalties and a recognition by most theater-goers in Britain and some in America that Macready was the more thoughtful and skillful actor. Forrest's rude reaction to his rival's success was to hiss loudly at Macready's performance of Hamlet in 1846 at the Edinburgh Theatre Royal and, astoundingly, to defend his action in a letter to the London *Times*. He was entitled to express his opinion of any actor's performance, Forrest insisted, by applauding the good and hissing the bad. Macready, he declared, had desecrated a scene in *Hamlet* by introducing "a fancy dance." The British press and public were outraged; the American press and public, on balance, defended Forrest.[10]

The showdown came on May 10, 1849 in New York, when a boisterous mob of Forrest's supporters refused to let Macready, early in his third American tour, complete *Macbeth* at the aristocratic Astor Place Opera House. The "Bowery Boys"—armed with vegetables, eggs, and insults—drove Macready from the stage, while an angry mob on the outside hurled paving bricks into the building. With thousands of rioters out of control, New York militiamen fired above the crowd but not high enough. At least 22 people died, many of them bystanders (the precise number has never been determined), and many more were wounded.[11] Macready fled to Boston and then to England and never returned. But Forrest had won a Pyrrhic victory. Despite the cheers of American Anglophobes, many moulders of American cultural opinion condemned Forrest and his supporters for disgracing the city and nation. Forrest continued to act and to draw partisan praise, but his sun was setting. The public was growing tired of disrupted performances and annoyed by histrionic acting. A more subtle, natural style, represented by yet another British itinerant, Junius Brutus Booth, was rapidly gaining favor.

Booth had arrived in the United States in 1821, only a year after Edmund Kean, whom he resembled in stature, appearance, and acting style, and with whom he had developed a bitter competition. Unlike Kean, Booth went to America to stay, having just abandoned his first wife and young son. Avoiding the limelight, Booth played for many years in the southern states but eventually made brief appearances in New York, Boston, and Philadelphia; more often he acted farther west—Pittsburgh, Nashville, New Orleans—and after the Gold Rush of the late 1840s, he performed briefly but to great applause in San Francisco. His death in 1852 on his way back east ended prematurely a career marked by great achievement but troubled by alcohol and insanity. Like many actors of his time, Booth was best known for his Shakespearian roles. Although he was adept in most of them, he excelled as the villainous Richard III, Macbeth, Shylock, and Iago rather than the flawed but heroic Hamlet, Othello, and Lear.[12]

Junius Brutus Booth, Sr. was in several respects a transitional figure. Although of English birth and training, he was an American by choice for most of his career. He was a long-time resident of the East, as were most major actors of that era, but his stage appearances spanned the continent. And, especially important for his adopted nation, he founded a theatrical dynasty that lessened the American theater's dependency on visiting British stars. British actors would continue to play on American stages to the present day, of course, but the era of almost total dependence on visiting talent to give American audiences high-quality Shakespeare ended not long after the Astor Place riot brought the Anglo-American rivalry to its bloody climax and, almost simultaneously, the Booth family's second generation of theatrical stars emerged.

The eldest son, Junius Brutus Booth, Jr. (usually called June), was better known as a theater manager and producer of shows than as an actor. His brother Edwin Thomas Booth also excelled at management, notably at the Winter Garden Theatre in New York City and the Walnut Street Theatre in Philadelphia, of which he was a co-owner. But Edwin was also a great actor, perhaps the best of his era, especially in "intellectual" roles such as Hamlet, Richard III, and Iago; while the youngest brother, John Wilkes Booth, who resented Edwin's success and argued bitterly with him about politics, gradually received recognition for his strong supporting roles and eventually for leading roles. On November 25, 1864 at the Winter Garden, the three brothers acted together for the only time (Fig. 2.2). It was a fateful

Figure 2.2. A photograph of (left to right) John Wilkes Booth as Mark Antony, Edwin Booth as Brutus, and Junius Brutus Booth, Jr. as Cassius in *Julius Caesar*, November 25, 1864. TS932.4F., vol. 2. Harvard Theatre Collection, Houghton Library, Harvard University.

event. In *Julius Caesar* Edwin played Brutus, June played Cassius, and John played Mark Antony, as their mother watched from the audience. The play was an artistic and financial success, raising $35,000 toward a statue of Shakespeare to be erected in New York's Central Park. But for John Wilkes Booth, who would assassinate President Abraham Lincoln at Ford's Theatre in Washington less than five months later, the drama's lasting message was the righteousness of deposing a tyrant, which the pro-South, pro-slavery actor believed Lincoln to be. During the next few months, John joined a conspiracy to abduct—and, nearer the event, to kill—the President and several members of his administration.

Lincoln, as many of his contemporaries knew, was also deeply influenced by Shakespeare, especially from his frequent reading of *Macbeth* and other tragedies. He had admired and absorbed the plays since early adulthood, both by reading—usually aloud—and by attending performances before and during his presidency, and there is abundant testimony that Lincoln had Shakespeare on his mind in his final days. A French diplomat who, five days before the murder, accompanied Lincoln from Richmond, Virginia, to Washington recalled: "Mr. Lincoln read to us for several hours passages taken from Shakespeare. Most of these were from *Macbeth*, and, in particular, the verses which follow Duncan's assassination." Among the lines Lincoln read and reread on that occasion were almost certainly "Better be with the dead/Whom we, to gain our peace, have sent to peace,/Than on torture of the mind to lie/In restless ecstasy" (III.ii.21–4). Although Lincoln is not known to have voiced the idea explicitly, he seems to have brooded over the play's implication that one should forfeit his life for having caused others to lose theirs. Two days later, Lincoln had a prophetic nightmare about his own death, a recurring dream, Lincoln said, that "has got possession of me, and like Banquo's ghost, it will not down." Nor would Shakespeare's lessons leave the fugitive Booth alone. His journal in the days after the assassination, while he frantically fled his pursuers, repeatedly invoked both *Julius Caesar* and *Macbeth* as he attempted to justify his heinous deed.[13]

Booth's family was shocked and embarrassed by John Wilkes's crime. Edwin, who had recently completed an unprecedented one-hundred performance run of *Hamlet*, immediately retired from the stage. But Edwin needed money. Perceiving that the public cast no blame on him for his brother's actions, in 1866 Edwin Booth returned triumphantly to the New York stage and resumed his stellar acting and managing careers. After a disastrous fire at the Winter Garden, Booth opened his own elegant and theatrically up-to-date Booth's Theatre at Sixth Avenue and 23rd Street, with a proscenium arch featuring Shakespeare's coat of arms and a statue of him with quill in hand. The initial performance was of *Romeo and Juliet*, with Edwin Booth and Mary McVicker, whom he later married, in the title roles. But despite Booth's acting and managerial skills, his shortcomings as a businessman proved disastrous, and in the Panic of 1873 he lost control of his own theater. A decade later it was demolished, but not before Edwin (if legend can be trusted), on a midnight visit to the basement, burned the remainder of John Wilkes's costumes, props, and personal papers—everything except his brother's racist rant of 1860.[14]

* * *

While Kean and Macready and the senior Booth were presenting the best of British Shakespeare to Americans, a handful of American actors displayed their talents in the British Isles. The trailblazer was James Henry Hackett, initially a comic actor from upstate New York who mimicked other comedians and sometimes serious actors. Hackett's first Shakespearian role, in New York City in 1826, was Dromio of Ephesus in *The Comedy of Errors*, in which he precisely and hilariously imitated the other Dromio. Two years later Hackett turned to Falstaff with so much success that he clung to the part for the rest of his career, though in the 1840s he attempted, far less successfully, Hamlet and Lear. Americans loved his Falstaff; Britons, who hosted him in 1827 and several times thereafter, were less enthusiastic, though they thoroughly enjoyed Hackett's caricatures of "shrewd or loutish American Originals." His Sir John Falstaff, British critics contended, was superficial, moralizing, and surprisingly dull. Hackett, who craved the approval of upper-class Britons, had to settle instead for praise from American dignitaries such as John Quincy Adams and Abraham Lincoln.[15]

Britons reacted more favorably to Boston's Charlotte Cushman. This failed opera singer found her métier on the stage, especially as

Lady Macbeth, a role in which she debuted in New Orleans on Shakespeare's birthday in 1836. After many years in New York and Philadelphia (where she also managed the Walnut Street Theatre), Cushman's big break came in 1843 at Boston when William Charles Macready asked her to play opposite him in *Macbeth*. Although the stage manager's daughter was instead given the part, Cushman learned from watching Macready act and eventually performed with him in Boston, New York, and Philadelphia. Then, at Macready's request, Cushman went to London, where she played Emilia to his Othello and Lady Macbeth to his Macbeth and bested him, according to some critics, in both plays. In the following years, divided between England and America, Cushman was a major attraction, performing many times with Macready, Forrest, and other male stars. Her tall stature and deep, strong voice were congenial also to breeches roles, especially Romeo, which she often played opposite her sister Susan's Juliet. "Never was courtship more fervent," one English reviewer proclaimed, "more apparently sincere, more reverential, and yet more impetuously passionate, than that which . . . ascended to Juliet's window." Cushman also played *King Henry VIII*'s Cardinal Wolsey and even Hamlet, which she acted several times in England and America. Cushman's performance of Queen Katherine in *Henry VIII* was generally considered her finest role.[16]

Virtually ignored by American critics but often praised in Britain and continental Europe was Cushman's contemporary, the African American Ira Aldridge. He started his theatrical career at the African Grove Theatre in lower Manhattan, where Shakespeare's plays were frequently performed by African Americans. In about 1823 Aldridge became a dresser for the touring English actor Henry Wallack and in 1824 accompanied Wallack's brother James to England as a personal servant, a position he quickly left. In London, Aldridge found a few non-Shakespearian roles for a black actor (the title role in Thomas Southerne's *Oroonoko*, for example), and soon was playing Othello in the provinces. Disguised in a wig and white body paint, he also played Shylock, Lear, and other "white" roles. Although Aldridge performed Othello at Covent Garden in 1833 to mixed reviews, the manager bowed to prevailing prejudice and cancelled the rest of the run.[17]

Determined to remain on the stage, Aldridge returned to the provinces, where he was appreciated as "the Negro tragedian," and in 1852 took his talents eastward to the Continent. In western and central Europe, the response to his acting was so favorable that he spent the balance of his career touring Europe, save for periodic returns to provincial Britain—but never to the United States. In Belgium, Hungary, Germany, Austria, Poland, Sweden, and Russia (Aldridge spoke English on stage, while the rest of the cast used the local language) he was lionized. Nation after nation bestowed its highest honors on the American actor who could not perform in America despite his mastery of major Shakespearian roles—not only Othello and *Titus Andronicus*' Aaron. Aldridge became a British citizen in 1863 and died in Poland in 1867, but knowledgeable Americans, especially African Americans, aware of his international success and New York roots, numbered the expatriate among the most influential promoters of Shakespeare in non-Anglophone nations. And like Edwin Forrest, James Henry Hackett, and Charlotte Cushman, Ira Aldridge demonstrated that by the middle of the nineteenth century, some American actors, including a few from African American communities, were skillful enough to perform Shakespeare abroad.

While touring British stars were dominating American stages and a few American actors were cheered abroad, other actors gained local recognition, such as John Howard Payne, a popular early Hamlet in East Coast theaters before he went to England in 1813, John R. Scott, who briefly rivaled the rising Edwin Forrest, and the melodramatic J. Hudson Kirby. Among female performers, Josephine Clifton ("the magnificent Josephine") played opposite Forrest in the early 1840s and was reputed to be as sturdy and nearly as talented as Charlotte Cushman, but her impressive career was ended by early death. Anna Cora Mowatt, who had read all of Shakespeare by age 10, was a popular playwright and actor throughout the 1840s and 50s. By then, Edward Loomis Davenport had emerged as a reliable (though unemotional, some critics complained) native-born performer who toured for a season with Mrs Mowatt in America and for two seasons in Britain. Back in America he starred for a decade or so as Hamlet, Brutus, and other major Shakespearian characters. Without such versatile actors, the pervasive demand for Shakespearian drama could not have been filled. In lead roles in cities and towns away from the metropolises, and in supporting roles to the great visiting

British actors at the major playhouses along the eastern seaboard, American born-and-bred thespians were essential to the ever-growing Shakespeare industry. A sign of their significance appeared in 1854–6: A lavish three-volume edition of Shakespeare's works, published in New York, featured dozens of engravings of "celebrated American actors, drawn from life," including, to cite a few examples, the unquestionably celebrated Forrest, Cushman, and Hackett in several roles (Fig. 2.3), but also many of the less prominent men and women of the antebellum American stage whose names no longer resonate.[18]

* * *

Although many Americans read Shakespeare's plays instead of—or in addition to—seeing them performed, the readers' texts often differed markedly from the actors' scripts. As in pre-Revolutionary America and Britain, the available editions of Shakespearian dramas in the late eighteenth and early nineteenth centuries, whether single plays or collected works, adhered quite closely to Shakespeare's quartos and folios; the newer editions differed especially in their annotations and ancillary materials. (Notable exceptions were John Bell's "acting editions" of 1773–4 and later, which reproduced the current stage versions.) Especially popular with American readers were English editions by Samuel Johnson and George Steevens, who succeeded their comprehensive ten-volume edition of 1773 with a new version in 1778, which in turn was revised by a heretofore unheralded editor, Isaac Reed, in 1785, the year after Johnson's death. But despite the Johnson–Steevens–Reed text's success, it had lively competition from updated versions of several older editions, and soon from Edmond Malone's of 1790.

In the absence of enforceable copyright protection, American printers were now free to reprint or rebind British editions with impunity and perhaps with profit, as Hugh Gaine may have done in 1761 with *The Tempest* and *King Lear.* Yet bibliographers' diligent scouring of printers' catalogues, library holdings, estate inventories, and newspaper advertisements have uncovered very few American imprints. After Gaine's possible contribution, there is a void until the 1780s, when there seems to have been a Philadelphia reprint of an adaptation of *The Comedy of Errors*, originally published in Edinburgh in 1780 (no copy has been found), and in 1794 the manager of

Figure 2.3. James Henry Hackett as Falstaff in *The Complete Works of Shakespeare*, featuring illustrations of "*celebrated American actors*" (1854–56). By permission of the Folger Shakespeare Library.

the first Boston theater printed abridged versions of Bell's Acting Editions of *Hamlet* and *Twelfth Night.* Not until 1795 did an edition appear that was forthrightly "American," and even that publication relied heavily on English materials. The anonymous new edition of Shakespeare's works has been attributed to a Philadelphia lawyer, Joseph Hopkinson, who cobbled together a slightly revised text by Samuel Ayscough, a British Museum librarian and author of the first Shakespeare concordance (1790), with Hopkinson's preface and very brief life of Shakespeare, a glossary largely plagiarized from a Scottish edition of 1792, and a sparse selection of notes by Samuel Johnson. The claim to Americanness rested on its being typeset and printed in Philadelphia and on local craftsmanship: "[T]he editors have exerted themselves as much as possible, by an elegant type and good paper, to do credit to the American press."[19] Americans could now keep the profits and take some pride in publishing Shakespeare on their side of the Atlantic.

Most subsequent editions out of Philadelphia, Boston, and New York for the next several decades followed Hopkinson's general pattern. In order to show *some* originality, most American editors—if that term can be applied to compilers of unauthorized reprints—chose a British edition different from the ones used by their immediate predecessors. Thus the first Boston edition (1802–7) was based on an Edinburgh edition of 1792, rather than Ayscough's, with notes from Johnson's edition of 1773 and the text of Shakespeare's poems from Bell's 1774 edition, which had in turn been taken from a flagrantly unreliable British edition. With so much reliance on other men's work, the Boston edition could be reasonably priced: each half-volume of about 200 pages, as it came off the press, cost subscribers 38 cents, non-subscribers 50 cents. Eventually, bound copies of individual plays sold for 25 cents. Most of the approximately 350 subscribers lived in Boston or its vicinity; many were affiliated with Harvard College, as were the subscribers to a second edition of the same set in 1807–9. A third Boston edition (1810–12) pretty much saturated the New England market. Assuming, as does the premier authority on early American editions, a press run of about 3,000 copies for each of the Boston editions, New England, with its relatively educated population, was a bastion of Shakespeare readership.[20]

Cost was also an important consideration to the compilers of another multivolume American edition. While a twenty-one-volume London edition was selling for $51, Joseph Dennie of Philadelphia announced that his would be half that price. Although based on the Johnson–Steevens–Reed edition of 1785, it would also be more original than its American predecessors and many of the English editions because Dennie, with help from other literary scholars, would add some annotations of his own. But the project went awry. Dennie's intention to publish one volume per month collapsed, largely because of multiple moves from one printing house to another, and the quality of some volumes did not match his promise of superior "neatness of mechanical execution" and a high degree of "fidelity and correctness." Yet Dennie persevered, and after five years' labor (1805–9) seventeen volumes were in print. Although it has been dubbed "the first American variorum" of Shakespeare's plays, Dennie's ambitious project falls short of the usual definition of a variorum as a text that includes the important notes by previous editors and explains variant readings of ambiguous words or passages.[21] In any case, it was a commercial failure.

During the next several decades, American editors and publishers of Shakespeare increased the tempo of new editions of single plays and collected works. Most of those editions remained heavily dependent on British texts, especially after 1817, when stereotype printing permitted the same pages to be reproduced again and again from metal plates that precisely duplicated the originals. The plates themselves, moreover, could be passed from publisher to publisher—for a suitable fee—so that the basic Shakespeare text remained the same, regardless of changes in ownership and variations in ancillary materials, including illustrations, and in packaging, which ranged from a single volume of the works to ten or more volumes. The first stereotype imprint of Shakespeare's works, published in New York in 1817, was reissued in 1818; another printer used the plates in 1821 and issued annual editions from 1823 to 1826; still another printer ran off an edition in 1835. At some point Harper and Brothers acquired the plates and issued at least eight editions of Shakespeare's works between 1839 and 1868. Also available to buyers in the United States were American imprints made from other stereotype plates, beginning with a Boston edition of 1836 based on a London edition of 1826.

Surviving evidence about the prices of the stereotype printings suggests that they were significantly cheaper than imported editions or reset local editions. And although no total sales figures for the many American imprints of Shakespeare are known, the sheer number of editions between 1795 and the 1860s—nearly 250, including reprints, have been identified, fifteen of them in the year 1850 alone—points to a remarkable demand for inexpensive versions of Shakespeare's writings that parallels the Shakespeare boom on the American stage. Shakespeare had become America's favorite playwright in print as well as performance, but always through books that were substantively more British than American.

* * *

America's lack of scholarly originality is largely explained by shortages of the necessary tools. American libraries lacked the quarto and folio editions for establishing Shakespeare's probable intentions, the manuscripts and rare books for reconstructing Shakespeare's sources and his life and times, and the community of scholars for debating new findings and theories and encouraging each others' endeavors. The practical effect of these shortcomings was an absence of men and women who spent the bulk of their adult lives engrossed in Shakespearian literature. Many Americans read and watched the plays; very few studied them.

A sea change came between the mid-1840s and the mid-1860s. During that span, three American editors issued multi-volume sets that not only printed accurate and thoughtful texts but also incorporated the fruits of serious Shakespeare scholarship based on rare books that had finally become available on the western side of the Atlantic. In those same years, a few well-read American commentators who were not editors published perceptive books or essays on Shakespeare. The nucleus of American Shakespeare criticism emerged.

In 1844–7 the New York lawyer, journalist, and (briefly) politician Gulian Crommelin Verplanck published three volumes—one each of Shakespeare's histories, tragedies, and comedies. Although Verplanck, like his American predecessors, took his text from an English edition, in this instance the recent one by John Payne Collier (1842–4), he reverted to early texts for many readings, and crafted explanatory notes from Collier's and his own interpretations. Verplanck also made original contributions to establishing the chronological sequence in which, he believed, the plays had been written, and although his publisher insisted on using the conventional organization of the three volumes based on the folios, Verplanck's introduction offered readers the option of having their copies printed according to Verplanck's preferred order. Few did. While Verplanck was not a Shakespeare scholar in today's sense of the term, his rigorous and often original editing set him apart from previous American editors and put him on a par with many in Britain. Had the plates for Verplanck's edition not been destroyed by a fire at Harper and Brothers offices in 1853, it might have retained much longer a leading position in the American market.

Instead, the edition by Henry Norman Hudson, published in eleven volumes between 1851 and 1856, briefly became the American standard. The remarkably versatile Hudson—farmer, coach-maker, school teacher, Episcopal clergyman, Civil War chaplain, and public lecturer—was one of the earliest Americans to make a living by teaching Shakespeare. Yet originality was not Hudson's strong suit; rather, he produced a solid compilation of the best foreign and American scholarship, with useful introductions to each play. His text relied on the English edition of S.W. Singer, which in turn was a revision of older English texts "carefully restored to the first editions." Hudson's edition would have a fairly long life in a revised version in 1871 and enjoy a rebirth in 1881 as the "Harvard Shakespeare."

Close on Hudson's heels was Richard Grant White, a New York journalist but lifelong student of Shakespeare. Volumes 2 through 11 of White's twelve-volume edition appeared between 1857 and 1861, while the final volume (meant to be number 1) was delayed by the Civil War until 1866. Availing himself of the impressive private libraries of Thomas Pennant Barton, the first serious American collector of Shakespeariana, and James Lenox, a more eclectic collector (Barton's books are now at the Boston Public Library, Lenox's at the New York Public Library), White based his text on the First Folio and on quartos for the plays not in the Folio. White's editorial notes, though brief, drew on a thorough assessment of the best English and American annotations. The result was an edition, the American critic James Russell Lowell observed, that has "almost the value of a *variorum*."[22]

White's scholarly reputation rested largely on his meticulous edition of Shakespeare's works (reprinted in 1883 as the "Riverside Edition") and a thoughtful biography of the writer in volume 1 (1865), and also on his early exposure of the forgeries of John Payne Collier. That English journalist, lawyer, and esteemed scholar published several books in the 1830s based partly on forged manuscripts that Collier himself had surreptitiously inserted in reputable collections, and his early 1840s edition of Shakespeare's works was well respected. Had he stopped there, his skulduggery might never have been discovered—at least in his lifetime. But in 1852 Collier claimed to possess a copy of the Second Folio (1632) that contained thousands of seventeenth-century annotations and emendations, many of which he incorporated into a new edition of the works (1853). White recognized immediately that certain words and phrases from the ostensible 1632 marginalia could only have been written much later. Assuming that Collier himself had been duped, White attacked the integrity of the Folio annotations and emendations, not Collier himself, in two articles in 1853 and a book in 1854. Meanwhile, English scholars raised technical questions about the manuscripts "discovered" by Collier as well as the 1632 folio, such as anachronisms in paper, ink, and handwriting. During half a dozen years' debate among scholars on both sides of the Atlantic, White's evidence was increasingly accepted. (Only after Collier's death in 1883 was his guilt irrefutably established.[23]) Although Richard Grant White had been a cautious but effective literary detective, he is nowadays more often cited for his advice to novice readers of Shakespeare: "[T]he first rule—and it is absolute and without exception, a rare rule indeed—is to read him only. Throw the commentators and editors to the dogs. Don't read any man's notes, or essays, or introductions.... Don't read mine. Read the plays themselves."[24]

* * *

The abundance and perspicacity of White's labors finally brought international respect to American Shakespeare scholarship. Americans had now at least one high-quality edition of Shakespeare's works, one reliable biography of Shakespeare's life, and one critic who ranked with the world's best. But although White was the leading light of antebellum American criticism, he was not completely alone. Before a new era in American politics and culture emerged near the end of the nineteenth century, several Americans contributed, however modestly, to Shakespeare studies through public lectures and published essays and books.

Several of Shakespeare's publicists were actors or editors. James Henry Hackett, for one, capped his long career with a catch-all book of *Notes, Criticism, and Correspondence upon Shakespeare's Plays and Actors* (1863), which remains valuable to the present day for his descriptions of the performance techniques of the great actors of his time, even if his chapters on Shakespearian characters—Hamlet, Lear—were unimaginative. Other actors who gave public readings from the plays or lectures on Shakespearian topics included Edwin Forrest, James E. Murdock, and especially Charlotte Cushman, of whom a publicity brochure in 1874 proclaimed, "'Cushman Readings' are as notable as 'Cushman Performances'." The most widely heard and read of the Shakespeare editors was surely the multi-talented H. N. Hudson, who spoke publicly about Shakespeare before and after he edited the complete works. As early as the 1840s, Hudson gave lectures that he subsequently published in his edition of the plays and separately in two volumes in 1848; in 1872 he published a two-volume biography of Shakespeare. Although Hudson's printed lectures have not stood the test of time in either substance or style, this "scholarly popularizer" undoubtedly persuaded many students and segments of the general public to enjoy Shakespeare, partly because the spoken lectures were lively, featuring, said a contemporary, "a kind of volcanic energy" that included "gestures, contortions and gyrations" as well as a thorough knowledge of the texts and the latest European and American criticism.[25]

Equally salient in enlightening Americans about Shakespeare were lectures and essays by men and women who were not primarily involved in performing or publishing Shakespeare's works. A list of such cultural spokespersons would include Richard Henry Dana, author of *Two Years before the Mast* (1840) and other nautical works, who spoke eloquently about Shakespeare in several eastern cities and to whom Hudson dedicated his *Lectures on Shakspeare.* Far more influential in the long run was the Massachusetts philosopher and essayist Ralph Waldo Emerson, who lectured around the United States and abroad in the 1840s on six of western civilization's "representative geniuses": Plato, Swedenborg, Montaigne, Napoleon, Goethe, and Shakespeare, each of whom, Emerson argued, exemplified a different human quality. Shakespeare was the greatest "Poet and Philosopher." In 1850 the essays were published as *Representative Men* and thereafter reached an even wider audience. Yet however much Emerson admired Shakespeare in print, he did not enjoy him in performance, even when acted by the inestimable Edwin Booth. Emerson's puritan heritage seems to have blunted his ability to appreciate the theater, its actors, and its literature. He attended very few plays of any kind, and lamented that Shakespeare's most acclaimed writings were dramas.

Yet Emerson idolized Shakespeare. Although a few of Emerson's comments have led critics to doubt his wholehearted belief in Shakespeare's greatness, his voluminous journals and especially the chapter in *Representative Men* (and the lectures that preceded and followed its publication) are emphatically praiseful. Emerson regretted that "the best poet led an obscure and profane life," but that did not, in Emerson's eyes, lessen the man's literary merit and influence. "No brain has dallied with finer imaginings than Shakespeare," he mused in his journal in 1853. Earlier, in the published version of his essay on the poet, he specified in the Romantic language of his era some achievements of the man he considered "inconceivably wise." Shakespeare

> wrote the text of modern life; the text of manners; he drew the man of England and Europe; the father of the man in America: he drew the man, and described the day, and what is done in it; he read the hearts of men and women, their probity, and their second thought, and wiles; the wiles of innocence, and the transitions by which virtues and vices slide into their contraries: he could divide the mother's part from the father's part in the face of the child, or draw the fine demarcations of freedom and of fate: . . . and all the sweets and all the terrors of human lot lay in his mind as truly but as softly as the landscape lies on the eye.

"If he should appear in any company of human souls," Emerson wondered, "who would not march in his troop?"[26]

Emerson's enthusiasm for Shakespeare's poetry, including the poetry of the plays, and his own popularity as a lecturer and essayist, made "the Concord sage" one of Shakespeare's most effective publicists. It was probably Emerson, for example, who spurred his Concord neighbor Louisa May Alcott to study Shakespeare's texts (she loved the theater, but her father, Bronson Alcott, neither liked nor understood Shakespeare), and it was certainly Emerson who inspired young Henry Clay Folger to launch a lifelong avocation as a collector of Shakespeare's works and, near the end of his life, to construct a magnificent library to make his treasures widely accessible.

Other American writers paid tribute to Shakespeare's greatness, usually through commentaries interspersed in books or essays on non-Shakespearian topics. Washington Irving often inserted the Bard into his *Sketch Book of Geoffrey Crayon* (1819–20), Irving's musings on England's history, literature, and people. James Fenimore Cooper, who grew up in a northern New York home that valued Shakespeare, quoted him more than 1,000 times in his *Leatherstocking Tales* of frontier America (1823–41). Louisa May Alcott's appreciation of Shakespeare is reflected in *Little Women* (1868–69) and more directly in "A Pair of Eyes," which owes much to *Macbeth,* and "Ariel, A Legend of the Lighthouse," strongly influenced by *The Tempest.* Another of Emerson's Concord neighbors, Henry David Thoreau, praised Shakespeare in *Walden Pond* (1854) and elsewhere, though Thoreau remained ambivalent. On the one hand Thoreau could refer to Shakespeare as a "transcendent genius" but on the other hand insist that "man is the great poet, and not Homer, nor Shakespeare." Herman Melville, while also somewhat ambivalent, often mentioned Shakespeare in *The Confidence Man* (1857), and the marginalia in his own copy of Shakespeare's works reveals the poet's substantial influence on *Moby Dick* (1851).[27]

Many of these intellectuals participated in America's Lyceum lecture movement, drawn from English experience and named for Aristotle's forums in ancient Greece. From the founding of the Boston Lyceum in 1828, sites for lectures and self-improvement programs spread nationwide into an informal chain of speakers' bureaus. Concord's Lyceum, the nation's largest, sponsored hundreds of lectures each year, of which Emerson regularly delivered dozens. Until the Civil War intervened, lyceums fostered interest in Shakespeare and many other topics, primarily among middle-class urban Americans from coast to coast but especially in the east. After the war, the Chautauqua movement would expand the lecturers' reach into rural areas and thereby provide Shakespeare and other cultural topics with a national audience.

Walt Whitman found Shakespeare on his own. From boyhood he read and pondered Shakespeare, attended numerous plays, and recited Shakespearian passages when he had time and place to himself: on New York stage coaches, along the streets of Washington, DC, and, as he later recalled, at Coney Island (before it became popular), where he would "race up and down the hard sand, and declaim Homer or Shakespeare to the surf and seagulls by the hour." But Whitman wrote sparsely and ambivalently about Shakespeare until near the end of his long career as a newspaper reporter, editor, essayist, and—beginning in 1855—a widely heralded but controversial poet. The problem for Whitman was not the quality of Shakespeare's poetry but its social and political context: "The great poems, Shakespeare included, are poisonous to the idea of pride and dignity of the common people, the life-blood of Democracy," he wrote in *Democratic Vistas* (1871); such writings "have had their birth in courts, and basked and grown in castle sunshine." By 1884 Whitman had had a change of heart. He now saw Shakespeare's overarching scheme—evident, perhaps, to Shakespeare's contemporaries, but hidden to nineteenth-century eyes—that began to emerge in the *Henry VI* trilogy, evolved though the other history plays, and reached fruition in *Macbeth* and *King Lear.* That historical lesson, Whitman now believed, showed that Shakespeare had "as profound and forecasting a brain and pen as ever appeared in literature." "[M]y maturest judgment," Whitman concluded, "confirm[s] the impressions of my early years that the distinctiveness and glory of the Poet reside not in his vaunted dramas of the passions, but those founded on the contests of English dynasties and the French wars" in which Shakespeare exposed the ruthlessness and arrogance of Europe's medieval aristocracy and thereby paved the way for the "inauguration of modern Democracy." It was a novel idea that found few followers among the writers of Whitman's day or beyond, although it generated its share of debate among Shakespeare specialists and, presumably, among ardent amateurs. Moreover, Whitman's musings enriched the search by American intellectuals for Shakespeare's place, if any, in the evolution of a democratic society.[28]

While Walt Whitman sought Shakespeare's central message for American democracy, the poet and editor William Cullen Bryant championed Shakespeare's implicit Americanness. Especially in speeches he delivered on Shakespeare's birthday in 1870 and at the dedication of a statue of Shakespeare in New York's Central Park in 1872, Bryant insisted that the English men and women who migrated to America brought along "not only their language but its literature"; thereafter "We Americans may...claim an equal property in the great English poet with those who remained in the Old World." Non-English immigrants might object that Shakespeare was not part of *their* pre-American culture, but if they accepted America as their new home and English as their new language, Bryant seemed to say, Shakespeare and his fellow poets were part of the package. It wasn't a truly new idea, of course. In the 1820s James Fenimore Cooper dubbed him "the great author of America," and in the year of the Constitutional Convention a Philadelphia poet insisted that Shakespeare was better attuned to America than to his homeland:

> Monopolizing Britain! Boast no more
> His genius to your narrow bounds confined;
> Shakespeare's bold spirit seeks our western shore,
> A gen'ral blessing for the world designed,
> And, emulous to form the rising age,
> The noblest Bard demands the noblest Stage.[29]

Yet Bryant in the 1870s articulated more precisely and publicly than any predecessor the notion that Shakespeare was a truly American writer—no matter where he had lived and written—and always would be. Subsequent writers, especially during the Anglo-American rapprochement in the decades between the late nineteenth century and World War I, would reinforce that theme.

Shakespeare's ties to the New World, some Americans believed, could be strengthened by forging material links, however superficial, between the man and the adopting nation. There is a hint of that notion in the sliver of wood carried home in 1786 by John Adams and Thomas Jefferson from the chair in the Stratford birthplace, which the Adamses kept until 1815 and probably much later. More ubiquitous were the souvenirs carved from a mulberry tree that Shakespeare planted (so it was claimed) soon after he acquired Stratford's "New

Place": statuettes, medallions, boxes, and other keepsakes—some of them surely bogus—that were sold for more than a century to visitors, including many Americans who wanted to own a piece of Shakespeare. Similar symbolic appropriations are suggested in the engravings of Shakespearian scenes from John Boydell and his nephew Josiah's Shakespeare Gallery in London, beginning in the 1790s, that graced many American homes. By the middle of the nineteenth century, the United States had become the principal market for Boydell prints. In the 1840s, the notorious master of humbug, Phineas T. Barnum, tried to go a giant step farther. To capitalize on the American fascination with all things Shakespearian, he offered to buy, transport in pieces to New York, and refurbish the dilapidated Stratford-upon-Avon birthplace. Contemporaneous reports of Barnum's scheme and England's reaction to it vary in many details, but the story's core seems valid: Barnum hoped to enhance dramatically his popular museum, to make a bundle by displaying the birthplace in America or selling it to Englishmen determined to keep it in Stratford, and to tweak English noses in either case. Whether in response to Barnum's audacity or for reasons of their own is unclear, but in 1847 English benefactors scooped Barnum by acquiring the building and restoring it to a presentable and profitable condition, as it remains, with further embellishments, to the present day. Despite—and partly because of—the brittle feelings between America and England in the 1840s, Barnum's expectation that Americans would flock to see a piece of Shakespeare on their side of the Atlantic Ocean—and that English spokesmen would take umbrage—was wholly realistic.[30] But even without the birthplace, Barnum contributed to the nineteenth century's Shakespearian craze by keeping the publicity pot boiling.

* * *

And then there was Delia Bacon, who occupied, in her day, a category of Shakespeariana all her own. The daughter of one New England preacher and the sister of another, Bacon was steeped in the classics but had little formal education other than a year at Catherine Beecher's school for young ladies. Yet she was undeniably intelligent, energetic, and determined to carve a career for herself. After several years of teaching and failed attempts to establish a school like Beecher's, she turned to writing fiction, with some success (she was only

20 when her first book was published), then to lecturing on history and literature, then, briefly, to writing plays, and finally to an intensive analysis of the corpus attributed to Shakespeare. Her enthusiasm was always compelling. Even Ralph Waldo Emerson and Nathaniel Hawthorne helped her explore the astonishing theory, broached to the public in 1856, that William Shakespeare of Stratford-upon-Avon did not write the plays that had appeared over his name for two and a half centuries. Rather, Bacon contended, there must have been several aristocratic authors, including Sir Francis Bacon and Sir Walter Ralegh, though she was less adamant about who should get the credit for the nearly forty plays than she was that the authors had been precursors of English and American liberty. (Delia Bacon's certainty that a mere "player" could not have composed *Hamlet* or *Lear* was not wholly original. In 1848 a New York lawyer, Joseph C. Hart, had published a book on yachting with a lengthy digression on the authorship of the plays. Hart accused the Stratford man of merely inserting bawdy passages into other men's texts and claiming them for his own. Whether Bacon was influenced by Hart's relatively obscure book, or Hart by Bacon's lectures, is unclear, and perhaps neither one knew of the other.) Delia Bacon's anonymous article of 1856 in *Putnam's Monthly,* "William Shakespeare and His Plays: An Inquiry Concerning Them," introduced her skepticism to the reading public but offered little supporting evidence. At this point she was content to ridicule the notion that the plays could have been authored by the "stupid, illiterate, third-rate play-actor" from Stratford. Bacon intended to clinch her case in subsequent essays, but Putnam's editors rejected the three she submitted for failing to produce any substantiation.[31]

Delia Bacon's exhausting book of 1857, *The Philosophy of the Plays of Shakspere Unfolded*, suffered from a similar deficiency. Although Hawthorne underwrote its publication and contributed a preface, he later called it "a ponderous octavo volume, which fell with a dead thump at the feet of the public, and has never been picked up." For good reason. Bacon attempted to demonstrate that *King Lear*, *Julius Caesar*, and *Coriolanus* encode critiques of the Tudor and early Stuart regimes, but she never showed why they could not have been written by Shakespeare other than for the reason she touted in her earlier essay and elaborated in the book: that the historical Shakespeare was incompetent. The plays, she insisted, must have been authored by men of refined culture and wide experience, who had (as she put it in the essay) "the highest Parisian breeding." They disguised their republican message in dozens of dramas to circumvent government censorship.[32]

The public's failure to accept her theory, or even to take it seriously, unhinged Delia Bacon. A year after the book's publication she was committed to an institution for the mentally ill; a few months later she died. Her legacy, however, is ongoing. Ever since she opened the authorship door, thousands of books and essays have promoted or refuted the notion that Francis Bacon wrote the Shakespeare canon, or, if not Bacon, then some other ghost writer or cluster of writers: Renaissance poets such as Christopher Marlowe, Philip Sidney, Thomas Dekker, Thomas Heywood, Thomas Middleton, John Webster, and Michael Drayton; or Renaissance gentlemen such as Walter Ralegh, Henry Melville, and William Stanley, the sixth Earl of Derby, or, especially, since 1920, Edward de Vere, the 17th Earl of Oxford. That endless authorial debate is Delia Bacon's long-range legacy. In the short range, from the first written statement of her theory in 1856 to the end of the Civil War and beyond, Miss Bacon sparked a new and often contentious element in America's fascination with all things Shakespearian. Although few American or European scholars initially accepted her argument or even read her writings, and most scholars, including Richard Grant White, disparaged her ideas as blatant nonsense, the flood of writings, pro and con, seeped into American literary discourse as her theory engendered a new category of enthusiasts.[33] Like most of the trends in America's love affair with Shakespeare, this one would survive the Civil War's profound distractions and re-emerge later in the century in new formulas and with renewed vigor.

A case in point is the Minnesota political reformer Ignatius Donnelly, whose public career included a term as his state's Republican lieutenant governor and three terms in the US House of Representatives in the 1860s, and a run for the Vice-Presidency of the United States on the Populist ticket in 1900. This "Great Apostle of Protest" also wrote several books that challenged popular beliefs, most notably *The Great Cryptogram: Francis Bacon's Cipher in the So-Called Shakespeare Plays* (1888). Donnelly claimed to have cracked the intricate verbal/mathematical code that proved (to his satisfaction) that the prolific Elizabethan–Jacobean intellectual statesman Sir Francis Bacon had written the plays attributed to Shakespeare as well as many dramas that had always been attributed to his contemporaries. But Donnelly's book was scarcely off the press before its mathematical calculations were undermined by several knowledgeable critics and his logic subjected to irrefutable counterattack. Like Delia Bacon, Ignatius Donnelly made few converts but nonetheless enlivened the American public's attention to Shakespeare from coast to coast. "The Pathology of Cryptology" had become an especially American ailment, as several amateur literary sleuths would demonstrate in the twentieth century.[34]

That Americans initiated the first major challenge to Shakespeare's authorship is ironic. A nation that applauded self-education and nearly apotheosized Benjamin Franklin, Andrew Jackson, Abraham Lincoln, and other self-made men should have shunned anyone who insisted that only an aristocrat, or cluster of aristocrats, had the upbringing and social connections to write plays about English or Continental courts and to discuss knowledgeably matters of law, medicine, heraldry, diplomacy, and the like. There is no simple explanation for this elitist notion; each advocate of Bacon or another candidate presumably had his or her own persuasive reasons. But part of the shared context behind Delia Bacon and her nineteenth-century supporters and emulators was the intellectual trend known as Higher Criticism, which, among other issues, challenged traditional explanations of sparsely documented classical authors such as Homer and the Old Testament and eventually Shakespeare. Another part of the context was America's ambivalence about British culture, admiring its accomplishments but annoyed by its dominance. Post-Revolutionary America merited a culture of its own, many intellectuals argued and Emerson articulated in *The American Scholar* (1837)—hailed by Oliver Wendell Holmes as "our intellectual Declaration of Independence."[35] Much earlier, Noah Webster had promoted American spelling and pronunciation. By the 1820s, American cultural commentators questioned the supremacy of British actors and urged American authors, including dramatists, to write on American subjects. The appetite for questioning certain authorships in particular and British cultural achievements in general may help to explain why Delia Bacon's theory, however awkwardly argued, resonated with Ignatius

Donnelly, Mark Twain, Henry James, and many other nineteenth-century Americans. Admiration for Shakespeare's plays and sonnets did not wane—they had been thoroughly incorporated into America's literary tradition, and even Delia Bacon had credited the authors of "Shakespeare" with fostering its political tradition—but the glover's son from Stratford could now be interrogated and found wanting.

Notes

1. Thomas Clark Pollock, *The Philadelphia Theatre in the Eighteenth Century, Together with the Day Book of the Same Period* (Philadelphia: University of Pennsylvania Press, 1933), 52–4, 161, 180, 181, 184, 352.
2. Charles H. Shattuck, *Shakespeare on the American Stage: From the Hallams to Edwin Booth* (Washington, DC: Folger Shakespeare Library, 1976), 82–3.25–9,50–54; *Cambridge Guide to American Theatre*, ed. Don B. Wilmeth and Tice L. Miller (Cambridge: Cambridge University Press, 1993), 106, 175, 182.
3. Shattuck, *American Stage*, 18–19.
4. Ibid. 21–2 (quotations).
5. Ibid. 22–3; Virginia Mason Vaughan, *Othello: A Contextual History* (Cambridge: Cambridge University Press, 1994), 96–7.
6. Our discussion of Cooke relies heavily on Shattuck, *American Stage*, 32–6; George C. D. Odell, *Annals of the New York Stage* (15 vols, New York: Columbia University Press, 1927–49), 2.353–63, 365–6, 368–9, 377–9; and esp. Don B. Wilmeth, "Cooke among the Yankee Doodles," *Theatre Survey* 14.2 (November 1973), 1–32 (quotations on 8, 10, 14).
7. Shattuck, *American Stage*, 37–43 (quotation on 38); Nigel Cliff, *The Shakespeare Riots: Revenge, Drama, and Death in Nineteenth-Century America* (New York: Random House, 2007), 30–33, 59–64, 72–8.
8. Ibid. 87, 95.
9. Ibid. 110–25; Frances Trollope, *Domestic Manners of the Americans*, ed. Donald Smalley (New York: Knopf, 1949), 404.
10. Shattuck, *American Stage*, 77–80; Cliff, *Shakespeare Riots*, 66, 84, 90, 94–5, 156–64 (quotations on 90, 95, 162).
11. Casualty figures are discussed in ibid. 240–41, 285–6 n. 7. Forrest had no direct role in the riot, and on the fatal night he had performed in *The Gladiator* at the Broadway Theatre.
12. The Booth family's careers are outlined in several biographical guides and in Shattuck, *American Stage*, 44–50, 131–48.

13. On Lincoln see Esther Cloudman Dunn, *Shakespeare in America* (New York: Macmillan, 1939), 274–83; and David Herbert Donald, *Lincoln* (New York: Simon & Schuster, 1995), 31, 569, 580. On J. W. Booth and the assassination see esp. Michael W. Kauffman, *American Brutus: John Wilkes Booth and the Lincoln Conspiracies* (New York: Random House, 2004), 149–227, and John Wilkes Booth, *Right or Wrong, God Judge Me: The Writings of John Wilkes Booth*, ed. John Rhodehamel and Louise Taper (Urbana: University of Illinois Press, 1997).
14. Ibid. 47–8. According to Kauffman, *American Brutus*, 377–8, 472 n.4, all of John Wilkes Booth's belongings perished in the Winter Garden fire of 1867 so nothing was left for Edwin to destroy later, a persistent myth notwithstanding.
15. Shattuck, *American Stage,* 56–62.
16. Ibid. 87–95 (quotation on 93).
17. Herbert Marshall and Mildred Stock, *Ira Aldridge: The Negro Tragedian* (New York: Macmillan, 1958; repr. Washington, DC: Howard University Press, 1993); Errol Hill, *Shakespeare in Sable: A History of Black Shakespearean Actors* (Amherst: University of Massachusetts Press, 1984), 17–27.
18. Shattuck, *American Stage*, 117–23; *The Complete Works of Shakespeare, from the Original Text;... Illustrated with new and finely executed steel engravings, chiefly portraits in character of celebrated American actors...* (3 vols, New York: Martin, Johnson & Co., 1854–56).
19. Alfred Van Rensselaer Westfall, *American Shakespearean Criticism, 1607–1865* (New York: Benjamin Blom, 1939), 84–95 (quotation on 94); Andrew Murphy, *Shakespeare in Print: A History and Chronology of Shakespeare Publishing* (Cambridge: Cambridge University Press, 2003), 145–6.
20. Our summary of early 19th-century editions in this and subsequent paragraphs is based principally on Westfall, *Shakespeare Criticism*, 96–184; and Murphy, *Shakespeare in Print*, 145–55.
21. *Port Folio* (1804), 46–7.
22. James Russell Lowell, "White's Shakspeare," *Atlantic Monthly* 3 (1859), 259.
23. A masterful retelling of Collier's hoax that omits White's role is S. Schoenbaum, *Shakespeare's Lives*, new edn. (Oxford: Clarendon Press, 1991), 245–66.
24. Presumably White voiced this advice long before it appeared in his *Studies in Shakespeare* (Boston: Houghton Mifflin, 1896), 3.
25. *Cambridge Guide,* 328–9; H. N. Hudson, *Lectures on Shakspeare* (New York: Baker & Scribner, 1848); [Charlotte Cushman,] *Steinway Hall. Morning and Evening Readings from Shakespeare and the Poets* (Philadelphia: Ledger job print, 1874), quotation from p. [2]; J. E. Rankin, *The*

Shakespearean Interpreter, with Memorial Words Respecting Henry Norman Hudson (Middlebury, VT: Printed by Register Co., 1886), 35–6.

26. R. W. Emerson, *Representative Men, Seven Lectures* (New York: James C. Derby, 1850), quotations on 208, 209, 213, 215; Emerson, *Journals and Miscellaneous Notebooks...*, ed. William H. Gilman et al. (16 vols, Cambridge, MA: Harvard University Press, 1960–82), 13.132; Dunn, *Shakespeare in America*, 252–60.
27. Kim C. Sturgess, *Shakespeare and the American Nation* (Cambridge: Cambridge University Press, 2004), 40–45, 149–51, 158–61; Thoreau, *Winter: From the Journal of Henry D. Thoreau*, ed. H. G. O. Black (Boston: Houghton, Mifflin, 1888), 279; Dunn, *Shakespeare in America*, 260.
28. Walt Whitman, *Autobiographia, or, The Story of a Life* (New York: C. L. Webster, 1892), 23–4; Walt Whitman, *Democratic Vistas* (New York: J. S. Redfield, 1871), 32; Walt Whitman, "What Lurks Behind Shakspere's Historical Plays?" *November Boughs* (Philadelphia: David McKay, 1888), 52–4.
29. William Cullen Bryant, *Prose Writings*, ed. Parke Godwin (New York: Russell & Russell, 1964), 305–9 (quotation on 305); Peter Markoe, "The Tragic Genius of Shakespeare: An Ode," in Markoe, *Miscellaneous Poems* (Philadelphia: Printed by W. Pritchard and B. Hall, 1787 [Evans #20482]), 23–7; James Fenimore Cooper, *Notions of the Americans: Picked Up by a Travelling Bachelor* (2 vols, London: Shackell & Bayliss, 1828), 2.148–9.
30. *The Boydell Shakespeare Gallery*, ed. Walter Pope and Frederick Burdick (Bottrop: Peter Pomp, 1996), 48; James O. Halliwell, *An Historical Account of the New Place, Stratford-upon-Avon, the Last Residence of Shakespeare* (London: Printed by J. E. Adlard, 1864), 222–34; Schoenbaum, *Shakespeare's Lives*, 108–9, 125. Abigail Adams told a grandson in 1815 that she still had the sliver of wood. It is not in the inventory of the Adams Homestead in Quincy but may survive elsewhere among the extended Adams family's possessions. On Barnum, see esp. P. T. Barnum, *Struggles and Triumphs or, Forty Years' Recollections...*, intro. Roy F. Dibble (New York: Macmillan, 1930), 258; and Frances Teague, *Shakespeare and the American Popular Stage* (Cambridge: Cambridge University Press, 2006), 41–51, which contributes new evidence.
31. Schoenbaum, *Shakespeare's Lives*, 385–94; Nina Baum, "Delia Bacon: History's Odd Woman Out," *New England Quarterly* 79 (1996), 223–49. Bacon's essay in *Putnam's* is conveniently reprinted in Peter Rawlings, *Americans on Shakespeare, 1776–1914* (Aldershot, UK: Ashgate, 1999), 169–99 (quotation on 199). The relevant portion of Hart's essay is in ibid. 140–50. Several other forerunners of Delia Bacon's theory, most

of them obscure, then and now, are discussed in Schoenbaum, *Shakespeare's Lives*, 395–404. For the possible influence of Hart on Bacon or Bacon on Hart, see ibid. 399–401, and Stanley Wells, "Plotting Against the Stratford Man," *New York Review of Books* 57.9 (May 27, 2010), 31–3 n. 3.

32. Nathaniel Hawthorne, "Recollections of a Gifted Woman," *Atlantic Monthly* 11 (1863), 43–58 (quotation on 55); Rawlings, *Americans on Shakespeare*, 169–99 (quotation on 190); Delia Bacon, *The Philosophy of the Plays of Shakespeare Unfolded* (Boston: Ticknor & Fields, 1857).
33. Schoenbaum, *Shakespeare's Lives*, 404–51.
34. Ignatius Donnelly, *The Great Cryptogram: Francis Bacon's Cipher in the So-Called Shakespeare Plays* (Chicago: R. S . Peale, 1888), esp. 505–629. We borrow "Pathology of Cryptology" from Schoenbaum, *Shakespeare's Lives*, 408, where it is attributed to David Kahn, *The Codebreakers: The Story of Secret Writing* (New York: Macmillan, 1967).
35. On Higher Criticism: James Shapiro, *Contested Will: Who Wrote Shakespeare?* (New York: Simon & Schuster, 2010), 69–79, 98–9, 102–3, 106; on "The American Scholar": Oliver Wendell Holmes, *Ralph Waldo Emerson* (Boston: Houghton Mifflin, 1885), 115.

3

Shakespeare and American Expansion

Anecdotes abound about the emergence of Shakespeare at improbable locations across America. There is, for example, the episode related earlier in this book about the British officer who in 1763 escaped almost certain death in Illinois territory because he was reading *Antony and Cleopatra* in a volume that had belonged several years earlier to another officer, then to one or more Indian warriors, and finally to the reader—just in time. A century later, along the Oregon Trail, the legendary frontiersman Jim Bridger illustrated Shakespeare's ubiquity when he swapped some cattle for a wagon train passenger's copy of the works and hired a German American lad to read it aloud. Bridger could speak several European and Indian languages but was illiterate. He was an attentive listener, however, and soon knew many Shakespeare passages by heart.[1]

These stories also illustrate Shakespeare's migration westward, from the east coast to mid-America to the Far West. Along the way, soldiers on garrison duty as well as civilians of diverse statuses and occupations read or acted Shakespeare's plays; and while many migrants besides Jim Bridger were illiterate, they generally enjoyed the performances of itinerant acting troupes that closely followed the advancing frontier or listened to better-educated companions read from the printed word. As in the East, Shakespeare spoke to migrating Americans through the stage or the page, or both.

Although by the early nineteenth century the East had substantial, sometimes elegant, theaters in its large (by American standards) cities, and numerous stores selling imported and domestic editions of Shakespeare's works, the interior and western regions made do with playing spaces whose principal functions were warehouses, saloons, or town halls and obtained copies of the plays without the help of traditional bookstores. Despite the hardships of travel and makeshift venues, eager performers, including English stage veterans, trekked westward, while copies of Shakespeare's plays often appeared on the shelves of general stores and in peddlers' wagons. In 1835 Alexis de Tocqueville, the peripatetic French author of *Democracy in America*, claimed (albeit hyperbolically): "There is hardly a pioneer's hut which does not contain a few odd volumes of Shakespeare. I remember reading the feudal drama of *Henry V* for the first time in a log cabin."[2] As America moved inexorably toward the Pacific Ocean, Shakespeare was seldom far behind.

This early transcontinental craving for Shakespeare in performance and print reflects, in part, the exposure to his works that most Americans had gained in school, where extracts from several of the most popular plays were standard fare in classroom lessons and widely distributed for home consumption in books on oratory. The essence of educational Shakespeare was declamation. School children recited, often memorized, speeches by Shakespeare's major characters—Hamlet, Macbeth, Mark Antony, Brutus, Portia—that were explicitly or implicitly accompanied by moral lessons the reader should imbibe with Shakespeare's words. Although familiarity with Shakespeare inevitably led to parodies and lampoons (themselves a sign of his popularity), the brief encounter most students had with a great writer encouraged many adults, especially upper middle-class women, to continue studying Shakespeare through voluntary local associations. Shakespeare's expansion in nineteenth-century America was as much social and intellectual as it was geographic.

* * *

Shakespeare was the favorite playwright at almost every location on the moving frontier. Starting in the back country of the eastern states and gradually advancing westward, new towns gave rise to new theatrical venues, as settlers flocked to see whatever entertainment had come their way. Shakespeare shared the stage, of course, with other playwrights and other performers—musicians, singers, dancers, magicians, acrobats, orators. The players, constrained by sparse performance spaces, small casts, and brief rehearsals, might give the audience only a few selected Shakespeare scenes from a well-known play; itinerant troupes often confined their entire Shakespearian repertoire to *Richard III*, *Hamlet*, *Othello*, *Romeo and Juliet*, and *Macbeth*. Whether it was a full play or a truncated version, it was almost always followed by one or more individual or small group entertainments and by a short farce or musical romance. David Garrick contrived many such afterpieces besides the popular *Catherine and Petruchio* and *Florizel and Perdita*—the only Shakespeare texts (if they can legitimately be called that) to be regularly relegated to second rank on American playbills.[3]

Wherever a troupe was available to perform, a temporary theater appeared. In the second decade of the nineteenth century, Shakespeare was played in Lexington, Kentucky, on the second floor of a brewery and later in the Masonic Hall; in Mobile, Alabama, shows were staged in a billiard parlour. Farther south in Alabama, the town of Miscaloosa's playhouse was the hotel ballroom. As towns grew larger and enjoyed a measure of prosperity, many marshalled civic pride and attracted visitors from the surrounding region by erecting bona fide theaters. In 1820 Cincinnati constructed a brick building that seated up to eight hundred. In the early Southwest, New Orleans led the way with several fine playhouses that frequently offered Shakespeare productions, most notably the St. Charles Theatre, which opened in 1835. Chicago and St Louis were not far behind in the construction of impressive auditoriums and the mounting of Shakespearian dramas.[4] Notable actors, both British and American, exhibited their skills on frontier stages: the elder Junius Booth, John Abthorpe Cooper, Charles Kean, Ellen Tree, Edwin Forrest, and James Henry Hackett, to name but half a dozen.

As westward migration reached, and briefly slowed, at the formidable Mississippi River, a new theatrical venue emerged that ran north to south rather than east to west. Beginning with the William Chapman family's purchase of a flatboat at Pittsburgh in 1831, floating shows brought Shakespeare to riverside hamlets and substantial cities from Cincinnati on the upper Ohio River to New Orleans at the mouth of the Mississippi. The seven Chapmans (William, Sr. and Caroline, their three sons and two daughters) were a troupe in themselves, already experienced Shakespearians in England and eastern America before they took their talents westward and eventually onto the river. When their flatboat, augmented by a simple house and flagpole and propelled by the current or by manual effort, drew enthusiastic audiences, the Chapmans converted a steamboat into a larger theater, with more reliable propulsion as well as better seating and other amenities. But the basic pattern of their peregrinations remained the same for nearly a decade: The Chapmans displayed their varied talents—which presumably included a hefty dose of Shakespeare, though no records survive of their specific showboat offerings—wherever a dock and a crowd were handy, then moved on. At the northern or southern end of the river, they reversed course. Other riverboat owners soon followed the Chapmans' example. Nearly a century later, the American critic Ashley Thorndike summarized several strands of Shakespeare's migration: "[I]n the West the travelling elocutionist, the lecturer, the company of actors on a Mississippi showboat became his emissaries and evangels. The frontier would not leave him to Europe and the East; no other writer was so quickly assimilated in the wilderness. Reverence for him became the symbol, the mark of culture, which united the frontiersman with Lowell and Emerson."[5] Shakespeare, implicitly, was an American cultural icon.

With the discovery of gold at John Sutter's sawmill near Sacramento, California, in early 1848, the irregular but seemingly predictable progression of the frontier from east to west gave way overnight to the settlement of California. Its American population jumped from 750 in 1845, to 92,000 in 1850, to 380,000 a decade later.[6] Some of those migrants came cross country by wagon but most traveled by ship around the horn of South America or to the Isthmus of Panama and again by ship up the western coast, as did the performers who followed close behind. With cash plentiful and almost no restrictions on how to spend it, theaters—often quite elegant—proliferated throughout the mining region, and handsome rewards were suddenly available for visiting performers. A vibrant theatrical culture quickly emerged in California and neighboring territories in which Shakespeare had a major role.

He had already played some minor roles in California before the gold boom. As early as the 1820s along the Yellowstone River, a party of trappers treasured a small collection of books that included "Byron,

Shakespeare, . . . Scott's works, [and] the Bible." In the summer of 1847, American soldiers on garrison duty in Santa Barbara performed *Richard III* in a house they revamped into a theater, and other soldiers in the spring of 1849, shortly before they left the army, put on acts one and five of *Hamlet* at Los Angeles and a truncated *Othello* at Monterey. By then the war against Mexico (1846–8) was over and the Gold Rush was on. Some of the discharged soldiers with theatrical aspirations moved to San Francisco or Sacramento, where new theaters had sprouted and actors were in short supply. Army veterans quietly merged with incoming professionals to form several acting companies of uneven merit.[7] But whatever their level of professionalism, most companies offered a lively mix of entertainment that included Shakespeare's better-known plays.

The first Gold Rush theater opened in Sacramento in the autumn of 1849, only a year and a half after the first gold strike. No record survives of a Shakespeare production in that sheet iron and canvas playhouse before a flood washed it away, but *Othello*, *Hamlet*, *The Merchant of Venice*, and *King Lear* were performed at San Francisco's first Jenny Lind Theatre in 1850 and early 1851. In the latter year, Junius ("June") Brutus Booth, Jr. arrived in San Francisco to manage the third Jenny Lind (the first two burned down) and to act major roles, especially Shakespearian. June wowed audiences as Iago in October 1851 and again, with a better Othello, in December and in the title roles in *Richard III* and *Macbeth* in November. The next July (1852), his father and 18-year-old brother Edwin joined June in San Francisco. The senior Booth played Richard III in August to rave reviews, and a night later he performed the title role in *Macbeth* with June as Macduff and Edwin as Malcolm.[8] Only four years into the gold boom, San Francisco enjoyed first-class Shakespeare.

Later in 1852 a combined troupe of the Booth family and some of the Chapman clan (George and Mary, relatives of the riverboat entrepreneurs, later joined by William ["Uncle Billy"] and Caroline and some of their kin) played *Hamlet*, *Macbeth*, *Othello*, and *Richard III* to packed houses at the Jenny Lind and put on *The Merchant of Venice* at San Francisco's new Adelphi Theatre. The two acting families then separately toured the mines around Sacramento and beyond—at towns such as Rough and Ready, Grass Valley, Marysville, and Nevada City—before Junius Sr. headed home to Maryland (and died on the way) and Edwin went still farther west to perform in Australia and Hawaii.

By then the Booths had done their share to make Shakespeare a fixture in California, with essential help from the many Chapmans, the Starks (James and Sarah), the Bakers (Lewis and Alexina), and other companies and individual stars who soon arrived in the West. The latter included Laura Keene, one of the era's most versatile and durable performers, admired especially for *Much Ado*'s Beatrice, and who accompanied Booth to Australia. James and Sarah Stark, who often joined forces with Edwin Booth, pleased numerous California audiences in comedies and tragedies in the early 1850s, with a fifteen-month gap in 1853–54 to tour Australia themselves. Among the Starks' most notable contributions to western theatrical life were the first professional productions of *1 Henry IV*, *King John*, *The Merry Wives of Windsor*, and *Pericles*. The Bakers introduced the West to *As You Like It*, *The Comedy of Errors*, and *Much Ado About Nothing*. Collectively these many troupers from the East performed twenty-two of Shakespeare's plays, most of them many times, during California's first decade of precious-metal prosperity. In the following decades, California audiences enjoyed tours of varying lengths from itinerant British actors such as the laconic Charles Kean; American favorites nearing life's end, such as James Henry Hackett and Edwin Forrest; Americans on the rise, including Forrest's vigorous protégé John McCulloch; and at least one distinguished performer from continental Europe, the Italian Tommaso Salvini.[9] Whatever the Far West's cultural shortcomings, a paucity of good Shakespearian theater was not among them.

But it was the West's version of the theater, not the east's. The relatively young, overwhelmingly male audiences of the western frontier favored the energetic action of *Richard III* (Cibber's version), *Hamlet* (with many local alterations), *Macbeth*, *Othello*, and *King Lear* (Tate's rewriting). Sword fights were popular. By and large, Shakespeare's histories and comedies were not, presumably because they were less familiar and generally less boisterous, except the always popular *Richard III* among the history plays and *The Merchant of Venice* and *The Taming of the Shrew* among the "comedies." Another exception was a lavish version of *A Midsummer Night's Dream* in San Francisco on the 300th anniversary of Shakespeare's birth in 1864.

The West's sudden wealth, moreover, allowed a surprisingly high level of staging at several theaters, even though the quality of acting did not always justify the set. Nor did the audiences' decorum. Back East, higher ticket prices at the "best" theaters and a new emphasis on silent participation (except for applause) was replacing the rowdy, outspoken behavior that had characterized much of the early British and American theatrical tradition. Gold miners and the other newcomers to the West insisted on their prerogatives as paying customers to speak out, often loudly, at any point in the performance, and, of course, to bombard inept actors with anything at hand. Visiting performers, however unhappy they might be with the West's atavistic rules, accepted them as the sacrifice they must make for occasional bags of gold dust tossed at their feet by appreciative patrons.[10]

One community in the West that adhered to genteel dramatic decorum was Salt Lake City, founded in the summer of 1847. Its leader, Brigham Young, favored wholesome productions for entertainment and moral enhancement. As early as 1848 an unpaid Mormon acting company staged light comedies and in 1856 added *Richard III* and *Othello* to its offerings, though with mixed success. In 1862 the opening of a 7,500-seat Salt Lake Theatre modeled on Drury Lane brought the Utah community into the theatrical mainstream. Visiting actors put on *Hamlet*, *Macbeth* (accompanied by the Mormon Tabernacle Choir), *Romeo and Juliet*, and *The Merchant of Venice.*[11] Although not a part of the Gold Rush movement but rather of western migration more generally, and especially of the Mormons' search for a religious and political haven, the residents of Salt Lake City and vicinity helped to make Shakespeare transcontinental.

From one perspective, California was the end of the western road until Hawaii became a new frontier in the second half of the nineteenth century. From another perspective, the American fascination with Shakespeare reached as far beyond the California coast as American thespians, professional or amateur, dared to venture. That point was made emphatically in October 1848 when sailors aboard the Nantucket whaling ship *Alpha*, "27 months out" in the South Pacific, performed the final scene of *Othello.* Their stage was the "Alphean Marine Theatre" on the ship's deck, with a huge curtain hanging from the rigging; the show would be performed "Wind, Weather, and Whales permitting." A letter from sailor William Macy, who played Desdemona, to his cousin on Nantucket Island incorporated a handwritten playbill that showed Shakespeare's scene as the featured event. Afterpieces included Macy singing "Wery Ridiculous," the sailor who had played Othello reciting "The Mariner's Dream," and a farce, "The Bosom Friends, or Unrequited Affection!," in which both sailor-actors again took prominent roles (Fig. 3.1).[12] Except for the all-male cast and audience and the brevity

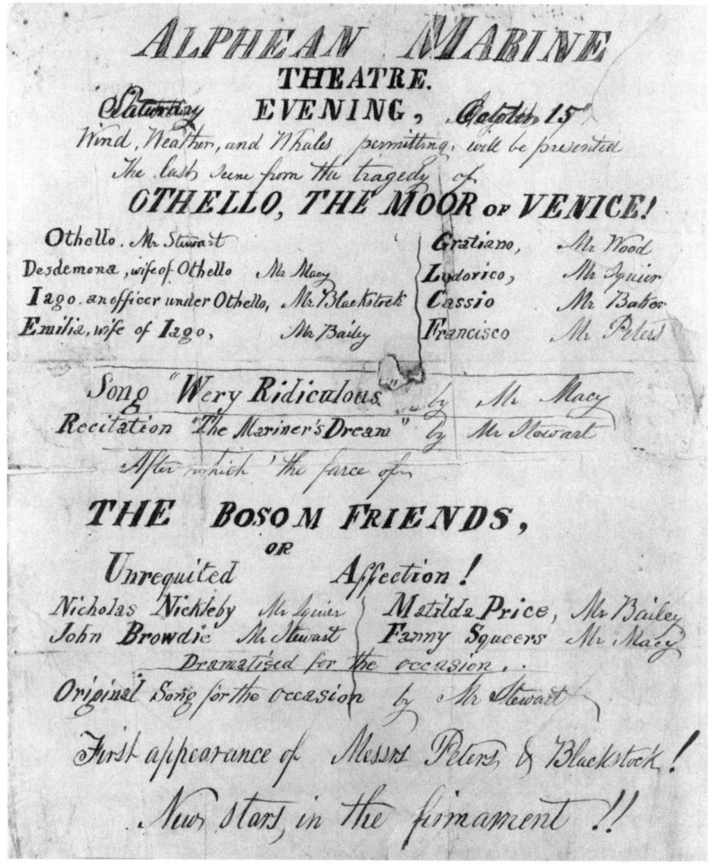

ALPHEAN MARINE
THEATRE.
Saturday EVENING, October 15th
Wind, Weather, and Whales permitting, will be presented
The last scene from the tragedy of
OTHELLO, THE MOOR OF VENICE!

Othello.	Mr Stewart	Gratiano,	Mr Wood
Desdemona, wife of Othello	Mr Macy	Lodorico,	Mr Squier
Iago. an officer under Othello,	Mr Blackstock	Cassio	Mr Baker
Emilia, wife of Iago,	Mr Bailey	Francisco	Mr Peters

Song "Wery Ridiculous" by Mr Macy
Recitation "The Mariner's Dream" by Mr Stewart
After which the farce of
THE BOSOM FRIENDS,
OR
Unrequited Affection!

Nicholas Nickleby	Mr Squier	Matilda Price,	Mr Bailey
John Browdie	Mr Stewart	Fanny Squeers	Mr Macy

Dramatised for the occasion.
Original Song for the occasion by Mr Stewart
First appearance of Messrs Peters & Blackstock!
New stars in the firmament!!

Figure 3.1. William Macy's handwritten playbill for the Alphean Marine Theatre's performance of a scene from *Othello* (1848). Collection of the Nantucket Historical Association.

of the main selection, the Alphean Marine Theatre presented a standard nineteenth-century Shakespearian show.

Despite Shakespeare's popularity among theater audiences and with many political and social leaders, a few influential segments of the American population in the early nineteenth century still considered the stage immoral and portions of his plays to be socially or sexually dangerous. Because America's schools were usually created, administered, and staffed by community or church officials, traditionalism prevailed. John Adams's frequent praise of Shakespeare notwithstanding, no Massachusetts school in his lifetime, secondary or collegiate, is known to have assigned for study in or out of the classroom any play—indeed any substantial passage—by William Shakespeare. Before he could be incorporated into American curricula, Shakespeare had to win over the nation's educators.

Shakespeare first entered American education as a rhetorician. British writers of books on elocution had long endorsed Shakespeare as a model writer and, at least implicitly, as a benign moral influence. Such sentiments resonated in post-Revolutionary America. An educational tract by Unitarian minister William Enfield of Liverpool and Norwich, England, *The Speaker: or, Miscellaneous Pieces Selected from the Best English Writers... with a View to the Improvement of Youth in Reading and Speaking*, went through several printings and revisions after its initial English edition in 1774; American editions appeared in 1798 and thereafter. Among the hundreds of selections from scores of prominent authors in Enfield's nearly 275 samples of admirable rhetoric from "*the Best English Writers*" (as well as, for comparison, translations of such "ancients" as Livy, Sallust, and Tacitus) were more speeches and dialogues by Shakespeare than any other author. Nearly a decade after the appearance of Enfield's *Speaker*, the Presbyterian preacher and Edinburgh professor of English literature Hugh Blair, who in 1753 had edited Shakespeare's works in eight volumes, published *Lectures on Rhetoric and Belles Lettres* (1783; first American edition 1784). Blair's essays quoted Shakespeare extensively and adjudged him and his works "great." Although Blair saw a number of shortcomings in Shakespeare's texts, he insisted that many passages exhibited "warm and genuine representations of human nature."[13] In an era that emphasized public oratory and encouraged its practice in schools and homes, American educators had to be impressed that two prominent Protestant clergyman had implicitly endorsed Shakespeare as an exemplar for American students.

The first American oratorical book to explicitly celebrate Shakespeare and take commercial advantage of his growing popularity appeared in 1810, when John Walker's *Elements of Elocution* concluded a long subtitle with the phrase "*Exemplified by a Copious Selection of the Most Striking Passages of Shakespeare.*" The implication that Shakespeare was the sole source of the illustrative passages stretched the truth: Walker included extracts from Milton, Addison, Pope, Dryden, and others, but passages from Shakespeare were the most numerous. Yet all quotations in Walker's book were subordinate to his text, serving as illustrations of elocutionary rules rather than as literary passages to be assessed and appreciated.[14]

That larger purpose came closer to realization three years later with the publication in New Haven, Connecticut, of Increase Cooke's *Sequel to the American Orator, or, Dialogues for Schools* (a follow-up to his earlier books with *American Orator* in the title). The caption to a frontispiece portrait of Shakespeare quoted Dr Samuel Johnson: "SHAKSPEARE has long outlived his century... and may now [Johnson had written many years earlier] begin to assume the dignity of an ancient, and claim the privilege of established fame, and prescriptive veneration." Cooke's text provided dozens of examples of Shakespearian rhetoric drawn from more than a score of his plays. Some of the excerpts were only a paragraph or two, such as Jaques' witty account of meeting a fool in *As You Like It* (II.vii.12–34) to illustrate mirth; Leonato's bitter response to charges against his daughter Hero in *Much Ado About Nothing* (IV.i.190–94) to illustrate revenge; and Prospero's promise to Ferdinand of Miranda's hand in marriage from *The Tempest* (IV.i.1–14) to illustrate "giving or granting." Much longer extracts from Shakespeare's dialogues covered several pages each in Cooke's octavo volume, such as Prince Henry's banter with Falstaff about his imagined battle with armed rogues in *1 Henry IV* (II.iv.113–60) to exemplify humor, and a condensed version of Shylock's excruciating trial in *The Merchant of Venice* (IV.ii.1–401) to show "Intercession—Obstinacy—Cruelty—Forced Submission, etc."[15] Here was Shakespeare as elocutionary example *and* an insightful guide to human behavior.

The potential value of Cooke's *Dialogues* for enlarging Shakespeare's role in American education suffered a serious setback when the author died in 1814. The book remained in use for many years, but it had no subsequent editions and competed with a growing number of English and American oratorical textbooks that gave less attention to Shakespeare than Cooke's had. Among them was William Scott's *Lessons in Elocution; or, A Selection of Pieces in Prose and Verse for the Improvement of Youth in Reading and Speaking* (Edinburgh, 1779), which was first published in America in 1791 and continued to be revised and reprinted long after Scott's death in 1804. Shakespeare was generously represented, though mostly in short extracts. Abraham Lincoln was among the many Americans who absorbed much of their Shakespeare from "Scott's lessons."[16]

Some of Scott's and Cooke's competitors ignored the dramatist altogether, thus depriving many early nineteenth-century American youngsters of the most likely place to encounter Shakespeare's words. The most conspicuous example of snubbing Shakespeare is the American-born Quaker Lindley Murray, whose *English Reader, or Pieces in Prose and Poetry: Selected from the Best Writers* was the best-selling schoolbook in both Britain and America between 1815 and about 1835. It had no selections from Shakespeare because Murray sought "to imbue [young] minds with the love of virtue," to which dramatic works, he believed, were antithetical—a point he argued vigorously in 1821 in an anthology of European and American anti-theatrical writings. Murray abhorred the "many profane, indecent, and irreligious sentiments [that] are to be found in the works of dramatic writers," and contended that "every sober and unprejudiced mind" must recognize "the corrupting influence, and fatal amusements, of the theatre." Ignoring Murray, most authors of instructional books included at least a few selections from Shakespeare on the grounds that his writings were substantively or aesthetically valuable, but rarely did the compiler identify the authors he borrowed from, or the plays from which the selections came, or the contexts in which the literary passages appeared. Enfield had at least cited the author, though not the play. Cooke had been far more helpful. Although he rarely provided contexts—many were self-evident—he almost always specified the author and the play and sometimes the act and scene. Cooke had also reprinted numerous notes by Samuel

Johnson, George Steevens, William Warburton, and other editors of the Shakespeare texts in the *Dialogues*, which reinforces the likelihood that Cooke's untimely death had temporarily dampened American efforts to promote the study of Shakespeare in his own right.[17]

By the mid-1830s, a few moderately successful books of oratorical selections emerged, with or without Shakespeare, before William Holmes McGuffey in 1836 launched the first of his vastly popular *Readers* for upper school grades. Over the long haul, McGuffey, more than anyone else, ensured Shakespeare's place in American scholastic education from his day almost to ours. Because he wanted everyone to study, appreciate, and recite effectively the great classical and modern orators—and, in the process, to learn industriousness, honesty, and moral probity—McGuffey urged the recitation and often the memorization of extracts from "the best American and English writers." Growing up in Ohio, McGuffey had himself displayed a prodigious memory, reciting large portions of the protestant Bible and many secular books. A remarkable career ensued. He became a rural school teacher at 14, a professor of philosophy and philology at 25, a Presbyterian minister (concurrently) at 29, and president of Cincinnati College at 36. Soon after financial troubles scuttled that institution, McGuffey accepted the presidency of Ohio University—a job that finally exceeded his talents. He was a rigid, tactless administrator and resigned under pressure. McGuffey spent the final twenty-eight years of his life as a professor of philosophy at the University of Virginia, while simultaneously revising his textbooks again and again, helped appreciably by his younger brother Alexander Hamilton McGuffey.[18]

The earliest *Readers* contained simple stories for young children. Their success encouraged McGuffey to launch a confusing sequence of new editions and revised older editions with curious titles and ever-changing contents aimed at various educational levels. Shakespeare first appeared in *The Eclectic Fourth Reader* (1937) in two excerpts in a book of more than 300 pages: Prince Arthur's appeal to Hubert to spare his life, from *King John*, and Mark Antony's incitement of the plebeians against Brutus and Cassius from *Julius Caesar*. In 1844 *McGuffey's Newly Revised Fourth Reader* offered 107 "lessons" in prose and poetry, of which two were again by Shakespeare: Prince Arthur's plea, as in the previous edition, and (supplanting Antony) a compressed version of the trial scene from *The Merchant of Venice.* These selections persisted through the next several revisions of the *Fourth Reader*, and even the otherwise innovative *McGuffey's New Fifth Eclectic Reader* and its subsequent revision, before a breakthrough came in *McGuffey's New Sixth Eclectic Reader* (1857), compiled almost entirely by Alexander McGuffey. It had nine passages from Shakespeare to only four each from Sir Walter Scott and Henry Wadsworth Longfellow, and only three from the King James Bible. Shakespeare's ascendance continued in the revised *Sixth Reader* of 1868, which contained 186 lessons in prose and poetry for students in the upper grades, of which eleven were by Shakespeare: predictably, Hamlet's most famous soliloquy and Henry V's oration to his troops at Harfleur, but also two selections each from *King John* and *Julius Caesar*, and one each from *Othello*, *Henry VIII*, *1 Henry IV*, *Richard III*, and (the longest of the Shakespeare selections) a patchwork piece from *All's Well That Ends Well* that combined parts of three scenes and altered many words and characters' names.

While later editions of the *Readers* added or subtracted selections and authors, several characteristics persisted. Extracts from Shakespeare were the most numerous; they were mostly from the tragedies; and some, notably the passages from *The Merchant of Venice* and *Othello*, were condensed and amended to reflect the McGuffey brothers'—and, presumably, many white middle-class Americans'—social biases. The McGuffeys, of course, viewed their editorial interventions from a different perspective. The preface to the *New Sixth Reader* explained: "Considerable liberty has been taken with the articles selected, in order to adapt them to the special purpose for which they are here designed. Much change and remodeling has been necessary." That "special purpose" was, they asserted, "to influence the heart by sound moral and religious instruction." Accordingly, in reproducing the trial scene from *The Merchant of Venice*, the McGuffeys omitted the most blatantly anti-Semitic passages and Shylock's condemnation of Christians for owning slaves, yet the resulting image of Shylock remains subtly but deeply derogatory. Portia's crucial contribution to the trial, moreover, is usurped by a male "Judge," who combines her role and the Duke's. Shakespeare's play thus retains a prejudicial view of Jews but is shorn of the original's irony and complexity, while the primacy of (arguably) the canon's most competent woman is effectively expunged. In these extracts, young Americans encountered Shakespeare's passages not as he had written them but as the McGuffeys wished he had.[19]

Despite considerable competition from other schoolbooks, *McGuffey's Readers* led the field for more than a century, especially in the South and West. (In the Northeast, educators preferred their time-honored English imports and such home-grown products as *The New England Primer* [1690], Noah Webster's *Spelling Book* [1782], and John Pierpont's *American First Class Reader* [1823] and *National Reader* [1827].) Before William McGuffey's death in 1873, his books had sold 47 million copies; by 1920 sales exceeded 122 million. Although not every student even in the South and West encountered the *Readers* (not every young American in any region, especially in rural areas, attended school in the nineteenth century), so many youths did use the *Readers*, and the rival schoolbooks so closely paralleled McGuffey's, that a vast number of Americans in the nineteenth and early twentieth centuries shared a common educational experience. Central to that experience was a familiarity with a rich variety of authors—European and American, ancient and modern—that virtually always included Shakespeare. American students read the selections repeatedly, usually aloud, and almost invariably memorized some of them for classroom recitation, which often meant retention (however imprecise) for life. In a tribute to William H. McGuffey and his books, the novelist Hamlin Garland spoke for several generations of Americans: "I got my first taste of Shakespeare from the selected scenes which I read in these books," Garland recalled in his autobiography of 1917. "[W]e were taught to feel the force of these poems and to reverence the genius that produced them.... Falstaff and Prince Hal, Henry and his wooing of Kate, Wolsey and his downfall, Shylock and his pound of flesh all became part of our thinking and helped us to measure the large figures of our own literature, for Whittier, Bryant, and Longfellow also had a place in these volumes."[20]

* * *

America's colleges lagged far behind its schools in the teaching of Shakespeare. College curricula stressed Latin and Greek, which were absorbed by classroom recitation from standard textbooks. As late as

1868–9, Harvard's catalog listed only a single course in "English" for each year of study after the freshman year, and their chronological coverage stopped at Chaucer. Only in foreign languages did instruction customarily include modern works. Departments of rhetoric, which included the study of English literature if the institution taught it at all, were primarily concerned with the structure of language (philology), pronunciation and effective delivery (oratory), and rules of composition (grammar). Little attention was paid to the content and style of individual works, especially English dramas, except in extracts, often anonymous, that illustrated good or bad writing. Until well past mid-century, Shakespeare rarely appeared in the college curriculum.[21]

American colleges did not try to thwart interest in Shakespeare, but they generally left students to their own devices. Some collegians, of course, attended amateur or professional stage productions; some participated in student-run literary clubs that promoted an interest in Shakespeare and other authors; and judging from publishers' subscription lists, many early nineteenth-century collegians owned copies of Shakespeare's works. The colleges owned sets of Shakespeare too, but they were often inaccessible. Campus libraries were usually tucked into a remote room or two, supervised by a part-time librarian, and open only a few hours a week. Two centuries after the founding of Harvard, freshmen at America's oldest college could borrow books only on Wednesdays, seniors on Mondays and Thursdays.

The teaching of Shakespeare and other post-Renaissance writers in American colleges emerged gradually, usually through one or more teachers of rhetoric on each campus who from personal preference emphasized aesthetic examples of writing and speaking but stopped short of assigning the whole work. An 1871 graduate of Columbia recalled that its one-semester class in English literature did not assign "the actual writings of any of the authors, nor was any hint dropped that we might possibly be benefited by reading them for ourselves."[22] Rather, college students encountered modern authors through college textbooks roughly analogous to McGuffey's for secondary schools, and rarely with as much attention to Shakespeare. The book assigned for many years at Yale and Michigan, William Spalding's *The History of English Literature, with an Outline of the Origin and Growth of the English Language* (1853), devoted only six of 413 pages to Shakespeare and had no extracts from his plays. Students at Columbia, Cornell, and Princeton fared no better with Thomas B. Shaw's *The Complete Manual of English Literature* (1846), though the same author's posthumous *Complete Specimens of English Literature* of 1870 reflected the growing interest in Shakespeare by including one of his sonnets and selections from ten of his plays. Also by 1870 Henry Norman Hudson was editing a series of Shakespeare's plays intended for use in schools and colleges, as was William J. Rolfe, a former Massachusetts schoolmaster. The latter's forty-volume set of Shakespeare's plays and poems featured substantial introductions and notes.[23] By the last quarter of the nineteenth century, school and college instructors could finally ask their students to read whole Shakespeare plays in affordable editions.

Initially, collegiate study of Shakespeare entered the curricula through the separate—and decidedly unequal—scientific schools that several colleges established to accommodate new emphases on practical science, such as Yale's Sheffield Scientific School and Harvard's Lawrence Scientific School. To make room for the scientific courses, attention to Latin and Greek was substantially reduced; into the void, along with science and modern languages came Shakespeare. Gradually and sometimes grudgingly, he was embraced by the faculties of the traditional colleges.

At first Shakespeare shared a semester's readings with other early English writers such as Chaucer, Spenser, Milton, Marlowe, and Ben Jonson. In 1857, Francis A. March at Lafayette College went a step further, devoting a course exclusively to *Paradise Lost* and *Julius Caesar*; a year later, Datus C. Brooks at the University of Michigan gave a course on Shakespeare alone, featuring *King Lear*, *Macbeth*, *Hamlet*, and *Othello*. By 1875, Michigan's Moses Coit Tyler, who later became an authority on American literature, taught those four tragedies as well as *Richard II*, *Richard III*, both parts of *Henry IV*, *Twelfth Night*, *The Merchant of Venice*, *A Midsummer Night's Dream*, and the sonnets. At about the same time—roughly the 1870s to 1890s—several colleges, including Harvard, Yale, Cornell, Princeton, Columbia, Pennsylvania, and Virginia initiated courses on Shakespeare. By the early twentieth century, students who wanted to study Shakespeare's works were almost certain to find one or more courses and qualified instructors; in 1906, twenty-five of America's thirty liberal arts colleges offered at least one course on Shakespeare. Although Shakespeare was not a required subject, he now had a foothold in college curricula that would strengthen and expand throughout the twentieth century. At Harvard, in many respects America's bellwether institution, Professor George Lyman Kittredge taught rigorous courses on Shakespeare, including a hefty dose of memorization, from 1888 until his retirement in 1936. In the latter year he published his own version of Shakespeare's *Complete Works.* Kittredge would be succeeded at Harvard by a long line of eminent Shakespearian teacher-scholars.[24]

* * *

The serious study of Shakespeare was not confined to academic institutions. Many adults considered him a lifelong companion to be appreciated by oneself or with like-minded friends. Some Shakespeare devotees acquired their attachment from learned parents, as had John Quincy Adams. Many others acquired it at school, as Hamlin Garland attested. Still others had been introduced to Shakespeare by outstanding stage performances or the lectures of Ralph Waldo Emerson, Henry Hudson, and other speakers in local auditoriums as part of the Lyceum movement or, after the 1870s, at outdoor assemblies in the upstate New York community of Chautauqua and similar rural venues. Often housed in large brown tents to distinguish them from the white tents of traveling circuses, Chautauquas increasingly abandoned the religious focus of the earliest meetings for a broad attention to cultural self-improvement that time and again involved Shakespeare.

Important expressions of that drive for self-improvement were the more-or-less formal "Shakespeare Clubs" that sprang up in cities and towns from Maine to California after mid-century. These increasingly popular gatherings for reading and discussing Shakespeare's plays had no national spokesmen, no established structure, and no common goal except the enjoyment of Shakespeare's works and the fellowship of other members. For the next half-century and beyond, Shakespeare clubs flourished. After many decades of experience, the 1898 pamphlet *How to Organize a Shakespeare Club* could claim, with some justification, "The pleasure and profit from the study of Literature increase if congenial persons meet together to read the same authors." Shakespeare's work, in particular, "encourages the formation of such clubs and classes by offering exceptional instruction and entertainment."[25] Between 1880 and 1940 nearly 500 Shakespearian clubs were founded in communities across America. Reading Shakespeare while socializing had become a national pastime. These self-generated associations mirrored in some respects the literary clubs that college students had formed half a century earlier.

Philadelphia, home of the first complete American edition of Shakespeare's plays, also spawned the first Shakespeare Club. In 1851 four Philadelphia lawyers decided to meet regularly to read Shakespeare together; by 1860 the club had twenty-six members and the next year was incorporated as The Shakspere [*sic*] Society of Philadelphia. On alternate Wednesday evenings from October to May, members gathered to eat, drink, and read aloud. On or near the Bard's birthday each April they celebrated at a lavish banquet, with a printed menu that featured quotations from the season's readings for each sumptuous course (Fig. 3.2). The society's enthusiasm for food and drink notwithstanding, the members took their educational mission seriously, collecting an impressive library of Shakespeariana: philological criticism, source studies, the latest editions, and even facsimiles of the early quartos. As they read the plays aloud, these amateur scholars argued over textual discrepancies and editors' emendations—forming, in effect, a foundation for the Variorum Shakespeare volumes on which their second president, Horace Howard Furness, would spend decades of selfless, fruitful labor.[26]

The Shakspere Society of Philadelphia was an elite, male preserve, as was the Shakespeare Society of New York City, founded in 1854. Like the Philadelphians, the New Yorkers collected and maintained a library, but they also sponsored a quasi-scholarly journal, *Shakespeariana*, which published essays on a wide variety of topics, including the ongoing authorship debate. The majority of Shakespeare clubs founded between 1851 and the 1920s may have been less systematic in their scholarship than the Philadelphians and New Yorkers, but they were no less serious. For the most part, Shakespeare clubs were organized by women who sought a social and educational venue where they could freely read, learn, and debate ideas.[27] In Michigan, for example, some members of the Ladies' Literary Club founded the Shakespeariana Society of Grand Rapids in 1887 and met the second

TWELFTH ANNUAL DINNER

OF THE

SHAKSPERE SOCIETY OF PHILADELPHIA

SHAKSPERE SOCIETY'S ROOMS No. 206 SOUTH FOURTH STREET

Lor. At dinner time
I pray you haue in minde where we must meete.—MERC. VEN., i., 1.

SATURDAY, APRIL 23, 1864

THE THREE HUNDREDTH BIRTH-DAY

——Feasts ſo ſolemne and ſo rare,
Since ſildom comming in the long yeares ſet,
Like ſtones of worth they thinly placed are
Or captaine Iewells in the carconet.—SONNET 52.

Nor *Mars* his ſword, nor warres quick fire ſhall burne
The liuing record of your memory.—SONNET 55.

1564, APRIL 26, GULIELMUS FILIUS, JOHANNES SHAKSPERE.
OBIIT ANO DOI 1616, ÆTATIS 53 DIE 23 AP.

Where euer the bright Sunne of Heauen shall shine,
His Honour and the greatnesse of his Name,
Shall be.—HEN. VIII., v., 4.

DINNER.

To. Does not our liues conſiſt of the foure Elements?
And. Faith ſo they ſay, but I thinke it rather conſiſts of eating and drinking.—TWELFE NIGHT, II., 3.
Sil. Ah ſirra (quotha) we ſhall doe nothing but eate and make good cheere, and praise heauen.—II HENRY IV., v., 3.

AT 5 P. M.

Mar. By this, I thinke the Diall points at fiue.—COM. OF ERRORS, v., 1.
Keeper. Is our whole diſſembly appeard?—MUCH ADOE, iv.
Lear. Let me not stay a iot for dinner.—LEAR, i., 4.

BILL OF FARE.

Which eyes not yet created ſhall ore-read.—SONNET 81.

OYSTERS ON THE HALF SHELL.

Cost. Easier ſwallowed than a flapdragon.—LOVES LAB., v., 1.
Brut. Kill him in the ſhell.—JULIUS CÆSAR, ii.

Figure 3.2. The first page of the Philadelphia Shakspere Society's menu for its annual dinner (1864). By permission of the Folger Shakespeare Library.

and fourth Wednesday of every month in members' homes to read and discuss the plays and poems. In California, the ladies of Pasadena's Shakespeare Club, which began the following year, met on Saturdays from October to July in their own clubhouse. Other groups, like the Shakespeare Club of Worcester, Massachusetts, brought together cultured ladies and gentlemen to read the plays scene by scene at bi-weekly meetings in members' living rooms.

Like many of its counterparts around the United States, the Worcester Shakespeare Club continues to thrive.

However socially focused Shakespeare clubs may have been—and it's clear from their many surviving scrapbooks that the gathering of "congenial persons" was a major element in their success—they kept a broad cross-section of middle class Americans reading the plays. Membership in a Shakespeare club provided cultural capital; it signaled an individual's learning and gentility. Moreover, as the impresario Augustin Daly argued in 1897, "Shakespeare clubs are the greatest of all factors for keeping the Shakespearean drama on the stage."[28] And if studying the plays whetted the appetite for formal and informal stage performances, it also, as the Philadelphia and New York clubs demonstrate, fostered the desire to collect a host of books that would allow members to illuminate Shakespeare's words and thereby enhance their enjoyment on stage and heighten the pleasures of informed dialogue.

* * *

Widespread American familiarity with Shakespeare's major plays—at least their plots, principal characters, and most memorable lines—encouraged good-natured mockery on stage and in print. Beginning in the seventeenth century and lasting to the foreseeable future, wherever Shakespeare's writings resonate widely, satirists and comedians subject his dramas to mangled soliloquies, linguistic puns, revamped characters, and topsy-turvy story lines. The resulting texts are variously dubbed parodies, caricatures, travesties, burlesques, lampoons, farces, or mockeries—nearly interchangeable terms for some writers but subtly distinct for others. In the absence of consensus, this book applies the first four terms to humorous but respectful adaptations of the original texts, the final three to adaptations that treat the originals with some degree of ridicule.[29]

This comic tradition began in England as early as 1675 when Thomas Duffett's *The Mock-Tempest, or, The Enchanted Castle* lampooned Dryden and Davenant's remaking of Shakespeare's original into *The Tempest, or, The Enchanted Island*, which in the early 1670s had supplanted the First Folio version on British stages. Duffett's farce is set in a prison for whores and vagabonds, where "Sir Prospero Whiffe," formerly "Duke of my Lord Mayors Doggkennel" (p. 10), presides over an obscenity-laden spectacle of music and sex that appealed to the boisterous tastes of Restoration London. In Duffett's rendition, for example, Ariel is a gutter version of Shakespeare's sprite, declaring in the second scene: "Hayl most potent Master, I come to serve thy pleasure/Be it to lye, swear, steal, pick pockets, or creep in at Windows" (p. 11); other characters, such as the wenches Beantosser, Mousetrappa, and Drinkallup, are comparably unscrupulous. (A character named "Murder" holds two bloody daggers as he sings "*Wake* Duncan! *would thou couldst*" (p.18), in unmistakable reference to *Macbeth*, thereby initiating a hallmark of the new genre: the incorporation of words, characters, and situations from one or more additional Shakespeare texts.) Since Duffett's day, hundreds of Shakespearian travesties have tickled English and American ribs, though rarely with *The Mock-Tempest*'s blatant bawdiness.[30]

The bellwether text for America, and arguably the first true Shakespeare burlesque since Duffett's, was *Hamlet Travestie: in Three Acts. With Annotations by Dr. Johnson and Geo. Steevens, esq. and Other Commentators*, by the prolific English comic dramatist John Poole. It was published repeatedly in London beginning in 1810 and in New York the following year.[31] Poole admitted "that any attempt to treat with levity the works of our IMMORTAL POET is in some danger of being received with displeasure," but insisted that he meant only "to afford an hour's amusement" (pp. [ii], v).

Much of the humor in Poole's lengthy text comes from whimsical stanzas set to familiar (at the time) English tunes. To the jingle "Derry Down," Hamlet sings:

> . . .
> Two months have scarce pass'd since dad's death, and my
> mother,
> Like a brute as she is, has just married his brother.
> To wed such a bore!—but tis all too late now:
> We can't make a silk purse of the ear of a sow. (p. 9)

Hamlet later foreshadows Gilbert and Sullivan's patter songs in this graveyard meditation:

> When deprived of our breath,
> By that harlequin, death,
> His pantomime changes fast follow:

First his magic displaces
Eyes and nose from our faces,
    And like this leaves them ghastly and hollow.
. . .
Next, without much delay,
We're converted to clay;
    But our next transformation's a lottery:
Some are changed into cans,
Some to pint-pots or pans—
    Some to tea-pots from Wedgwood's famed pottery.
By this rule may we trace
Julius Caesar's bold face,
    Till we find it i'th' form of a jug;
And renown'd Alexander,
The world's great commander,
    A two-penny earthenware mug! (p. 47)

A few pages of pseudo-annotations follow the text of *Hamlet Travestie.* Some are brief explications of a word or phrase, others are pedantic exchanges between Johnson, Steevens, Pope, and other eminent editors. An instance of the former is Johnson's gloss on Queen Gertrude's description of Hamlet as "Mad as butter in the sun" (p. 37). "Amongst the popular superstitions," Johnson explains, "is one, that butter is mad twice a year; viz in summer, when its liquidability renders it tenable only in a spoon; and in winter, when, by the adhesion of its parts, it almost resists the knife" (p. 59). The subsequent paucity of annotated burlesques suggests that however amusing *Hamlet Travestie* may have been to some readers and audiences, it appealed most strongly, perhaps, to those familiar with scholarly editions rather than to the public at large.

The success of Poole's parody spurred new efforts: a rival version of *Hamlet* entirely in prose (1811), travesties of *Romeo and Juliet* (1812), *Macbeth* (1813), *Othello* (1813, sometimes attributed to Poole), and two of *Richard III* (1816 and 1823).[32] Apparently none of these plays was initially printed or performed in America, although imported copies may have circulated in eastern American cities where increasingly popular variety shows often included a short farce as the final installment of a three-part program. The estimated "Time of Presentation" in acting editions of many Shakespeare burlesques (though not

Poole's and some other early texts) ranged from twenty minutes to an hour and ten or fifteen minutes, making them likely choices to conclude a three-part show. But the predicted duration was only a guess: at many theaters, calls from the audience for repeats of favorite songs or even audience participation in well-known skits might considerably delay the closing time.

Colonial Americans as early as 1770 had enjoyed perversions of Hamlet's "To be or not to be" and quipped about "Old Shakespeare, a poet who should not be spit on,/Although he was born in an island called Britain," and colonists laughed at Garrick's *Catherine and Petruchio.* (Although the adaptation was humorous in its own right, only the viewers familiar with Shakespeare's *The Taming of the Shrew* were likely to recognize Garrick's distortions.) Not until the 1820s, it seems, were Shakespeare's major plays so widely known that unabashed burlesques could be frequently and profitably staged in New York and other nascent cities; by mid-century they were immensely popular from coast to coast, in large communities and small. High-spirited California miners loved the locally produced caricatures of plays they hazily remembered from their eastern schooldays. In the early 1850s, San Francisco's Adelphi Theatre staged a parody of *Richard III*, starring some of the Chapman clan, who were especially adept at light comedy. Touring companies treated mining camps to impromptu burlesques of *Hamlet* and *Macbeth.*[33]

The most-often satirized plays were, of course, the ones Americans knew best. Judging from the number of surviving texts, *Hamlet* was the favorite, *Macbeth* a respectable runner-up, with *Romeo and Juliet*, *Othello*, and *The Merchant of Venice* not far behind. (The number of amateur and professional burlesque performances—a truer measure of popularity—defies measurement, because many skits were never published and performance records are notoriously incomplete.) The absence of American imprints did not, of course, preclude American performances. British imprints of Shakespeare parodies could readily be transported to America, and since many texts were short, manual transcriptions must have been common. The thirty-page *Shylock; or, The Merchant of Venice Preserved... a Jerusalem Hearty-Joke*, for example, is not known to have had an American edition, but it amused theater audiences in New York before and after it was published in London in 1855. At least one burlesque, Charles Selby's

Kinge Richard ye Third, seems to have been published simultaneously in London and New York in 1844.[34] Most of the parodies printed in America came from presses in New York or Boston, sometimes Chicago or St Louis, but distribution was nationwide.

American comic authors may have been slow to parody Shakespeare partly because British texts were so prevalent but mainly because American humorists gravitated to the emerging minstrel genre (discussed below). By the middle of the nineteenth century, however, home-grown conventional burlesques appeared with some frequency. Notable early examples are William Knight Northall's *Macbeth Travestie*, performed in 1843 but not published until 1852; an anonymous travesty of *King John* in 1846, George Edward Rice's *An Old Play in A New Garb (Hamlet, Prince of Denmark)* in 1853; George M. Baker's *Capuletta; or, Romeo and Juliet Restored. An Operatic Burlesque* in 1868, and the Englishman John Brougham's *Much Ado about A Merchant of Venice* in the same year, written and published during the author's extended visit to the United States.[35] In the 1870s a Missouri author, Charles Carroll Soule, was popular with relatively sophisticated audiences. His fifty-three-page *New Travesty on Romeo and Juliet* appeared initially at the University Club of St Louis in January 1877, where Soule's pedestrian songs and happy ending were well received. A few months later a handbill in Worcester, Massachusetts, hailed Soule's play as "The Most Successful Burlesque Performance ever given in Worcester."[36]

Such praise encouraged Soule to write *A Travesty Without a Pun! Hamlet Revamped, Modernized, and Set to Music* (1879) in a fusion of Shakespeare's story with songs that evoked the newly popular Gilbert and Sullivan operettas.[37] In Soule's rendition, Polonius is a professor at Wittenburgh University, where Hamlet and Horatio are students. A boisterous dormitory party, intended to cheer up Hamlet ("What is there, man, to make you blue?/You're on the Nine, you're in the Crew" [p. 6]), is interrupted:

> . . . We'll drink a toast:—
> To Hamlet,—classmate, friend, and host! (Knocks)
> That awful knock! the faculty!
> Conceal these signs of revelry,
> Throw gloves and foils behind the chairs;

The glasses hide beneath the table!
The pipes, tobacco—No, who cares?
Don't make a noise so much like Babel!
Pile lexicons, in careless bunch,
Above, round, the bowl of punch!
Each take a book, and when they speak,
Appear absorbed in learning Greek!

The queen arrives and is not amused.

Horatio: Your majesty, we kneel before you!
Queen: Has consciousness at length come o'er you?
Prefer that Greek to us? Aha!
We'll teach you, youngsters, who we are.
Professor P., expel them all! (p. 8)

But harmony is soon restored, with the chorus reminding the audience that:

The queen gets her king back
From the ghostly, mysterious shades of the dead;
While Hamlet and Ophelia
Won't die, but will happily wed:
For we jolly students so helped them along,
With counsel and song, they couldn't go wrong; and
We've turned the whole play
From a tragic affray to a comedy gay.—a comedy gay[.] (p. 48)

This frothy burlesque, borrowing hoary tunes like "Pop Goes the Weasel" and "Three Blind Mice," had four American editions between 1879 and 1894. Their greatest appeal was, presumably, to college theatrical groups.

A few American parodies remained quite faithful to Shakespeare's plots. *Katherine, A Travesty* (1888), for example, adhered roughly to *The Taming of the Shrew*, with five acts—rather than the typical burlesque's one to three—and the original's cast of characters. But *Katherine* included songs intentionally modeled on Gilbert and Sullivan, such as "Two Little Dudes from Pisa We" (*The Mikado* had debuted three years earlier) and enough puns to make it a quintessential burlesque. Far more common were the radically condensed and revamped shows that also, almost always, featured popular music and humorous wordplay, as in Alice Gould's *The Merchant of Venice. A Burlesque Operatic Version* (1929), which relied heavily on songs and sight gags. And many pastiches, whether musical or not, dispensed with Shakespeare's plots altogether. In *A Shakespearean Fantasy* (1901), for example, Prospero is surrounded not only by characters from *The Tempest* but also by Hamlet and Ophelia, Romeo and Mercutio, Falstaff, and Lear, to name the most notable. In Hope Moulton's *Hamlet, A Burlesque in One Act* (1927) Ophelia elopes with Horatio; Hamlet, eager to reunite with a girl he married at the university, drives the getaway car at a daring 40 m.p.h. Even less faithful, if possible, to Shakespeare's text is Sara Hawkes Sterling's *Hamlet's Brides* (1900), in which the title character woos Portia, Rosalind, Juliet, Beatrice, and Viola in Salt Lake City; all of the women are widowed or divorced and welcome Hamlet's advances. Portia advises that in Mormon territory he can marry them all, to which Hamlet intones "Oh blessed, blessed Brigham Young!" (p. 18).[38]

America's favorite and most indigenous Shakespearian burlesque is surely Mark Twain's in *Adventures of Huckleberry Finn* (1884).[39] During Huck and Jim's travels down the Mississippi, they encounter a self-styled "king" and a "duke" who rehearse the balcony scene from *Romeo and Juliet* and the sword fight from *Richard III* to swindle naïve riverside audiences. The duke tries to teach Hamlet's principal soliloquy to the king for an encore, but with no copy of the play for reference, he "call[s] it back from recollection's vaults" in a flurry of facial and bodily contortions.

> By and by he got it [Huck remembers]. He told us to give attention. Then he strikes a most noble attitude, with one leg shoved forwards, and his arms stretched away up, and his head tilted back, looking up at the sky; and then he begins to rip and rave and grit his teeth; and after that, all through his speech he howled, and spread around, and swelled up his chest, and just knocked the spots out of any acting ever *I* see before. This is the speech—I learned it, easy enough, while he was learning it to the king:
>
> To be, or not to be; that is the bare bodkin
> That makes calamity of so long life;
> For who would fardels bear, till Birnam Wood do come to Dunsinane,
> But that the fear of something after death

Murders the innocent sleep,
Great nature's second course,
And makes us rather sling the arrows of outrageous fortune
Than fly to others that we know not of.
...
...But soft you, the fair Ophelia:
Ope not thy ponderous and marble jaws,
But get thee to a nunnery—go! (pp. 114–15)

Styling themselves "The world renowned tragedians, David Garrick the younger...and Edmund Kean the elder" (p. 116), the two rapscallions strip their Arkansas audiences of nearly $500 before fleeing for their lives. Twain accomplishes a double burlesque: Duke and the king's manipulation of Shakespeare's dramas to gull rural audiences, and the book's spoof of the Shakespearian parody tradition itself. By the 1880s that tradition was already a century old in America and shows no sign of flagging more than a century and a quarter later.

* * *

A notorious subgenre of the travesty tradition, blackface minstrelsy, flourished for more than a century as a major American entertainment vehicle. Its principal progenitors were the early "Ethiopian delineators," including a few mainstream actors like the American Edwin Forrest and the visiting Englishman Charles Mathews, who occasionally mimicked African American accents, dress, dance, and behavior as perceived by white performers and audiences. The most notable and durable mimic was Thomas Dartmouth ("Daddy") Rice. In the 1830s he sang and danced "Jump Jim Crow" to enthusiastic crowds in taverns and circuses as well as, increasingly, at legitimate theaters in America and Britain. By the early 1840s a number of immensely popular "Ethiopian Minstrels" had branched off from the traditional family-based minstrel shows in which whites played whites; in the new "darky shows," whites in black makeup (initially burnt cork, later grease paint) portrayed imaginary African American characters in shows written specifically for the new genre. Later in the nineteenth century and lasting into the twentieth, some black actors applied similar makeup to achieve a comparable exaggerated effect.[40]

Black minstrelsy's heyday began in 1843 with the almost simultaneous formation of the Virginia Minstrels in New York City, featuring Dan Emmett and three colleagues, and Edwin C. Christy's Minstrels in Albany, New York, organized by Christy and featuring his stepson George Christy (a former one-man Ethiopian delineator). Christy was soon joined by George W. H. Griffin, who wrote many of the scripts, often took the leading role, and assumed leadership of the company after George Christy's death in 1868. Meanwhile, scores of other blackface minstrel companies emerged to meet the insatiable demand; in 1860 New York had ten such companies. Shakespeare, not surprisingly, was fodder for writers of blackface farces who sought readily recognizable plots and characters for their coarse humor. Only a dozen or so published skits borrowed principally from Shakespeare (including only six of 100 titles in an 1874 list of Christy's Minstrel "Ethiopian Dramas"—two versions of *Othello,* one each of *Comedy of Errors*, *Hamlet*, and *The Merchant of Venice*, and a pastiche of quotations, *De Darkey Tragedian*), but they were among the audience favorites. The basic version often spawned several published or unpublished variants.[41]

Hamlet was the favorite. A comic opera version was performed in New York as early as 1843; by 1863–4 a blackface burlesque had appeared, and in 1866 George Griffin's very popular *Hamlet, the Dainty, An Ethiopian Burlesque* was playing at New York's Fifth Avenue Opera House (Fig. 3.3). Griffin's text had numerous additional American editions between 1870 and 1894, plus a London edition in 1877. Like the other minstrel shows, this skit (some of it paraphrased from John Poole's much earlier *Hamlet*) exaggerated everything—clothing, props, accents, and acting, with racist stereotypes intruding from the outset. Hamlet opens with "The air bites shrewdly—it is very cold," to which Horatio responds, "I never saw a darky half so bold." Upon the appearance of the elder Hamlet's ghost, smoking a long cigar and his face covered with white flour, Horatio and Marcellus react with slapstick antics, as Hamlet exclaims: "He's from the South! Oh, grace defend us!/Prithee! No more such frightful specters send us!" (p. 4). The play closes with the queen warning Hamlet: "I'm poisoned! Your old uncle, here,/Has mixed a deadly poison with the beer./It's now too late—I took too many swigs—/He put the poison in, to kill off all you nigs" (p. 8).[42]

Othello was the other prime blackface Shakespearian text. "Daddy" Rice wrote and acted in one of the earliest, *Otello*, and some years

Figure 3.3. The cover of *Hamlet the Dainty* in the Happy Hours Company's Ethiopian Drama series (*c.*1870). By permission of the Folger Shakespeare Library.

later "*Othello*," *A Burlesque* (*c.*1870), performed by Griffin and Christy's Minstrels, became a widespread favorite, replete with pejorative language and actions. Iago opens with a song: "When first I Desdemona saw, I thought her very fine,/And by the way she treated me, I thought she'd soon be mine;/But she's cleared out and left me now, with a nasty, dirty fellar,/As black as mud—a white-washer—a nagur called Othello" (p. 3). In the end, Griffin's Othello stays true to the original plot: "How beautiful she looks—and yet I'll kill her—/Not shed her blood—but choke her wid dis pillow" (p. 10).

Another caricature of *Othello*, titled *Desdemonum* (1874) and perhaps also by Griffin, is a musical set in "Wennice," where "Oteller" plays the tambourine and "Roderigum" the banjo. In the opening duet, Desdemonum replies to Oteller's invitation to join him: "Tel, my duck, I hear you; daddy's gone to bed./Fotch along your ladderum, I'm de gal to wed!/Since burnt-cork am de fashion, I'll not be behind—/I'll see Oteller's wisage in his highfalutin' mind." Together they sing, "De hour am propitious—come, my darlin' flame!/Dey say dat in de dark all cullers am de same" (pp. 3–4).[43]

Griffin insulted America's racial and ethnic minorities with fine impartiality. His "*Shylock,*" *A Burlesque* (1874), had Griffin impersonating "Shylock (Dealer in Old Clothes)" and reciting his rhymed speeches in a mock-Yiddish accent. Although this play is listed among the company's Ethiopian dramas, there is no indication that the actors used blackface or pseudo-African American speech, and unlike the other "Ethiopian" publications by the Happy Hours Company, the title page identifies it as *A Burlesque* rather than *An Ethiopian Burlesque*. In other respects, however, this skit fits the minstrel genre. It opens with "Two hooked-nose gentlemen" on the Rialto, where Shylock insists that Antonio repay his loan: "If at the time he doesn't come and pay—/I'll cut his liver out, the very day!/If he's a liver then, he shall not prate,/He must die early, so he shan't di-late!" (pp. 3–4). There follows a very condensed version of Shakespeare's plot that ends with "The Dook" querying Shylock about the pound of Antonio's flesh:

> Well, what say you, Jew, will you consent
> To take it from his hide? the cash you lent
> Is clearly lost, so do what you think better,
> To rid yourself of an insolvent debtor.

Portia interjects:

> Hold you willain! I'm not *willin* yet
> Antonio's buzzum shall be upset;
> But, now wade in! like a duck in the mud,
> But remember, you *draw not one drop of blood!*

To which Shylock laments:

> The game is up, I cannot solve this riddle,
> I'm trembling like a cat-gut on a fiddle;

> I've lost my *flesh*, my *monish*, and my *daughter*,
> Now I'll sneak out like a lamb to the slaughter. (p. 8)

Shylock is seized and tossed up and down on a large canvas until the curtain drops.[44]

Griffin and Christy's Minstrels were the most prominent promoters and performers of Shakespearian blackface but never the only ones. In an undated burlesque, probably from the late 1850s, the American author and manager John F. Poole presented *Ye Comedie of Errours: A Glorious, Uproarious Burlesque... with Many a Chorus, Warranted not to Bore Us, Now for the First Time Set before Us.* Andy Foolus and Dummy-o of Ephesus and their counterparts of Syracuse speak in mock African American dialects. Some years later, the anonymous *Dar's de Money (Burlesque on "Othello")* was performed in New York at Wood's Minstrel Hall but not printed until simultaneous London and New York editions in *c.*1880. This twenty-minute skit consists of two comically dressed pseudo-black men who scheme to make easy money by performing the deathbed scene from "Othello, and Dars-de-money" (p. 24).[45] *Julius the Snoozer, or The Conspirators of Thompson Street* (1876) borrowed *Julius Caesar*, very loosely, to mock the recently deposed New York "Boss," William Marcy Tweed.[46] The brevity of these and other blackface shows—usually ten pages or fewer—appears to reflect the authors' intention, in response to audience preferences, to use such skits in the three-part minstrel format established by Christy's Minstrels.

Although blackface minstrels had a long life, their greatest popularity came in the 1840s through 1870s; thereafter they persisted unevenly until the civil rights movement of the 1960s exposed their blatant bigotry. Much earlier, however, Shakespeare fell from favor. He remained a recurring theme in white burlesques well into the twentieth century, with a cluster of new titles in the few years prior to World War I and in a scattering in the 1920s through 1940s. But tellingly, few blackface Shakespeare texts are recorded after 1880, even if some of the older works were still occasionally performed and vestiges of minstrelsy emerged from time to time in vaudeville songs and eventually in radio programs. But the earlier voracious appetite for spoofs of Shakespeare, it seems, had largely been exhausted for the many audiences that still enjoyed blackface entertainment. That several of the new whiteface burlesques of the twentieth century mocked women's Shakespeare clubs suggests that when Shakespeare appeared in parodies, he appealed mainly to genteel audiences.

Minstrel shows, whether enacted by whites in burnt cork or African Americans with blackface highlights, bear no affinity, of course, to the serious performance of Shakespeare's plays by African American actors. That topic is addressed in the next chapter.

Notes

1. Among the many accounts of the Bridger tale is Jennifer Lee Carrell, "How the Bard Won the West," *Smithsonian* 19.5 (August 1998), 99–107.
2. Alexis de Tocqueville, *Democracy in America*, ed. J. P. Mayer and Max Lerner, trans. George Lawrence (New York: Harper & Row, 1966), 438.
3. Esther Cloudman Dunn, *Shakespeare in America* (New York: Macmillan, 1939), 176. Louis B. Wright, *Culture on the Moving Frontier* (1955; repr. New York: Harper & Bros., 1961), 78, gives a different list of frontier favorites.
4. Dunn, *Shakespeare in America*, 178–80; Charles H. Shattuck, *Shakespeare on the American Stage: From the Hallams to Edwin Booth* (Washington, DC: Folger Shakespeare Library, 1976), 50–54.
5. Dunn, *Shakespeare in America*, 202–4; Ashley Thorndike, *Shakespeare in America* (London: Oxford University Press, 1927), 10.
6. Dunn, *Shakespeare in America*, 205–6.
7. Wright, *Moving Frontier*, 75 (quotation), 116; Helene Wickham Koon, *How Shakespeare Won the West: Players and Performances in America's Gold Rush, 1849–1865* (Jefferson, NC: McFarland, 1989), 20–23.
8. Koon, *How Shakespeare Won the West*, 35–40, 61–5; Louis Marder, *His Exits and Entrances: The Story of Shakespeare's Reputation* (Philadelphia: J. B. Lippincott, 1963), 303–4, says that *Othello*, *Macbeth*, and *Richard III* were performed in 1850; Dunn, *Shakespeare in America*, 209, says *Macbeth*, *Hamlet*, and *Much Ado.*
9. Koon, *How Shakespeare Won the West*, 39–74.
10. Dunn, *Shakespeare in America*, 205–12; Koon, *How Shakespeare Won the West*, 12–15.
11. Ibid. 29–31; Leonard J. Arrington, *Brigham Young: American Moses* (New York: Knopf, 1985), 287–93.
12. The original letter is at the Nantucket Historical Association.

13. William Enfield, *The Speaker: or, Miscellaneous Pieces, Selected from the Best English Writers . . . with a View to the Improvement of Youth in Reading and Speaking*, new edn (London: J. Johnson, 1803); Hugh Blair, *Lectures on Rhetoric and Belles Lettres* (2 vols, London: W. Strahan & T. Cardell, 1783), quotations on 2.523, 524; Henry William Simon, *The Reading of Shakespeare in American Schools and Colleges: An Historical Survey* (New York: Simon & Schuster, 1932), 11–13; Marder, *His Exits and Entrances*, 276–7.
14. John Walker, *Elements of Elocution; in which the Principles of Reading and Speaking Are Investigated . . .* (Boston: D. Mallory & Co., 1810).
15. Cooke had a three-volume sequence: an *Introduction to the American Orator* (1812) for beginners; *The American Orator, or Elegant Extracts in Prose and Poetry* (1811) for more advanced students; and *Sequel to the American Orator, or, Dialogues for Schools* (New Haven, CT: Increase Cooke & Co., 1813), which we discuss.
16. Douglas L. Wilson and Rodney O. Davis (eds.), *Herndon's Informants: Letters, Interviews, and Statements about Abraham Lincoln* (Urbana: University of Illinois Press, 1998), 129, 138.
17. Simon, *Reading of Shakespeare*, 13–15; Lindley Murray, *Sentiments of Several Eminent Persons on the Tendency of Dramatic Entertainments . . .* (New York: Mahlon Day, 1821), quotations from 20, 24. For examples of footnotes in Cooke, *Dialogues*, see 183–4, 206–7, 324–5, 378.
18. For McGuffey's career see Simon, *Reading of Shakespeare*, 26–44; Henry H. Vail, *A History of the McGuffey Readers* (Cleveland, OH: Burrows Brothers, 1911), 4–7, 18, 61–4; and Harvey C. Minnich, *William Holmes McGuffey and His Readers* (New York: American Book Company, 1936), 71–82.
19. See the various editions of McGuffey, as cited, and Simon, *Reading of Shakespeare*, 26–9; and for tampering with *The Merchant of Venice*, Jonathan Burton, "Lay On, McGuffey: Excerpting Shakespeare in Nineteenth-Century Schoolbooks," in *Shakespearean Educations: Power, Citizenship, and Performance*, ed. Coppélia Kahn, Heather S. Nathans, and Mimi Godfrey (Newark: University of Delaware Press, 2011), 95–111.
20. Sales of 122 million by 1920 are cited by Simon, *Reading of Shakespeare*, 26, based on the estimate by McGuffey's publisher. Hamlin Garland, *A Son of the Middle Border* (New York: Macmillan, 1917), 112–13.
21. Simon, *Reading of Shakespeare*, 45–59.
22. Brander Matthews, *These Many Years: Recollections of a New Yorker* (New York: Scribner's Sons, 1917), 108.
23. Simon, *Reading of Shakespeare*, 59–76; Marder, *Exits and Entrances*, 288–9; Andrew Murphy, *Shakespeare in Print: A History and Chronology of*

Shakespeare Publishing (Cambridge: Cambridge University Press, 2003), 152–3, 155, 359.

24. Simon, *Reading of Shakespeare*, 77, 84–7; Frederick Rudolph, *Curriculum: A History of the American Undergraduate Course of Study since 1636* (San Francisco, CA: Jossey-Bass, 1977), 104, 134–44; Marder, *Exits and Entrances*, 284–5.
25. *How to Organize a Shakespeare Club* (New York: Doubleday & McClure, 1899).
26. See Henry L. Savage, "The Shakspere Society of Philadelphia," *Shakespeare Quarterly* 3 (1952), 341–52.
27. Katherine Scheil documents the growth of women's Shakespeare clubs in *She Hath Been Reading: Shakespeare's Women Readers* (Minneapolis, MN: University of Minnesota Press, 2012).
28. Quoted from Anna Randall-Diehl, *The American Shakespeare Magazine* (1897).
29. On definitions see the note to "caricature" in the *Oxford American Writers Thesaurus* (New York: Oxford University Press, 2004), 124, and Stanley Wells (ed.), *Nineteenth-Century Shakespeare Burlesques* (5 vols, London: Diploma Press, 1977–78), 1.xiii–iv.
30. T[homas] Duffett, *The Mock-Tempest: or the Enchanted Castle* (London: Printed for William Cademan, 1675).
31. John Poole, *Hamlet Travestie: in Three Acts. With Annotations by Dr. Johnson and Geo. Steevens, esq. and Other Commentators* (New York: David Longworth, 1811 [Early American Imprints, 2 ser. 23712]). See also Henry E. Jacobs and Claudia D. Johnson (eds.), *An Annotated Bibliography of Shakespearean Burlesques, Parodies, and Travesties* (New York: Garland, 1976), #50–55, 63; and Wells, *Shakespeare Burlesques*, 1.xvi–xxi.
32. Arthur Murphy, *Life of Hamlet, with Alterations: A Tragedy, In Three Acts*, in Jesse Foote (ed.), *The Life of Arthur Murphy* (London: John Nichols & Sons, 1811); Richard Gurney, *Romeo and Juliet Travesty. In Three Acts* (London: T. Hookham, Jr., et al., 1812); John Poole, *Othello Travestie; In Three Acts. With Burlesque Notes In the Manner of the Most Celebrated Commentators* (London: Printed for J. J. Stockdale, 1813); William By, *Richard III. Travestie in Three Acts, with Annotations* (London: Sherwood, Neely & Jones, 1816). See also Wells, *Shakespeare Burlesques*, 1.xxii–vi, and Anon., *King Richard III Travestie. A Burlesque, Operatic, Mock Terrific Tragedy, in Two Acts* (London: E. Duncombe, 1823), repr. in Wells, *Shakespeare Burlesques*, 1:[199]–235.
33. For parodies of Hamlet passages, see above, Ch. 1, 25–6; for "Old Shakespeare," see Marder, *Exits and Entrances*, 295; Koons, *How Shakespeare Won the West*, 50.

34. Francis Talfourd, *Shylock, or The Merchant of Venice Preserved. An Entirely New Reading of Shakespeare, from an Edition Hitherto Undiscovered by Modern Authorities, and Which it is Hoped May be Received as the Stray Leaves of a Jerusalem Hearty-Joke* (London: Thomas Hailes Lacy, 1855); Charles Selby, *Kinge Richard Ye Third* (London and New York: Samuel French, 1844).
35. W. K. Northall, *Macbeth Travestie. A Burlesque in Two Acts. With the Stage Business, Cast of Characters, Costumes, Relative Positions, Etc.* (New York and Baltimore: Wm. Taylor & Henry Taylor, [1852]), with a brief performance history in the preface; Jacobs and Johnson, *Annotated Bibliography*, #117; Anon., "King John," in *Judy* 1.2 (December 5, 1846), 17–21, and Jacobs and Johnson, *Annotated Bibliography*, #85; George Edward Rice, *An Old Play in a New Garb (Hamlet Prince of Denmark in Three Acts)* (Boston: Ticknor, Reed, & Fields, 1853); Jacobs and Johnson, *Annotated Bibliography*, #56, 138. George M. Baker, *Capuletta; or, Romeo and Juliet Restored. An Operatic Burlesque*, repr. in Baker, *The Mimic Stage* (Boston: Lee & Shepard, 1869), 79–105; John Brougham, *Much Ado About A Merchant of Venice. From the Original Text—A Long Way* (New York: Samuel French, 1868).
36. [Charles C. Soule,] *A New Travesty of Romeo and Juliet as Originally Presented before the University Club of St. Louis* (Chicago: G. I. Jones, 1877); handbill for Worcester performance of May 14 [1877], American Antiquarian Society, Worcester, MA.
37. Charles C. Soule, *A Travesty Without A Pun. Hamlet Revamped, Modernized, and Set to Music* (St Louis: G. I. Jones, 1879); for subsequent editions see Jacobs and Johnson, *Annotated Bibliography*, #60, 61, 132, 187.
38. John Kendrick Bangs, *Katherine, A Travesty* (New York: Gilliss Brothers & Turnure, 1888); Alice Gould, *The Merchant of Venice. A Burlesque Operatic Version* (Boston, MA: Walter H. Baker, 1929); Oscar Fay Adams, *A Shakespearean Fantasy*, in *A Motley Jest. Shakespearean Diversion* (Boston: Samuel French, 1901), 1–48; Sara Hawkes Sterling, *Hamlet's Brides. A Shakespearean Burlesque in One Act* (Boston, MA: Walter H. Baker, 1900), repr. with *The Shakespeare Wooing* (Boston, MA: Walter H. Baker, 1915); Hope H. Moulton, *Hamlet, A Burlesque in One Act* (Boston: Walter H. Baker, 1927).
39. Mark Twain, *Adventures of Huckleberry Finn* (New York: Modern Library, 2001), 101–17, 126–9.
40. The substantial literature on this topic is discussed below in "Further Reading." A good starting point is Robert Toll, *Blacking Up: The Minstrel Show in Nineteenth-Century America* (New York: Oxford University Press, 1974).

41. See the list on back cover of George W. H. Griffin, *Desdemonum, An Ethiopian Burlesque in Three Scenes* (New York: Happy Hours Company [1874]). Among 34 "Parlour Plays for Home Performance" (implicitly not in blackface) in the same advertisement is *Katherine and Petruchio.*
42. G. W. H. Griffin, *Hamlet the Dainty. An Ethiopian Burlesque on Shakespeare's Hamlet, Performed by Griffin & Christy's Minstrels* (New York: Happy Hours Company, *c.*1870). For evidence of earlier and later editions, see Gary D. Engle, *This Grotesque Essence: Plays from the American Minstrel Stage* (Baton Rouge: Louisiana State University Press, 1978), 85–6; and Jacobs and Johnson, *Annotated Bibliography*, #32–6.
43. George W. H. Griffin, "*Othello,*" *A Burlesque as Performed by Griffin and Christy's Minstrels* (Clyde, OH: A. D. Ames [*c.*1870]), but see also Jacobs and Johnson, *Annotated Bibliography*, #164, 166–8; Griffin, *Desdemonum.*
44. "*Shylock,*" *A Burlesque, as Performed by Griffin and Christy's Minstrels, arranged by G. W. H. Griffin* (New York: Happy Hours Company, 1874). The skit was performed as early as 1867, according to Engle, *Grotesque Essence*, 91–2.
45. John F. Poole, *Ye comedy of Errours....* (New York: Samuel French [*c.*1858]), in Wells, *Shakespeare Burlesques*, 5.57–76; Anon., *Dars de Money (Burlesque on "Othello")* (London: Samuel French; New York: Samuel French and Son, [*c.*1880]); Jacobs and Johnson, *Annotated Bibliography*, #149.
46. Add[ison] Ryman and Charles White, *Julius the Snoozer, or, The Conspirators of Thompson Street. An Ethiopian Burlesque in Three Scenes* (New York: R.M. De Witt, 1876), reprinted in Engle, *Grotesque Essence*, 162–72.

4

Multicultural Shakespeare

To celebrate the three hundredth anniversary of Shakespeare's death, the New York City Shakespeare Tercentenary Celebration Committee hired the playwright and poet Percy MacKaye to write a memorial masque. The resulting outdoor extravaganza, *Caliban by the Yellow Sands*, was mounted May 24 to June 6, 1916 in the City College of New York's mammoth Lewisohn Stadium, with thirty professional actors in the speaking parts and as many as 2,500 mute participants in pantomimes and choreographed interludes. MacKaye had been especially chosen for the task because he advocated community theater as an uplifting experience for spectators of all classes and ethnicities. In the Appendix to the published text of *Caliban by the Yellow Sands*, MacKaye lists the participating ethnic groups from New York's teeming immigrant population: Egyptian, Greek, Italian, German, French, and Spanish, as well as Anglo-American, and he asked that the masque be translated into Italian, German, and Yiddish.[1] For MacKaye, Shakespeare was the great moral teacher who could inspire New York's non-English speaking immigrants to join their Anglophone neighbors in a new, multiethnic American community.

The theme of the masque, MacKaye explained, is "Caliban seeking to learn the art of Prospero." Caliban is "that passionate child-curious part of us all, groveling close to his aboriginal origins, yet groping up and staggering—with almost rhythmic falls and back-slidings—towards that serener plane of pity and love, reason and disciplined will, where Miranda and Prospero commune with Ariel and his Spirits."[2] The masque displays a contest for Caliban's soul between the forces of evil (Setebos, Lust, War, and Death) and the forces of virtue (Prospero). It also conflates Prospero's artistic powers with Shakespeare's. Using ten inner scenes taken from Shakespeare's plays, MacKaye's masque chronicles the rise of western civilization, using each vignette to teach Caliban a moral lesson. The message is clear. In order to assimilate into the American community, non-English-speaking immigrants should embrace the primary English-speaking poet, Shakespeare, and all he had come to represent. MacKaye's *Caliban*, argues a modern theater historian, "may well be read as an ambitious effort to reassert America's status as a bastion of Anglo-Saxon culture at a moment in time when that status was being threatened both from within and without."[3]

While assimilation was the favored pattern for European immigrants, separate but not equal was the norm for black Americans. They had been integral to American culture since the colonial era but were barred from white institutions because of their perceived (by many white Americans) racial inferiority. In 1916 black actors could only perform serious Shakespeare in New York's segregated black theaters. On April 24, 1916 an all-black amateur cast under the leadership of Edward Sterling Wright performed a production of *Othello* at Harlem's Lafayette Theatre.[4] Downtown from Harlem, black performers could participate in travesties of Shakespeare. Ziegfield's Follies, for example, featured the African American comedian Bert Williams in a travesty sketch of *Othello* that culminated in his beating Desdemona with a sledgehammer.[5]

The tercentenary celebrations of 1916 illustrate a tension still felt by America's minorities, who are caught between the widely accepted assumption that American culture is one huge melting pot where disparate ingredients simmer into a tasty stew, and their own experiences of continuing discrimination. By fashioning Shakespearian productions based on their own traditions and the challenges they faced in America, earlier generations of immigrant groups as well as African Americans helped to shape a hybrid Shakespeare that often strayed far from its British models. In the years since World War II, Asian American and Latino writers have expressed some resistance to Shakespeare as a symbol of America's white power elite and put less emphasis on assimilation than had earlier generations of immigrants. Yet, more recently, Asian American and Latino theater practitioners have included some of Shakespeare's best known plays in their repertoires, often in hybrid productions. In the twenty-first century, Shakespeare, the most celebrated bastion of Anglophone culture, continues to provoke debate about the complications ethnic minorities face in crafting their own American identity.

* * *

The great age of Europe's migration to America began in the mid-nineteenth century. Faced with starvation at home, especially after the famine of 1846, the Irish followed earlier migrations of Germans and Sephardic Jews. After the Civil War, new waves of migrants from central and southern Europe who had come to America in search of economic and political opportunities sought relief from their daily toil in theatrical entertainments spoken in their own language and geared to their own experiences. Shakespeare, whether in translation, adaptation, or travesty, was not as popular as comedy and variety shows, but he was nevertheless a staple in dramatic repertoires. Sometimes productions toured the United States from the homeland, such as the German actor Bogumel Dawson's *Hamlet* in New York (1866) with a German acting company. More often, Shakespeare performances were hybrids of the Old World and the New, as in Fanny Janauschek's *Macbeth* of 1867 in which she played Lady Macbeth in German while Edwin Booth, as her husband, spoke English. Many in the audience were familiar with Shakespeare's plots if not his language, and they could also purchase an inexpensive "libretto." The Italian community flocked to bilingual Shakespearian performances by celebrated Italian actors, regardless of the linguistic mix. Adelaide Ristori appeared as Lady Macbeth in the major cities of the eastern seaboard in 1866, speaking all of her lines in Italian, although in her 1884–5 tour, which ranged from coast to coast, she switched to English. Tommaso Salvini brought an Italian ensemble on his American tour in 1873–4, but in subsequent visits he spoke Italian while local actors used English. Throughout the Northeast, into the Midwest, and eventually in San Francisco, Salvini portrayed Othello (often to Edwin Booth's Iago), Hamlet, King Lear, and Coriolanus. In 1881–2, Ernesto Rossi tried to build on Salvini's success.[6] From the end of the nineteenth century into the twentieth, productions of Shakespeare's major tragedies in German and Italian enabled immigrant communities to partake of America's affection for the English poet.

A full-fledged Yiddish acting company developed in New York City during the 1870s, and by 1917 the city could boast three more. In the early twentieth century, Newark, Baltimore, Chicago, Cleveland, and Detroit also had Yiddish theaters.[7] While Jewish immigrants from Eastern Europe may not have been familiar with Shakespeare at first, they soon recognized earlier American immigrants' high regard for his writings and the popularity of his plays.[8] Up to two million Eastern European Jews fled pogroms and other forms of persecution and arrived on the east coast between 1880 and 1917; from the 1890s until World War I, Yiddish theater professionals mounted adaptations of Shakespeare's major tragedies suited to their audience's experience.

The most prominent adaptation was the Russian-born playwright Jacob Gordin's *Jewish King Lear*, first performed at New York's Union Theatre in 1892. Not content to follow earlier Yiddish authors who, he complained, "take a foreign play, squeeze every drop of juice out of it, change the Gentile names to Jewish ones, slap on manly beards and *peyes* [sideburns] and let them parade across the stage as Jews," Gordin recast Lear's story from the perspective of contemporaneous Eastern European Jews. The noted actor Jacob P. Adler took the lead role of Dovid Moysheles, a rich businessman from Vilna who divides his wealth among his three daughters and moves to Palestine. The plot roughly continues the Lear storyline: Dovid's two oldest daughters praise his decision while the youngest daughter, Taybele (Little Dove), resists. Taybele rejects the orthodoxy practiced by her sisters as the sons-in-law suck dry the estate, leaving Dovid penniless. Yaffe, the plain-speaking Kent figure who marries Taybele, makes the connection between Dovid and King Lear explicit:

> The old king, like you, divided his kingdom and also like you sent away the loving daughter who told him the truth. Oh! How dearly he paid for that! Yes, you are a Jewish King Lear! May God protect you from such an end as that to which King Lear came.[9]

Gordin omits the Gloucester plot and instead has Dovid go blind, and in his suffering he reassesses his daughters. Dovid realizes at last that although the elder daughters and their husbands follow the letter of Jewish law, they violate its spirit; their opponents emerge as the more honest and compassionate characters. After Dovid reconciles with Taybele, Yaffee (who has been trained in medicine during Dovid's absence) cures his blindness. Unlike *King Lear*, Gordin's play has a happy ending comparable to Nahum Tate's long-running English adaptation. For the Yiddish immigrants in the audience, the message was apparent: the younger generation's accommodation with American values is to be commended, not condemned. Dovid's fortunate outcome bodes well for the audience. They have suffered poverty, uprooting, and sometimes an incomprehensible new environment, but by blending the best of the old ways and the best of the new, they may flourish in America.[10]

Yiddish theaters also adapted Shakespeare's *Hamlet*, *Othello*, and *Romeo and Juliet* to meet their audiences' needs, accentuating conflict between the generations and the challenges faced by outsiders. Hamlet, for example, was cast as a rabbinical student, Friar Lawrence as a Reform rabbi. Unsurprisingly, the treatment of a Jewish outsider in *The Merchant of Venice* especially attracted the Yiddish community's attention; in 1899 it became the first Shakespearian play to be translated into Yiddish and published in the United States. Two years later Jacob Adler starred in its first successful production, speaking in Yiddish while the other actors spoke English (Fig. 4.1). Adler modeled his Shylock on the English actor Henry Irving's, but Adler made him even more sympathetic. And in the aftermath of World War II, Maurice Schwartz's new adaptation, *Shylock and His Daughter* (1947), highlighted the Christian community's anti-Semitism and made Shylock vengeful only after the loss of his daughter.[11] Like other Yiddish adaptations of Shakespeare, *Shylock and His Daughter* recast the original text in ways that reflected its audience's Jewish American identity. Instead of assimilating—performing Shakespeare in the same way he was presented in America's mainstream theaters—Yiddish actors grafted their own, quite different experiences onto his plots and characters to produce a hybrid Shakespeare, a tactic that would later be used by other minorities as well.

* * *

A celebrated Yiddish actor like Jacob Adler could cross over to perform for mainstream audiences, especially if he had mastered spoken English. The barriers to African American performers were less easily overcome, and it was not until the middle of the twentieth

Figure 4.1. The Yiddish actor Jacob Adler as a sympathetic Shylock. Courtesy Yivo Institute for Jewish Research.

century that Canada Lee and Paul Robeson successfully broke the color bar. Until then, even the audiences in "white" theaters were customarily segregated. Patrons of African descent sat in the least desirable section of the main floor or in the upper balcony. More often, black Americans were restricted to the black-owned theaters in their own communities.

The first such theater, founded by the West Indian immigrant William Henry Brown on New York's lower Broadway in 1821, drew on Brown's African Grove tea garden (or pleasure garden, loosely modeled on London's Vauxhall) that for several years had offered light entertainment to the community. The African Company, using a theater on the African Grove grounds with 300–400 seats, relied on some of the performers from the tea garden and a few newcomers. The ensemble sought to replicate with a black cast, black management, and black ownership the repertoire offered at white theaters. When Brown opened with America's favorite Shakespearian play of the time, *Richard III*, the actors included James Hewlett, perhaps the first African American Shakespeare actor, and soon added Ira Aldridge.[12] The popularity of Brown's African Theatre with both black and white audience members (the latter seated in a special section), led Brown to acquire a larger theater on Mercer Street, where Hewlett and others put on several Shakespeare plays in a diverse repertoire. Such success increasingly annoyed Stephen Price, the white manager of New York's prestigious Park Street Theatre. Price did whatever he could to close his rival down, most effectively by encouraging the African Company's neighbors to complain about noise and disorderly conduct. Eventually the police interrupted an African Company performance and jailed the actors until they gave assurances that they would not again perform Shakespeare.[13] The African Company closed its doors after barely three years of tumultuous existence. The talented Hewlett continued to offer his versions of Shakespeare's great monologues in one-man recitals in New York and elsewhere, while Ira Aldridge migrated to Europe to make his name as Othello and Lear. By the late 1820s, the United States had no formal venue for an African American to act Shakespearian drama.[14]

As Hewlett demonstrated, although an accomplished black actor could not star in full-scale Shakespeare productions, he or she might find a place in informal venues or on the lecture circuit. Hewlett's skill at acting and the cleverness of his imitations of major Shakespearians of the day earned him the sobriquet "the celebrated tragedian," yet his career was short, ending mysteriously in 1831. For the next several decades, talented black actors who craved Shakespearian roles headed for England. Ira Aldridge was by far the most conspicuous and successful. "The colored tragedian," Samuel Morgan Smith, arrived a year before Aldridge died in 1867 and in some respects filled the great actor's shoes. Smith had studied acting, especially Shakespearian roles, in Philadelphia, Boston, and New York but, like his contemporaneous thespians, could find no consistent venue for his talents. In England, on the other hand, he quickly found a niche in a small theater in Gravesend, where he played Othello, Hamlet, Macbeth, Shylock, and Richard III, and was universally appreciated. Smith continued in those and other roles throughout Britain, including London, until his death in 1882. A third American expatriate, Paul Molyneaux (real surname Hewlett), performed in Britain for about a decade before his death, back in America, at age 35 in 1891. He had played Othello in Boston before mixed audiences, but his prospects for steady employment were slim; in England he performed Othello in London and the provinces, with some praise but not enough to assure a prosperous career even in relatively tolerant Britain.

The only viable theatrical opportunities for aspiring black actors intent upon playing Shakespeare were joining underfunded black community theaters or touring as solo elocution performers who read or recited selections from the canon. Henrietta Vinton Davis (1860–1941) chose the latter route, touring extensively in the 1880s and 90s with her one-woman Shakespearian monologues, including Juliet's soliloquy before she takes the potion, Portia's discussion of mercy, Cleopatra's deathbed reverie, and some of Rosalind's witty remarks from *As You Like It.* Having studied elocution and dramatic art in Washington, DC, Boston, and New York, she was a true professional in training and performance.

Davis began her public recitations at the YMCA in Boston in 1883, then toured eastern cities, and later western cities as well, to growing applause. In addition to her solo performances, Davis sometimes combined with the impressive black actor Powhatan Beaty in selections from *Macbeth*. But despite almost unanimous praise and a coast-to-coast reputation among integrated audiences, the color bar kept Henrietta Vinton Davis out of every legitimate theater company. Under different circumstances, Davis would have had a distinguished career as an full-fledged actress of serious drama, but throughout the nineteenth century and far into the twentieth, the professional American theater considered no black actor or actress qualified to play a standard character in any white-controlled productions of a

Shakespeare play.[15] In a mix of idealism and frustration, Davis had by 1919 joined Marcus Garvey's black separatist movement, to which she devoted the remainder of her working life.

Davis's contemporaries who cast their lot with organized companies rather than solo performances had two options that sometimes overlapped: black minstrelsy (discussed in Chapter 3, pp. 97–102) or impecunious performance in black theaters. After the Civil War, a handful of black acting groups developed in urban areas along the east coast, as well as San Francisco, Chicago, and Louisville. Supported by amateurs, these companies hosted visiting professionals in single productions of Shakespeare's major plays. Best known is the Astor Place Company of Colored Tragedians, based in New York, which flourished in the 1880s, performing at neighborhood venues like the Brooklyn Atheneum. Its most illustrious performer was J. A. Arneaux, whose Iago and Richard III won wide praise. He modeled the latter on Edwin Booth, but added some light touches to emphasize Richard's mercurial nature. In late 1888 Arneaux left America to study acting in Paris, where he fell into obscurity. Nevertheless, his contributions to all-black companies in New York, Brooklyn, Providence, Philadelphia, and Baltimore had made their mark, inspiring lesser-known African American thespians like Benjamin J. Ford, Charles Van Buren, and Alice M. Franklin to assay Shakespeare in amateur productions.[16]

Opportunities for serious African American actors to perform the classics improved in 1935 when the Federal Theatre Project, under the auspices of the New Deal's Work Progress Administration, established viable African American acting companies. The FTP's goal was to provide work for unemployed theater professionals and, in the process, to bring theatrical performances to audiences outside major urban centers. At the height of the Depression some 25,000 theater professionals were unemployed, at least 3,000 of them African American. Black units of the FTP were formed in twenty-two cities across the country.[17] Although the FTP only lasted until 1939, during its short life black acting companies performed Shakespeare in a variety of venues, including Harlem's Lafayette Theatre, where "Voodoo *Macbeth*" was one of the most successful plays sponsored by the FTP.

Produced by John Houseman and directed by Orson Welles, "Voodoo *Macbeth*" opened on April 9, 1936, ran for fourteen weeks, and toured for thirteen more. As many as 120,000 people saw it.[18] Welles hired four professional African American actors for the lead roles: Jack Carter as Macbeth, Edna Thomas as Lady Macbeth, Canada Lee as Banquo, and Eric Burroughs as Hecate, whose role as a male witch doctor was expanded from Shakespeare's original. The rest of the 100-member cast came from the Harlem community and had little acting experience.[19] Welles set the play in Haiti, using as a template the history of Jean Christophe, who rose in the military ranks during Toussaint L'Ouverture's late eighteenth-century slave revolt. Christophe subsequently led a second revolt, declared himself king, and ruled despotically until—threatened by his subjects' unrest—he committed suicide in 1820. Welles's version was a decidedly New World *Macbeth*, with the natives' animistic customs of witchcraft and voodoo opposing the hero's attempt to mimic European monarchy. Welles substituted a jungle setting for Shakespeare's heath and made the witches into voodoo priestesses. He also employed a musical score composed by Virgil Thomson that alternated voodoo drums with European waltz music. "The *primitive* violence of the drums," observed one student of the play, "either added dimension to the images of *civilized* violence onstage, or served as ironic counterpoint when the action of the play fell into a momentary calm." The banquet scene, staged as a coronation ball, is a case in point: "While the waltz music was playing (and, incidentally, establishing the play's period), the sound of the voodoo drums rose slowly, only taking over once the transition from one scene to the other had been completed."[20] The rhythmic pounding of drums underscored the primitive forces lurking beneath the civilized façade of Macbeth's court

Although "Voodoo *Macbeth*" played to sell-out crowds, many of the reviewers complained that it wasn't sufficiently Shakespearian; the actors, they argued, couldn't speak Shakespeare's lines properly, while spectacle and special effects overtook Macbeth's heroic role. As one African American critic noted at the time, white audiences accustomed to mainstream productions could hardly be sympathetic to a black production: "We therefore warn downtown visitors that the play is purely for Harlem consumption, and is geared and produced accordingly."[21] But both the white and black reviewers missed the point. The actors' low-key verse-speaking "was due neither to ineffective actors nor to defiant Negroes, but rather to a deliberate, artistic decision by Welles," who, as Houseman later explained, wanted an end to the "glib English Bensonian [Frank Benson, one of England's leading actor/managers] declamatory tradition of Shakespearian performance and a return to a simpler, more direct and rapid delivery of dramatic verse." Welles wanted his *Macbeth* to capture the natural rhythms of American speech.

The FTP's "Voodoo *Macbeth*" maintained the color line, in that the men in charge, Orson Welles and John Houseman, were white while the cast was entirely black. Nevertheless, the production's success demonstrated to some viewers, if not all, that black actors could indeed do Shakespeare. Ten years later Canada Lee, Welles's Banquo, became the first black actor to play a traditionally white role in a major Shakespearian production when Margaret Webster cast him as Caliban in *The Tempest*. Although the First Folio describes Caliban as "a savage and deformed slave," and while slavery might suggest the history of black Americans, Lee emphasized instead the character's monstrousness, consistent with his costume of fish scales, long fingernails, and grotesque facial mask. (Webster assured the press, "I do not intend to make Caliban a parable of the current state of the American Negro."[22]) Like those who had criticized the verse-speaking of "Voodoo *Macbeth*," the *Saturday Review*'s critic had trouble with Lee's delivery: "Canada Lee's Caliban is a monster; earth-sprung; fearsome, badgered and pathetic. His only trouble is that he keeps all of Caliban's poetry earth-sprung too" (February 10, 1945). But Rosamund Gilder, writing for *Theatre Arts*, praised Lee for capturing Caliban's language: "His voice has a rumbling strength that gives the poetry which Caliban, like all true inhabitants of the magic isle must speak, a very special quality, an unconventional rhythm and emphasis which has a melody of its own" (March 1945). Lee, way ahead of his time it would seem, gave Caliban's speech the inflection of a colonial subaltern, leaving Prospero to speak the King's English.

Two years before casting Lee as Caliban in her production of *The Tempest*, Margaret Webster had made an even greater historical breakthrough by directing Paul Robeson in the Theatre Guild's *Othello*, the most successful Broadway production of Shakespeare to date. A powerful athlete (four-sport standout and twice a football all-American at Rutgers), an outstanding student (Phi Beta Kappa, valedictorian of the class of 1919) who subsequently earned a law degree from Columbia, Robeson began his professional stage career in 1924 with acclaim for his performance in Eugene O'Neill's *All God's Chillun Got Wings* and *The Emperor Jones.* Othello, which he played in three separate productions during his career (1930, 1943–5, and 1959), was his signature (and only) Shakespearian role.

The Theatre Guild production broke all records, with 296 performances during its 1943–44 New York run, a tour to 45 cities across the United States and Canada in 1944–45, and a two-week return to Broadway (Fig. 4.2). As Webster explained in her autobiography, "The Robeson *Othello* became more than just a successful revival; it was a declaration and its success an event in which the performance itself was of less importance than the public response."[23] Performed during the height of World War II, this *Othello* embodied American ideals. Actor Earle Hyman, who played Othello five times in his

Figure 4.2. Othello (Paul Robeson) and Desdemona (Uta Hagen) in Margaret Webster's Theatre Guild production of *Othello*. Photograph by Richard Tucker (1943). ©Billy Rose Theatre Division, The New York Public Library for the Performing Arts.

career, believes that Robeson "simply *was* Othello" because "the majesty—there is no other word for it—of his sheer presence on stage was electric. When Paul Robeson kissed his Desdemona [Uta Hagen] full on the mouth, an audible gasp went through the entire audience at the sold-out Schubert Theater on Broadway...I feel certain that all of us in the audience knew we were seeing *Shakespeare's Othello* for the first time."[24] Robeson's Othello was indeed a revelation, for except for Ira Aldridge's European appearances, no professional black actor had ever before played the Moor in a major theatrical venue.

Just as Jacob Adler successfully conveyed the difficulties of Jewish life in *The Jewish King Lear*, Robeson wanted to convey through Othello the dignity and humanity of his race as well as the African American's sense of isolation in his own country. Robeson himself reflected in 1930 when he first undertook the role in London that "Othello in the Venice of that time was in practically the same position as a coloured man in America to-day. He was a general, and while he could be valuable as a fighter he was tolerated, just as a Negro who could save New York from a disaster would become a great man overnight. So soon, however, as Othello wanted a white woman, Desdemona, everything was changed, just as New York would be indignant if their coloured man married a white woman" (*Pearson's Weekly*, April 5, 1930). Webster later explained,

> When Paul Robeson stepped onto the stage for the very first time, when he spoke his very first line, he immediately, by his very presence, brought an incalculable sense of reality to the entire play. Here was a great man, a man of simplicity and strength; here also was a black man. We believed that he could command the armies of Venice; we knew that he would always be alien to its society.[25]

Robeson agreed: "Shakespeare's Othello has learned to live in a strange society, but he is not *of* it—as an easterner today might pick up western manners and not be western."[26]

The postwar years were particularly hard on Robeson. He was hounded by the FBI, which accused him of Communist affiliations and revoked his passport. When he was finally able to travel in 1959, he appeared again as Othello in a Shakespeare Memorial Theatre production at Stratford, but by then his romantic, dignified Moor was out of tune with a flashy, modernized production. His performance for the Theatre Guild, however, remains his greatest theatrical triumph, and it opened the way for subsequent African American actors such as Earle Hyman, James Earl Jones, and Lawrence Fishburne to perform Othello in a play that many consider uniquely appropriate to the United States because of America's persistent legacy of slavery and institutionalized racism.

Robeson's success as Othello, combined with a widening American sensitivity regarding racial stereotypes in the aftermath of the civil rights movement of the 1950s and 60s, virtually guaranteed that no white American actor would ever again play Othello in blackface. Yet one white British actor—Patrick Stewart—longed to play the Moor. In 1997 Stewart proposed to Michael Kahn, Artistic Director of The Shakespeare Theatre in Washington, DC, a "photo-negative" *Othello*, in which Othello would be white, the rest of the cast black. The director, Jude Kelly from the West Yorkshire Playhouse, decided on a modern dress production with contemporary military costumes. The Venetians were portrayed by African American actors, the Cypriots by Hispanic or mixed-race actors. Sometime during rehearsals, Kelly decided not to change the play's many references to Desdemona's whiteness or Othello's blackness, and as a result, the production's visual and verbal cues often contradicted each other. Stewart's Othello was "lean, cerebral and humorous," while Ron Canada's "black Iago was heavy-set, obsessed with rules, and a wife-abuser."[27] Riveting as Stewart's performance was, the "photo-negative" *Othello* repressed exploration of the tragedy's racial implications in favor of an interrogation of the play's claustrophobic military milieu and its representation of the abusive gender dynamics between Iago and Emilia, as well as Othello and Desdemona.

Less heralded than Canada Lee's and Paul Robeson's pioneering Shakespeare performances on stage was the work of African American composer Duke Ellington, who brought Shakespeare to swing music in 1957 with a jazz suite, *Such Sweet Thunder*, composed of eleven numbers, each meant to represent a Shakespearian character. In his program notes Ellington suggested a link between jazz and Shakespearian drama: both art forms were originally intended for popular audiences, but through changing cultural contingencies, by the mid-twentieth century they came to be perceived by many as "highbrow" despite their origins. Ellington placed black characters—Othello and Cleopatra—at the beginning and ending of the suite, and midway through he included "Sonnet in Search of a Moor," suggesting a further link between African Americans and Britain's premier dramatist, particularly the music's affirmation of black sexuality.[28]

* * *

By the time Washington's Shakespeare Theatre presented the photo-negative *Othello* in 1997, the taboo against integrated casts broken by Margaret Webster in the 1940s had been lifted; minority actors could now take ownership of some of Shakespeare's most exciting roles. But the transition took decades. It wasn't until the 1950s that Joseph Papp insisted that the casts for his New York Shakespeare Festival's productions in Central Park should be multiracial and multiethnic. The son of Jewish immigrants from Eastern Europe, Papp (born Papirofsky) studied at the Actors' Laboratory Workshop in Los Angeles after World War II, then worked in New York for CBS-TV. In 1956 he began to mount free outdoor Shakespeare at the East River Park Amphitheater, and in 1957 he moved to Central Park, where a permanent outdoor amphitheater, the Delacorte, opened in 1962. From the beginning, Papp argued that the people's Shakespeare should look and sound like the people, and that the actors on stage should reflect the city's diversity. In the aftermath of Papp's pioneering casting decisions, the majority of Shakespeare festival theaters across the United States, not to mention many British acting companies, have adopted "colorblind" casting. Productions that are genuinely colorblind adopt the policy that "neither the race nor the ethnicity of an actor should prevent her or him from playing a role as long as she or he was the best actor available."[29]

Such a policy is not without controversy. A continuing dispute over the pros and cons of colorblind casting reflects a fundamental tension between separatist and assimilationist impulses. In a widely disseminated discussion Robert Brustein, who for many years directed the American Repertory Theatre in Cambridge, Massachusetts, advocated the assignment of actors in Shakespearian productions without regard to race; opposed was the African American playwright August Wilson, who contended: "Colorblind casting is an aberrant idea that has never had any validity other than as a tool of the Cultural Imperialists who view American culture, rooted in the Icons of European culture, as beyond reproach in its perfection." Black actors, Wilson argued, should perform in a black theater in plays that realistically depict the black experience in America.[30] For Wilson, explains a student of the debate, "Colorblind casting amounts to assimilation, effective displacement and erasure while misappropriating the black actor to investigate white culture through its preferred texts, a travesty that renders the black body subject once again to the interests of a dominant racial elite."[31] Despite Wilson's fervent embrace of a separate black theater, today's American Shakespeare is predominantly multiracial, if not always colorblind. In productions across the United States, from Ashland, Oregon, to Washington, DC, to Boston and Lenox, Massachusetts, actors of African American and Hispanic heritage frequently appear in integrated performances, often in leading roles.[32] When a play such as *Titus Andronicus* or *Othello* calls for black characters, the roles are routinely assigned to minority actors. More striking are productions that cast a minority actor in a traditionally European role, such as Denzel Washington's Don Pedro in Kenneth Branagh's film of *Much Ado About Nothing*. Even when such casting startles a predominantly white audience, it ensures Shakespeare's participation in America's ongoing interrogation of its racial heritage.

* * *

Since the eighteenth century the color bar has often prevented African Americans who were born and raised in the United States from full participation in classical theater. Despite the success of actors like Paul Robeson, James Earl Jones, and Denzel Washington, many in the African American community remain ambivalent about Shakespeare and the cultural hierarchy he has come to represent. The barriers seem even higher for America's newest immigrants—Latinos and Asian Americans—because Shakespeare is the premier poet of the English language and his vocabulary is more difficult to master than colloquial American speech. In recent immigrant communities, the push for bilingualism is an everyday reality, and to many newcomers the demand to "learn English" can seem oppressive. As a result, for many Latino and Asian American artists Shakespeare has come to stand for Anglo-America's cultural hegemony.

"Japanese Hamlet," Toshio Mori's short story of 1939, artfully uses Shakespeare to explore the challenges of being a minority American. Mori, a Japanese American who was interned at Topaz War Relocation Center in Utah during World War II, tells the story of young Tom Fukunaga, a Japanese American in Piedmont, California, who loved Shakespeare: "And as his love for Shakespeare's plays grew with the years he did not want anything else in the world but to be a Shakespearean actor."[33] The narrator, Tom's boyhood friend, reports that Fukunaga carries *The Complete Works of William Shakespeare* with him wherever he goes. Instead of getting a job, as his relatives insist, Tom spends his days studying Shakespeare. Even at age 31, Tom remains a schoolboy, living off $5 a day (the story never indicates its source) and reciting Shakespeare. At first the narrator assists him by following the text as Tom recites, but suggests that if Tom really wants to be an actor, he should contact an acting company. Tom says he is not yet ready. As time goes on, the narrator becomes increasingly frustrated. "I began to dread his presence in the house as if his figure reminded me of my part in the mock play that his life was.... One night I became desperate. 'That book is destroying you, Tom. Why don't you give this up for awhile?'" In this story Shakespeare—epitomized by the Shakespeare "book"—represents America's dominant white culture. Lurking underneath Tom's desire to become a great Shakespearian actor is the conviction that Shakespeare is universal and that anyone can access his greatness, but Tom's relatives and the narrator know better. What the narrator represses is the unspoken barrier that keeps Tom from becoming a successful Shakespearian actor—he is Japanese. At the same time, Mori's story artfully embraces Shakespeare, because as a 31-year-old man in a protracted adolescent state who seems unable to accomplish anything, Tom indeed becomes a sort of Japanese American Hamlet. Mori thereby "grounds the moral, transcendental dilemma of Hamlet in a specifically racial problematic."[34]

The interplay of culture and identity is also apparent in Paisley Rekdal's memoir, *The Night My Mother Met Bruce Lee: Observations About Not Fitting In* (2000), where Shakespeare again becomes the vehicle for reflection. Born in Seattle, Washington, to a Chinese American mother and Anglo-American father, Rekdal recounts her memories of coming to grips with biracialism in a painful adolescence as well as the difficulties she had as a young woman accepting her Chinese American identity. After teaching English in Korea for a year, she spent a month traveling in China, where she reports feeling conflicted: "Are they [the Chinese] the savages I once believed them—and me—to have been? At times they are the example of what I love most about my family, its strange exoticism and history." But then she recalls a college production of *The Tempest* she once saw, in which Caliban was portrayed by a black woman, who scuttled "on all fours, her head never extending beyond the mid-thigh point on Prospero.... How degrading! I thought watching her... the woman's crouch told me that the native is the animal, no matter how justified her anger, how cultivated her speech." When at the play's finale Caliban simply disappears, Rekdal sees herself "stuck in a place that has confounded what we perceive to be ourselves, cheated out of a claim to cultural ownership, shunned. Caliban is savage because she is seen as savage and, in the end, it is almost impossible for her not to believe she is by nature that way, too."[35]

Mori and Rekdal's ambivalence perhaps explains why there are fewer Asian American appropriations of Shakespeare than there were for earlier immigrant groups. The occasional film—*Romeo Must Die*, a 2000 film based on the plot of *Romeo and Juliet* that figures the Montagues as a powerful Chinese gang and the Capulets as African American—draws on well known Shakespearian themes. And more recently, Young Jean Lee, a Korean-American experimental playwright, used *King Lear* as the template for New York's Soho Repertory Company's *Lear*, a contemporary meditation on death and loss articulated solely from the younger generation's viewpoint, in which neither Lear nor Gloucester appears. Such appropriations are the exception.

In contrast, Shakespeare remains the coin of the realm for theater practitioners, and any repertory company desiring to establish its credentials as a venue for classical theater must include his work in its repertoire. But often it is Shakespeare with a difference. In order to reach a younger, more multicultural audience John R. Briggs created a hybrid version of *Macbeth* in 1985 that incorporated elements of Japanese theater in *Shogun Macbeth*. Briggs's goal was to reinvigorate a Shakespearian classic with Japanese performance culture by adding language and stage business for his Asian American actors to perform: the witches were transformed into bunraku puppets, the three murderers into ninja warriors, and the interlude of the drunken porter into a kyogen comic routine. First staged at the Shakespeare Festival of Dallas, *Shogun Macbeth* moved to the Pan Asian Theatre in New York the following year.[36]

New York's National Asian American Theater Company, founded in 1989 by Richard Eng and Mia Katigbak, aims to "promote and support Asian American actors, directors, designers, and technicians through the performance of European and American classics." NAATCO mounted productions of *A Midsummer Night's Dream* in 1995 and in 2000 produced the Asian American equivalent of Jude Kelly's "photo-negative" *Othello*. Othello, played by Joshua Spafford, was white, while the rest of the cast were of Asian descent. Like the Shakespeare Theatre, NAATCO's production of *Othello* kept Shakespeare's original language with its references to the characters' skin color, creating cognitive dissonance that worried some reviewers.[37] In 2007 Chicago's Silk Road Theatre Project transferred *The Merchant of Venice* to Bollywood, shifting Shakespeare's conflict between Christians and Jews to one between Hindus and Muslims in contemporary Southern California. *Merchant on Venice*, written by American playwright Shishir Kurup, also enlivened Shakespeare's dark comedy with music and dance.[38]

Shakespeare's language remains an obstacle in many minority communities. When Caliban first appears in *The Tempest*, he blames Prospero for teaching him language: "my profit on't/Is I know how to curse" (1.ii.366–7). Except perhaps for his chant, "Ca, Ca, Caliban," we never learn what his original language was, but presumably he had one in common with Sycorax and perhaps Ariel. Not surprisingly, actors who come to Shakespeare from the Latino community sometimes seek a bilingual approach to his language. Perhaps America's best-known Hispanic Shakespearian was Raul Juliá, a bilingual Puerto Rican who worked with Joseph Papp in the New York Shakespeare Festival and later went on to film stardom in *The Kiss of the Spider Woman*. His performances of Proteus in *Two Gentlemen of Verona*, Petruchio (to Meryl Streep's Katherine) in *The Taming of the Shrew*, and Kalibanos in Paul Mazursky's film, *Tempest*, received much acclaim. But earlier in his career Juliá had also played Macduff in a Spanish version of *Macbeth* and participated in the Puerto Rican Traveling Theatre.

New York is also home to the Latin American Theater Experiment & Associates (LATEA), founded in 1982 by Nelson Tamayo, Mateo Gomez, and Nelson Landrieu, which provides opportunities to Latino artists in a repertoire that is "relevant to the life experiences of its multicultural audiences." LATEA's website explains that it "was founded in the principle that no one could define or tell us as Latinos what roles we could or could not play," and proudly announces: "We now tackle Shakespeare and have garnered awards for our work."[39] During the last decade, in addition to productions written in Spanish, LATEA includes a major Shakespearian drama in its repertory each year, but with an experimental twist. For example, *Hamlet* (2006), set in contemporary New York, represented the young prince and his family as Latinos. The following year, LATEA alternated between a male actor (David Beckles, Jr.) and a female actor (Cheryl D. Hescott) in *Othello*'s title role. The 2008 *Macbeth* was set in the year 2029 after the Apocalypse and performed by a multi-ethnic cast. LATEA's 2010 production of *Romeo and Juliet*, which set the Capulet–Montague rivalry on the contemporary Lower East Side between Latinos and Chinese, won four awards from the Hispanic Organization of Latin Actors (HOLA), including best director for José Esquea (Fig. 4.3).[40] These productions demonstrate both LATEA's legitimacy as a repertory theater company and its commitment to experimentation appealing to ethnically diverse audiences.

If Shakespeare in English lends credibility to Asian American and Latino theatrical practitioners, what about Shakespeare in translation? Antonio Ocampo-Guzman, who first studied Shakespeare in the Anglo-Colombian School in Bogotá, wrote of his desire to experience Shakespeare in English and Spanish at the same time—a dream that was realized in 2005 when he directed a bilingual production of *Romeo and Juliet* at Florida State University. Ocampo-Guzman had studied verse speaking during three years of training at Shakespeare and Company in Lenox, Massachusetts, and coached his Spanish-speaking students through some sections of the play in English; other parts were translated into Spanish. While the production was enriching for Ocampo-Guzman and his student actors, his relationship to Shakespeare remains complicated. On the

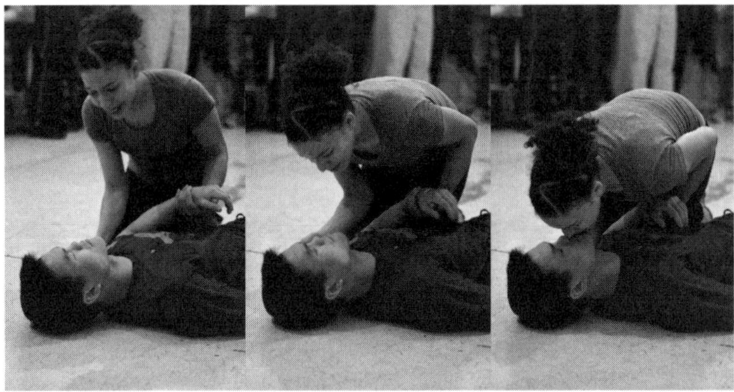

Figure 4.3. "The Death of Romeo." Romeo (Chester Poon) and Juliet (Carissa Jocett Toro) in the Latin American Theater Experiment Associates (LATEA) production of *Romeo and Juliet* (2006), directed by José Esquea. Photograph by Joe Macaldo.

one hand, he explains, "For a Latino actor, mastering Shakespeare is an additional source of self-esteem, because I am able to master a language that so many native English speakers find challenging." On the other hand, he confesses: "making Shakespeare one's own is more than just mastering the language, stories, and characters. In order for socially defined minorities to make Shakespeare our own, we must address how playing with Shakespeare affects our complex contemporary lives."[41]

Many in Ocampo-Guzman's audience no doubt understood Spanish and could easily follow a bilingual *Macbeth*. Anita Maynard-Losh's 2003 production of the same play in Tlingit, first performed at the Perseverance Theatre in Juneau, Alaska, and later at the National Museum of the American Indian in Washington, DC, must have been more challenging. Maynard-Losh explains that her production tapped into the kinship she observed between Tlingit and medieval Scottish clan systems, Tlingit and Scottish beliefs in supernatural influence over human events, and both societies' history of tribal warfare. All of her performers were Alaskan natives, some part-Tlingit but others from other tribes as well. The characters spoke Tlingit "when observing traditional group values, and English when following individual desires." Reflecting on her production's success, Maynard-Losh concludes:

> Shakespeare could be considered the ultimate "white" playwright, and thus a symbol of the dominant culture that stripped away so much from the Tlingit. We all felt the transformational power of art shifting our world view as the play was illuminated by setting it in this cultural context. It became more than a play to us, more than art—it became a mission, an invocation of ancestors.... Native audience members spoke of how moving and healing it was to them to see that their culture "made Shakespeare better".[42]

Because *Macbeth* is one of the best-known Shakespearian plays, audience members who did not know Tlingit could follow the action in Maynard-Losh's bilingual production. Having some knowledge of the original text also helped audiences at a production directed by Paul T. Mitri at the Kennedy Theatre at the University of Hawaii, Manoa, in 2008. Mitri's *Macbeth* challenged his audience with a multicultural production that was also multilingual. "The witches spoke several different languages; Duncan and his clan spoke a great deal of Japanese...; Macduff and his family spoke Russian. There was a smattering of Gaelic (the Gentlewoman in 5.1) and Arabic (the Doctor). The Macbeths spoke Spanish as well as English." William C. Carroll observes that for an English speaker who knows the play quite well, the different languages created an alienation effect, forcing greater attention to the play's power dynamics. For those less familiar with the play, the feast of languages invited confusion.[43]

Repertory theaters like NAATCO and LATEA, as well as committed directors like John R. Briggs, Anita Maynard-Losh, and Paul T. Mitri, have not abandoned Shakespeare, but they believe that the plays should be made interesting and relevant to America's minority communities. The challenge of presenting Shakespeare to minority high school students is even more daunting. In New York City, R. Evolucion Latina, an organization formed to foster the arts within the Latino community through educational support programs and performance work, brought Shakespeare into the lives of Spanish-speaking students with *Ser o no Cer Vantes* (To be or not to be... Cervantes), a whimsical drama based on the contention that Cervantes and Shakespeare were the same person. Playing with the historical fact that Cervantes and Shakespeare both died on April 23, 1616 (albeit ten days apart because of the difference between Spain's Gregorian and England's Julian calendars), this comedy gives Shakespeare a decidedly Latino aura by exploring connections between Cervantes' work and Shakespearian drama, thereby making the greatest early modern Iberian writer equal to—the same as—England and America's foremost poet. Whether or not the experience will inspire the youngsters to study Shakespeare, the play underscores the equal cultural authority of Spanish literature.

* * *

In contrast to productions that feature a particular ethnic group, Peter Sellars's 1994 *Merchant of Venice* at Chicago's Goodman Theater was perhaps the ultimate multicultural production. Sellars moved Shakespeare's comedy to a southern California beach town, where tension abounds among blacks, whites, Hispanics, and Asian Americans. Shylock was portrayed by a black actor, Portia and her entourage by Asian Americans, and Bassanio and Antonio by Latinos. Sellars's casting was not colorblind because he sought a particular racial mix. At the same time, his innovative *Merchant* provided minority actors with the opportunity to perform important Shakespearian roles. Such hybrid productions shift Shakespeare's plots and characters to contemporary American culture in order to reach heterogeneous audiences. Colorblind casting has also enabled minority actors to take roles in major Shakespearian productions across the country. Still, while many minority Americans seem to need Shakespeare to prove their legitimacy, an essential ambivalence remains.

It may be that Gloria Naylor, a celebrated African American novelist, says it all in *The Women of Brewster Place.* Naylor conveys African American ambivalence about Shakespeare's cultural hegemony in an impoverished, single African American mother, Cora Lee, who takes her children to see an all-black performance of *A Midsummer Night's Dream.*

On the way home, Cora's son asks, "Shakespeare's black?" Cora Lee replies, "Not yet."[44]

Notes

1. Percy MacKaye, *Caliban by the Yellow Sands* (New York: Doubleday, 1916), 152–4.
2. Ibid. xvii and xv.

3. Thomas Cartelli, *Repositioning Shakespeare: National Formations, Postcolonial Appropriations* (London: Routledge, 1999), 77.
4. See Errol Hill, *Shakespeare in Sable: A History of Black Shakespearean Actors* (Amherst: University of Massachusetts Press, 1984), 92–6.
5. Ibid. 88.
6. See Marvin Carlson, *The Italian Shakespearians: Performances by Ristori, Salvini, and Rossi in England and America* (Washington, DC: Folger Shakespeare Library, 1985).
7. Weldon B. Durham (ed.), *American Theatre Companies, 1888–1830* (New York: Greenwood, 1987), 134–5.
8. Joel Berkowitz, *Shakespeare on the American Yiddish Stage* (Iowa City: University of Iowa Press, 2007), xii and 1; Iska Alter, "When the Audience Called 'Author! Author!': Shakespeare on New York's Yiddish Stage," *Theatre History Studies* 10 (1990), 141–61.
9. Quoted from Jacob Gordin, *The Jewish King Lear: A Comedy in America*, trans. Ruth Gay (New Haven, CT: Yale University Press, 2007), 19.
10. Berkowitz, *Shakespeare on the Yiddish Stage*, 31–49 (quotations from 27 and 47).
11. For a full account, see ibid. 198–205.
12. Hill, *Shakespeare in Sable*, 12.
13. Ibid. 14.
14. See ibid. 11–16; and Joyce Green MacDonald, "Acting Black: *Othello*, *Othello* Burlesques, and the Performance of Blackness," *Theatre Journal* 46 (1994), 231–49.
15. Hill, *Shakespeare in Sable*, 77.
16. See ibid. 44–63.
17. See ibid. 103–8.
18. See John S. O'Connor, "'But was it 'Shakespeare?': Welles's *Macbeth* and *Julius Caesar*," *Theatre Journal* 32 (1980), 337–48, esp. 338.
19. See Richard France, "The Voodoo *Macbeth* of Orson Welles," *Yale/theatre* 5 (1974), 66–78, esp. 75.
20. Ibid. 68.
21. Quoted from Rena Fraden, *Blueprints for a Black Federal Theatre, 1935–1939* (Cambridge: Cambridge University Press, 1994), 153.
22. Quoted from Glenda E. Gill, *White Grease Paint on Black Performers* (New York: Peter Lang, 1988), 41.
23. Margaret Webster, *Don't Put Your Daughter on the Stage* (New York: Alfred A. Knopf, 1972), 107.
24. Earle Hyman, "Othello: Or Ego in Love, Sex, and War," in Mythili Kaul (ed.), *Othello: New Essays by Black Writers* (Washington, DC: Howard University Press, 1997), 23–8 (quotation from 23).

25. Margaret Webster, *Shakespeare Without Tears* (New York: Capricorn Books, 1975), 178–9.
26. From an interview with Marvin Rosenberg recorded in *The Masks of Othello* (Berkeley: University of California Press, 1961), 195.
27. Lois Potter, *Othello: Shakespeare in Performance* (Manchester: Manchester University Press, 2002), 179–84 (quotation from 183–4).
28. See Douglas Lanier, "Jazzing up Shakespeare," in Virginia Mason Vaughan and Alden T. Vaughan (eds), *Shakespeare in American Life* (Washington, DC: Folger Shakespeare Library, 2007), 83–6.
29. Ayanna Thompson (ed.), *Colorblind Shakespeare: New Perspectives on Race and Performance* (New York: Routledge, 2006), 6.
30. August Wilson, "The Ground," *American Theatre* (September 1996), 72. See also Stephen Nunns, "Wilson, Brustein and the Press," *American Theatre* (March 1997).
31. Ian Smith, review of Thompson, *Colorblind Shakespeare*, in *Shakespeare Quarterly* 59 (2008), 354–6 (quotation from 355).
32. The Oregon Shakespeare Festival in Ashland, Oregon; The Shakespeare Theatre of Washington, DC; The Actors' Shakespeare Project of Boston; and Shakespeare and Company in Lenox, Massachusetts, all have policies of multiracial or colorblind casting.
33. Toshio Mori, "Japanese Hamlet," in Wesley Brown and Amy Ling (eds), *Imagining America: Stories from the Promised Land* (New York: Persea Books, 1991), 125–7 (quotation from 125).
34. David Palaumbo-Liu, "The Minority Self as Other: Problematics of Representation in Asian-American Literature," *Cultural Critique* 28 (1994), 75–102 (quotation from 84).
35. Paisley Rekdal, *The Night My Mother Met Bruce Lee: Observations on Not Fitting In* (New York: Pantheon, 2000), 150–51.
36. Alexander C. Y. Huang, "Asian-American Theatre Reimagined: *Shogun Macbeth* in New York," in Scott L. Newstok and Ayanna Thompson (eds), *Weyward Macbeth: Intersections of Race and Performance* (New York: Palgrave Macmillan, 2010), 121–5. See pp. 241–52 for a list of productions of *Macbeth* that used non-traditional casting.
37. http://naatco.org/index/html?productions/2000_othello (accessed October 4, 2010).
38. http://www.srtp.org/blog/category/merchantonvenice/ (accessed October 4, 2010).
39. http://www.teatrolatea.com/about.html (accessed October 18, 2010).
40. See also José A. Esquea, "A Post-apocalyptic *Macbeth*: Teatra LATEA's *Macbeth 2029*," in Newstok and Thompson, *Weyward Macbeth*, 133–5.

41. Antonio Ocampo-Guzman, "My Own Private Shakespeare; or, Am I Deluding Myself?" in Thompson, *Colorblind Shakespeare*, 125–36.
42. Anita Maynard-Losh, "The Tlingit Play: *Macbeth* and Native Americanism," in Newstok and Thompson, *Weyward Macbeth*, 127–31.
43. William C. Carroll, "Multicultural Multilingual *Macbeth*," in Newstok and Thompson, *Weyward Macbeth*, 238–41 (quotations from 238 and 239).
44. Gloria Naylor, *The Women of Brewster Place* (New York: Viking, 1982), 127.

5

Professional Shakespeare and Its Discontents

Philadelphia lawyer Horace Howard Furness spent the summer of 1862 compiling a large notebook on *Hamlet* for the Shakspere Society of Philadelphia's fall season. Since its founding in 1851, the Society had based its lively discussions on the multivolume 1821 variorum edition by James Boswell the younger, but Furness had become increasingly frustrated at its limitations. Boswell's text included the "various opinions" of prior editors, commentators, and critics, but by 1862 it was conspicuously out of date. Furness bemoaned that after spending an evening of impassioned debate with his colleagues over a particular textual crux, he would later discover that an editor or commentator writing since 1821 had cleared up the difficulty. Furness resolved to create a new variorum. At the top of his notebook's blank pages, Furness pasted lines of text from Karl Elze's 1857 edition of *Hamlet*; underneath he recorded textual variants; below them he copied by hand all the relevant commentary he could find. When the club met later in the fall of 1862, Furness had at his fingertips all the information he needed to make an informed opinion. His cohorts listened with admiration.[1]

After the Shakspere Society scheduled *Romeo and Juliet* for its 1866 meeting, Furness arranged with Philadelphia publisher J. B. Lippincott to print a more formal variorum than his *Hamlet* workbook. For the next several years, the Philadelphia lawyer spent his off hours meticulously addressing every detail of the book's content and format, including different print fonts for text, textual variants, and commentary.

In 1871 Lippincott published Furness's *New Variorum Romeo and Juliet*, thereby launching America's New Variorum edition of Shakespeare's plays. Under the sponsorship of America's Modern Language Association since 1936, it remains a work in progress well into the twenty-first century.

In 1866, while Furness was buried in notes for *Romeo and Juliet*, an anonymous critique of Richard Grant White in the periodical *Round Table* explained (albeit tongue-in-cheek, given Grant's status as a respected editor of Shakespeare's plays) that America had no Shakespearian scholars because it was "a new and half-formed country... not exactly and in all respects up to the mark of an old and mature one." Fortunately, the writer hoped, "we shall all improve together."[2] Forty years later, while Furness was finishing the *New Variorum Antony and Cleopatra*, in an address of 1906 to the German Shakespeare Society on "Shakespeare in America," George B. Churchill reflected that while the work of American scholars still could not compare with that of the Germans and English, it had "ceased to be provincial" and shared "in the full current of the world's enthusiasm and knowledge."[3] By the early years of the twentieth century, Shakespeare studies in America had grown from a handful of academic specialists and informal clubs of enthusiastic amateurs to an expanding class of professional scholars.

More than any other American Shakespearian, Horace Howard Furness exemplifies that shift. A self-taught amateur who quit his law practice to edit Shakespeare as a full-time occupation, Furness was arguably America's first professional Shakespearian scholar.[4] To support his editing endeavor, he built an impressive reference library of rare and modern books. In the 1880s and 90s he also served on the University of Pennsylvania's Board of Trustees, where he helped the English Department revise its curriculum to include Shakespeare. Furness's friendship with actors like Edwin Booth and theater impresarios like Augustin Daly was symptomatic also of his broad interest in Shakespeare on stage. With his enthusiasm for collecting, editing, teaching, and performance, Furness embodies the many directions the study of Shakespeare would take in America from the late nineteenth century to the present.

While American actors and theater managers are unquestionably "professionals," the concern here is primarily with the development of

Shakespeare studies in the academic world. American colleges and universities began to encourage such professional Shakespeare in the late nineteenth and early twentieth centuries, when they shifted the focus of their English curricula from rhetoric and philology to literature (see Chapter 3, pp. 84–7). The intensive study of Shakespeare soon became an academic sub-discipline in which college and university professors would make their mark. The explosion of scholarly commentary on all things Shakespearian was followed shortly by the founding of academic journals, associations, and summer institutes. But none of this could happen until American scholars had access to the early modern books and manuscripts that underlay their work.

* * *

To complete his collation of the early printed texts of *Romeo and Juliet*, Horace Howard Furness needed the four folios printed in the seventeenth century (1623, 1632, 1663, and 1685) and the early quarto versions of the plays for which they existed. The Shakspere Society's library included some facsimiles of the quarto texts, and Furness owned a copy of the fourth folio; he had borrowed the second and third folios from the actor Edwin Forrest. Furness's library would improve exponentially when his father-in-law died in 1870, leaving a substantial fortune to Furness's wife, Helen Kate Furness. The lawyer-turned-scholar soon relinquished his law practice and began to build a library worthy of his variorum project. Over the next several years he acquired copies of all four folios, a substantial number of early quartos, and every important edition since Nicholas Rowe's (1709). By 1873 he boasted more than 2,000 volumes centered on Shakespeare. Besides editions, his library included most of the dramatist's source materials, plays written by his contemporaries, modern criticism from England and Germany, and theatrical memorabilia. Upon the death of his son, Horace Howard Furness, Jr., in 1930, the library they had assembled so painstakingly was moved to the University of Pennsylvania, where it continues to be a resource for the university's students and faculty, and for visiting scholars from around the world.

During the 1890s Furness became acquainted with a New York executive from the Standard Oil Company who shared his passion for collecting Shakespearian materials. Henry Clay Folger, born in

Brooklyn, New York, in 1857 and graduated from Amherst College in 1879, spent the bulk of his adult life acquiring Shakespeariana. His notebooks reveal that he was an avid reader,[5] and after attending a visiting lecture at Amherst by Ralph Waldo Emerson, Folger explored the Concord sage's published essays. He was particularly impressed by Emerson's advocacy of Shakespeare as a "representative man" whose moral insights were universal. On the title page of his copy of Emerson's book, Folger wrote a line from the "Essay on Nature": "Build therefore your own world."[6] As a young man beginning to make his own way in the world, Folger found in Shakespeare, channeled through Emerson, an inspirational source of American idealism.

After college, Folger worked at an oil company while he attended the Columbia University Law School. During this period he also met and married Emily Clara Jordan, a graduate of Vassar College who shared Folger's intellectual pursuits. She, too, was passionate about Shakespeare and began work on a master's degree in Shakespeare for which she sought guidance from Furness. He advised her to read a play every day from a facsimile of the First Folio, eschewing modernization and editorial commentary. "At the end of the thirty seven days," he wrote, "you will be in a Shakespearian atmosphere that will astonish you with its novelty and its pleasure, and its profit. Don't read a single note during the month."[7] Emily completed her thesis, "The True Text of Shakespeare," and was awarded her Master of Arts degree from Vassar in 1896. By this time Henry had begun collecting early editions of Shakespeare's plays, beginning with a copy of the Fourth Folio he bought in 1889. Eventually the Folger Library would hold 79, plus fragments, of the First Folio; 58 of the Second; 24 of the Third; and 37 of the Fourth.

Collecting rare and expensive items was not unusual in late nineteenth-century America. While Folger in New York employed English booksellers to search for folios, quartos, manuscripts, and all the essential modern books on Shakespeare, in California a railroad magnate spent much of his fortune on the books and manuscripts that would later constitute the Henry E. Huntington Library in San Marino; sometimes the two wealthy bibliophiles competed for the same book or cache of books. Meanwhile in Boston, Isabella Stewart Gardner collected art, while another rich New Yorker, J. P. Morgan, assembled his own superlative collections of books and art. Folger's collecting was unusual only in that it was devoted to one subject and that, unlike Furness, he was not assembling a library to support his own scholarship. Rather, Henry Clay Folger purchased for his own satisfaction—primarily in England—an unparalleled assemblage of rare books and manuscripts devoted to Shakespeare and his contemporaries. As the collection grew, Henry and Emily decided it should be housed in a special but accessible library as a public trust for the American people.

Until the library was built, most of the Folgers' collection was virtually inaccessible in several New York warehouses. Some advisors suggested that the obvious place for such a resource would be Stratford-upon-Avon, but the Folgers wanted their Shakespeare Memorial Library to be in America, and eventually they chose Washington, DC, because it was the nation's capital. Behind the scenes, Henry bought up parcels of land next to the Library of Congress. When Henry Clay Folger died unexpectedly in 1930, soon after the cornerstone was laid on East Capitol Street between Second and Third Streets, Emily continued his work. In 1932, at the formal opening of the Folger Shakespeare Memorial Library, she presented the keys to President Herbert Hoover on behalf of the American people, although the administration and endowment were assigned to the trustees of Amherst College (Fig. 5.1). Located two blocks from the United States Capitol, even closer to the Supreme Court and Library of Congress, "the Folger" remains the world's most valuable and accessible collection of Shakespeare materials.

* * *

John Bartlett, a nineteenth-century Cambridge, Massachusetts, bookseller and printer and later a Boston editor and publisher, was, like Henry Folger, an avid promoter of Shakespeare scholarship but in a very different way. Early in his career, Bartlett seems to have caught the enthusiasm for Shakespeare from wide reading and his proximity to Emerson and other eastern Massachusetts intellectuals who championed Shakespeare's writings. Initially Bartlett was more of a popularizer than a student of the subject, although in the long run he would facilitate the professional study of Shakespeare. In the former role, Bartlett probably did more than any other American of

Figure 5.1. The east end of the Main Reading Room at the Folger Shakespeare Library. By permission of the Folger Shakespeare Library.

his time, aside from William Holmes McGuffey, to disseminate a reverence for Shakespeare to a nationwide audience. Like McGuffey, Bartlett promoted Shakespeare by publishing extracts from the plays and poems rather than complete texts, and like McGuffey, Bartlett gave increasing attention to Shakespeare in successive editions of his frequently reissued book. The principal difference between the two men was that McGuffey almost exclusively addressed young students while Bartlett principally addressed adults, identifying for them the passages from the works of Shakespeare and other great writers that they *should* recognize and revere.

With a print run of 1,000, the first edition of Bartlett's *Collection of Familiar Quotations* (1855) included dozens of extracts from Shakespeare. The book was an instant success and quickly embraced by commercial presses, most notably Boston's Little, Brown and Company, of which Bartlett became an employee in 1863 and eventually a senior partner; Little, Brown has published all editions of *Familiar Quotations* since the fourth (1863). The number of Shakespeare quotations in the successive editions held steady or increased through the eight versions Bartlett compiled before his death in 1905, and continued to escalate thereafter in the many editions under other editors. The seventeenth edition of *Familiar Quotations*, edited by the Pulitzer Prize biographer Justin Kaplan (with advice from selected Shakespeare scholars), appeared in 2002, with nearly 2,000 passages from Shakespeare. In 2005 Little, Brown published separately *Bartlett's Shakespeare Quotations* from that edition.[8]

But Bartlett's contributions to Shakespeare popularization and scholarship went well beyond the premier position the poet held in *Familiar Quotations*. In 1861 a London publisher issued Bartlett's *Choice Thoughts from Shakspere* in 333 pages of substantial selections from each play "specially adapted to the youth of both sexes, and for use in the family circle." In accord with nineteenth-century America's penchant for individual moral improvement, Shakespeare's plays were to be mined for specific passages of sage advice and moral wisdom. Twenty years later, Little, Brown issued his *Shakespeare Phrase Book*—"a concordance of phrases rather than words," the preface explained, arranged alphabetically by each phrase's key word. Some phrases had more than one entry. "Misery acquaints a man with strange bedfellows" (*The Tempest*, II.ii.36–7), for example, appeared under both the first and last words. Conversely, many key words had dozens, even hundreds of entries. "World," for example had five and a half pages of entries; "Love" had six pages, and "Heart" nearly eight pages. Counting each phrase only once, the number of entries in Bartlett's *Phrase Book* still exceeded 50,000, on 952 pages of 57 lines per page, with most phrases crammed into a single line. On an additional 80-odd pages Bartlett compared the quotations, all drawn from the Cambridge edition (1863–6), with the slightly different versions in five other scholarly editions of the complete works. The *Shakespeare Phrase Book* was an impressive undertaking, for Bartlett had included every Shakespearean phrase that was coherent by itself, firmly believing, as his title page proclaimed (with—what else?—a Shakespearian phrase): "Good phrases are surely, and ever were, very commendable" (*2 Henry IV*, III.ii.64–5).[9]

Near the end of the nineteenth century Bartlett completed the final step in his sequence of Shakespeare handbooks, this one aimed principally at scholars: a massive *New and Complete Concordance or Verbal Index to Words, Phrases, & Passages in the Dramatic Works of Shakespeare* (1894). It had taken Bartlett, with considerable help from his wife, Hannah Stanifield Willard, almost twenty years to compile the nearly 2,000 pages that listed alphabetically *every word* in the canon, except definite and indefinite articles and a few interjections, with their location(s) in the texts. Although of course not a best-seller like *Familiar Quotations*, the *Concordance* was nonetheless frequently reprinted and is still a standard reference for scholars and laymen, even after the publication in 1973 of the computer-assisted *Harvard Concordance.*[10] Thanks to John Bartlett's tireless efforts, in the latter part of the nineteenth century and far beyond, American households, public libraries, and scholars' studies have had readily accessible and impeccably reliable handbooks to Shakespeare's works in which to find the source or refresh the memory of a half-forgotten line. And from 1855 to the present day, there has always been a recent edition of Bartlett's *Familiar Quotations* to remind readers of what one omnivorous editor and his successors believed were Shakespeare's most affecting passages.

* * *

Horace Howard Furness's transformation from an amateur Shakespearian and proud member of Philadelphia's Shakspere Society into a professional editor and critic is characteristic of the development of Shakespeare studies in the United States. As the twentieth century began, Shakespeare clubs had become a vibrant cultural force in communities across America. In particular, the 1916 tercentenary of Shakespeare's death was a watershed year, as Shakespeare clubs from New York to California celebrated with parties, plays, and pageants. Two years earlier, a select group of delegates from Shakespeare clubs across the country had met at the New York Public Library to consider the creation of a national organization, and their efforts came to fruition in 1916 in Washington, DC, with the establishment of a nation-wide Shakespeare Society. The advent of World War I brought the project to a sudden halt. After the Washington effort formally ended in 1923, an alternative society in New York, the Shakespeare Association of America (SAA), emerged in 1932. Membership consisted mostly of New York's Shakespeare Club members and aficionados, but some faculty in the New York area also joined. Soon the organization began its own newsletter, the *Shakespeare Association Bulletin*.

With a comparatively small membership based, for the most part, in the New York area, the SAA survived the pressures of another world war, but in the postwar era, when veterans under the G.I bill crammed the halls of academe, the organization was ripe for a major overhaul. With Professor Robert Metcalfe Smith of Lehigh University assuming the editorship of the *Bulletin* in 1947, the substance of the articles shifted toward academic scholarship. Under Smith's leadership, a new, improved publication began in 1950 with the first issue of the *Shakespeare Quarterly*. The next year, with James McManaway, librarian of the Folger Shakespeare Library, succeeding Smith as the journal's editor, the emphasis on serious scholarship continued and gradually strengthened.[11]

The SAA continued to be the *Shakespeare Quarterly*'s official sponsor until 1972, when control of the journal was transferred to the Folger Shakespeare Library; Richard Schoeck, the library's head of research, took over as editor. That same year in New York, a dwindling treasury and reduced membership caused the Shakespeare Association of America to disband, though it retained its legal designation as the SAA in case the society might reorganize at a later date under new auspices. When J. Leeds Barroll, Professor of English at the University of South Carolina and editor of *Shakespeare Studies*, learned of the SAA's demise, he contacted its former trustees, and after some negotiation, one of them, Dr. Mary C. Hyde, led the effort to transfer the old name to a new organization. Late in 1972 the newly incorporated second iteration of the Shakespeare Association of America met at the Folger Library at the invitation of Director O. B. Hardison, Jr. The Board of Trustees included a cross-section of American academics, among them distinguished professors from San Francisco State University, the University of South Carolina, the University of Nebraska, the University of Georgia, and Yale University. Princeton's G. E. Bentley was selected to be President, with founder Leeds Barroll serving as Executive Secretary. In March 1973 the first annual meeting of the newly constituted SAA met in Washington, DC, with an attendance of about 250; it has met every year since in cities across North America. What had been a loose cadre of amateur Shakespearians developed into a professional association comprising mainly academic Shakespearians, many of whom identify their field as "Shakespeare studies" and who attend annual conferences to share the results of their research. The number of participants has grown impressively, and SAA now boasts well over 1,000 members.

What made this organization distinctly "American," as opposed to the International Shakespeare Conference begun in postwar Britain that meets at Stratford-upon-Avon in alternate years, was the democratic policy that every member was entitled to present his or her work and, space permitting, to be on the conference program. After the SAA's second annual meeting, Leeds Barroll became Deputy Director of the National Endowment for the Humanities and could not continue as SAA's Executive Secretary because the organization was applying to NEH for a special grant to underwrite a World Shakespeare Congress in 1976. The trustees selected Ann Jennalie Cook of Vanderbilt University as Barroll's replacement. Working with the World Congress's program committee, Cook designed an innovative system of two-hour seminars, centered on topics of interest to many in the field. Instead of waiting to be invited to give a paper, scholars who enrolled in a seminar pre-circulated their work to the other seminar participants and participated in the seminar's remarkably egalitarian discussions. Whether they were advanced graduate students or full professors, each participant's name was in the program (often the only means of procuring travel funds from a home institution) and could rightly feel part of the larger Shakespearian enterprise. Over the years, the SAA's inclusiveness has fostered the professional careers of younger scholars even as its membership has expanded beyond North America to include substantial representation from European institutions. More than one hundred years after George B. Churchill's 1906 confession that American scholarship did not compare favorably with that of Germany and England, the situation has altered dramatically.

* * *

Perhaps the most often encountered but least understood branch of Shakespeare scholarship is textual editing. Well into the nineteenth century, Americans relied on British editors to provide authoritative versions of individual plays and complete sets of Shakespeare's dramas. American editing grew slowly with the pioneering efforts of Gulian Crommelin Verplanck, Henry Norman Hudson, and Richard Grant White, among others (see Chapter 2, pp. 55–7), and finally

Horace Howard Furness. By the early twentieth century, after the great collectors of America's gilded age had used their wealth to bring rare materials from England to the United States, a new generation of American editors began to rival their English counterparts for mastery of Shakespearian textual scholarship.

In the twentieth century as in the nineteenth, access to the earliest printed versions of Shakespeare's plays was essential to crafting new and better texts, and with the opening of the Folger Shakespeare Library in 1932, scholars could find in one location most of the essential rare books. American editors now had access to all early versions of each Shakespearian text, could compare variants, and could select what in their judgment was the most convincing interpretation. By mid-century editing had taken on the mystique of hard science, partly because it depended so heavily on rational deductions made from a material (as opposed to a theoretical) text, but mostly, perhaps, because a new generation of college and university professors found it easier to receive funding if they could lard their applications with the mantra of science. From the late 1920s until the 1950s, England's Sir Walter W. Greg, sometime librarian at Trinity College, Cambridge, but mostly an independent scholar, spearheaded what was known as the "New Bibliography"—the effort to discover the content and format of an author's lost original by analyzing the "corrupted" versions produced by early English print shops. The modern editor's task was to determine as fully as possible what sort of manuscript material lay behind the printed text, what errors had been introduced during the printing process, and to infer from that evidence what the author had intended. Editors might thereby overcome the "barriers between the ideal text, or the mind that produced it, and the individual reader."[12]

After Greg died in 1959, the mantle of "Editor-in-Chief" fell to Fredson Thayer Bowers, Professor of English for most of his professional life at the University of Virginia in Charlottesville. Educated at Brown University (BA 1925) and Harvard (Ph.D. 1934), and using the theoretical tools of the New Bibliography, Bowers during a long career edited over 60 volumes of works, some by Shakespeare but most by his contemporaries. While Bowers worked at Charlottesville, his contemporary Charlton K. Hinman of the University of Kansas worked principally at the Folger Library in Washington,

Figure 5.2. The Hinman Collator. By permission of the Folger Shakespeare Library.

where he had access to its 79 copies of the 1623 First Folio—the largest collection in the world. Hinman subjected each folio to meticulous scrutiny by comparing word by word the fifty-five most complete folios with each other, and, displaying some Yankee ingenuity, inventing a machine—the "Hinman Collator"—that could mechanically superimpose images of nearly identical pages to highlight their variations (Fig. 5.2). In 1963 Hinman published his findings in *The Printing and Proof-Reading of The First Folio of Shakespeare*, followed in 1968 by the *Norton Facsimile of the First Folio of Shakespeare*. That relatively inexpensive facsimile edition allowed Shakespeare scholars everywhere, as well as public and private libraries, to have an exact copy of the 1623 folio, with one essential qualification: the Norton edition did not reproduce an entire copy, as had earlier facsimiles, but rather the best version of each page from the Folger's copies. After much comparison, Hinman selected pages from twenty-nine of them. The result was a book that had never existed before and was probably more accurate and certainly more legible overall than any surviving copy. Without Henry Clay Folger's insistence on collecting as many copies of the First Folio as possible, Hinman's collation would have been far less representative.

The influence of Bowers' and Hinman's scholarship and Hinman's optical invention went beyond Shakespeare studies to affect scholarly editions of major English authors, mainly from Shakespeare's era, and American authors, mainly from the nineteenth century. Ben Jonson and John Dryden typify the former category, James Fenimore Cooper and William Dean Howells the latter. But the New Bibliography that Bowers and Hinman had championed came into question by the 1970s, when doubts emerged about the viability of ever finding the author's original intention. By the 1980s a direct challenge to Bowers's "scientific" editing coalesced around a group of Shakespearians, most of them based in the United States, who suggested that Shakespeare probably revised his work from time to time so that variants in a play's substantives could indicate a change of authorial conception. Gary Taylor, the American co-editor of the *Oxford Shakespeare*, was among those who argued, for example, that the folio version of *King Lear* altered the final scenes from the quarto text so that Cordelia seemed less like a French queen invading Britain and the battle seemed more like a civil war than an invasion. The publication in 1983 of *The Division of the Kingdoms: Shakespeare's Two Versions of King Lear*, edited by Taylor and Michael Warren, renewed scholarly debates about editing procedures and textual authority—debates that continue to the present.

The first decades of the twenty-first century suggest as well that there is no longer much of a distinction between "American" and "British" editing. Since the 1980s North American editors have worked together with their British counterparts on major editing projects, including the Third Arden Series, the New Cambridge Shakespeare, and the Oxford Shakespeare. While Horace Howard Furness concluded each of his many variorum volumes with large swaths of critical commentary, modern editorial practices reverse the sequence. Editors now customarily preface a new edition with a lengthy overview of critical approaches to the play and explain their rationale for choosing their authoritative text and the alterations they have made to it (e.g. modern spelling, modern punctuation, additional stage directions), then provide the text itself with explanatory notes. On both sides of the Atlantic, scholars generally recognize that the texts that have come down to us are mediated by practices in the playhouse and printing house that we don't yet fully understand and perhaps never will. American editors share in the quest for persuasive explanations.

* * *

Shakespearian scholarship, broadly defined, encompasses the vast number of editions, articles, essays, book chapters, monographs, and dissertations produced every year on Shakespeare's plays and poems. The output is substantial: the World Shakespeare Bibliography, published under the auspices of *Shakespeare Quarterly*, lists 125,576 items published in the half century between 1960 and 2010, written by authors around the world but especially, inevitably, in Britain and the United States.

Although the history of Shakespeare criticism in America parallels for the most part, and is intertwined with, the intellectual and cultural currents of the United Kingdom, by the mid-twentieth century there came to be some noticeable differences. From the last half of the nineteenth century well into the twentieth, British and American scholars shared similar emphases. The investigation and dissection of Shakespeare's major characters, which reached its British apogee at the dawn of the twentieth century with the first holder of a chair in English at Oxford, A. C. Bradley (1851–1935), was the predominant discursive thread in the nineteenth century, particularly on the lecture circuit and in Shakespeare clubs. The closest American counterparts to Bradley were arguably Henry Norman Hudson (1814–86) and George Lyman Kittredge (1860–1941). The former scholar's career as an editor, author, and lecturer has already been addressed (Chapter 2, pp. 56–8); the latter's academic career has also been briefly introduced (Chapter 3, p. 87). At Harvard, Kittredge's interpretations of Shakespeare's plays influenced battalions of undergraduates before his retirement in 1936. Among his favorite topics were "Falstaff's courage, Hamlet's hesitation, [and] Iago's motivelessness," always relating the plays to real life situations.[13] "Kitty," as he was known (behind his back) by generations of Harvard students, represented an older style of undergraduate teaching as well as an older approach to the plays. Like Bradley and Hudson before him, Kittredge discussed Shakespeare's dramatis personae as if they were real human beings, emphasizing the reader's role as empathizer.

At the time Kittredge was ending his career, literary studies in both Britain and America often represented Shakespeare as the supreme spokesperson for conservative Anglo-American values. Scholars who practiced what is now known as "Old Historicism" argued that Shakespeare was a loyal supporter of the Tudor monarchy; Cambridge's E. M. W. Tillyard, for example, contended that Shakespeare's history plays conveyed the official Tudor doctrine of non-resistance and the importance of "order and degree" for a stable, prosperous society. In the United States, a different kind of conservatism appeared in "New Criticism," as it was often called, which pervaded American scholarship in the years after World War II. Originally fostered in the south by critics such as Cleanth Brooks at Louisiana State University, later at Yale, this "formalist" approach eschewed contingencies outside the text. The text's historical context, the author's biography, the play's staging practices—all were devalued in the attention paid to a drama's formal structure. To professional Shakespearians of this new persuasion, the plays were not scripts for performance but timeless poems whose language needed to be decoded, their ambiguities explained, and their figurative images unraveled. Once this was done, the astute reader could find "unity" in the plays, where each part related organically to the whole.[14]

While the followers of New Criticism claimed to be above politics, their reverential treatment of Shakespeare's language barely cloaked a conservative brand of anglophilia. That changed in the aftermath of the political unrest that beset America's universities during the height of the Vietnam War. By the 1980s a "culture war" for control of the curriculum raged in English departments across the United States, and Shakespeare was often the largest bone of contention. Younger faculty, educated during the tumultuous 1960s, demanded a more diverse curriculum that included women and writers of color instead of the "dead white males" that were routinely taught; Shakespeare was the supreme "dead white male." Few departments abandoned Shakespeare—although a course in Shakespeare might no longer be required of English majors—but the "culture wars" affected the way he was taught. As American professors began to challenge Shakespeare's universal wisdom and deconstruct his meaning, groups that had felt excluded by academia's predominantly male establishment began a reassessment of the dramatist's work.

After sharing ideas at an annual meeting of the Modern Language Association in 1976, Carolyn Ruth Swift Lenz, Gayle Greene, and Carol Thomas Neely assembled a collection of critical essays by women academics who approached Shakespeare from a feminist perspective.[15] They were especially interested in the dramatist's representations of female characters that had been overlooked or underrated in traditional criticism. Irene Dash of Hunter College, New York, Carol Thomas Neely of the University of Illinois-Champaign, and Marianne Novy of the University of Pittsburgh, among others, re-examined Shakespeare's women in light of their own experience of patriarchy.[16] As feminist criticism of Shakespeare matured, the emphasis moved from women *per se* to the construction of gender in early modern England, as well as the ways his works have been used to reinforce gender inequality in contemporary America. Using a variety of critical approaches, whether historical, psychoanalytic, linguistic, or performance-oriented, twenty-first century feminist criticism of Shakespeare in America now freely interrogates his work's patriarchal underpinnings.

In the aftermath of the 1960s civil rights movement, some American scholars turned their attention to Shakespeare's conspicuous "others": characters like Shylock, Aaron, Othello, Cleopatra, and Caliban, who are neither white nor British. Like the early feminist critics, American scholars with an interest in race and ethnicity began by identifying characters who are black, Moorish, or, in Shylock's case, Jewish, and then made a case for Shakespeare's comparative open-mindedness in his representation of their common humanity. In the early 1990s, spurred in part by the quincentennial commemoration of Columbus's first voyage to America, scholars began to reassess *The Tempest* in the context of European colonialism, with particular emphasis on Caliban's relationship with Prospero. Stephen

J. Greenblatt, for example, placed Caliban's declaration, "You taught me language, and my profit on't/Is I know how to curse" (1.ii.366–7) in juxtaposition with Spanish conquistadors' mistaken assumption that American Indians had no language of their own.[17] For many scholars writing in the 1990s, including American historians, Caliban seemed to be Shakespeare's representation of a Native American, akin to the Powhatans that British settlers confronted in Jamestown.

While some British Shakespearians have also explored Shakespeare's representations of non-English peoples, the preponderance of work in this sub-field has been conducted by American scholars. Kim F. Hall's *Things of Darkness: Economies of Race and Gender in Early Modern England* broadened the discussion from analysis of individual characters to examine the factors contributing to the formation of racial attitudes while focusing primarily on the imbrication of race and gender.[18] In *English Ethnicity and Race in Early Modern Drama* Mary Floyd-Wilson analyzed Renaissance geohumoral theories that linked differences in racial characteristics to geographical changes affecting climate.[19] More recently Lara Bovilsky and Ian Smith have seen the formation of English racial attitudes as emerging, in part, from an entrenched discourse regarding the "barbarousness" of peoples outside the city, whether Rome or London.[20] Although Turks are only addressed peripherally in Shakespeare's plays, the importance of religious difference as an "othering" catalyst is outlined in work on early modern English views of the Ottoman empire in general and Turks in particular in works by American scholars Daniel Vitkus, Linda McJannet, and Benedict S. Robinson.[21] James Shapiro's *Shakespeare and the Jews* (1996) investigates the English attitudes toward Jews that inform *The Merchant of Venice*. In the United States, where ethnic and racial identities play such a crucial role in political discourse, the representation of non-English peoples by Shakespeare and his contemporaries remains a focal point of critical inquiry.

New Criticism had largely ignored the overt discussion of social or political issues in its close readings of Shakespeare's poetry and had also eschewed historical contextualization. That, too, was to change after the 1980 publication of Stephen Greenblatt's *Renaissance Self-Fashioning from More to Marlowe*.[22] Influenced by French historical theorist Michel Foucault, Greenblatt insisted that Shakespeare (or any other Renaissance writer) needs to be understood within his own historical episteme, particularly the political institutions, beliefs, and social conditions that shaped the culture at large. Whereas early twentieth-century scholars—"Old Historicists"—had attributed a monological "Elizabethan world view" to Shakespeare, Greenblatt called for a newer historicism that located the plays within the dynamic interaction of subversive and dominant ideologies. Unlike its counterpart in Britain, "Cultural Materialism," a movement influenced by the Marxist scholar Raymond Williams that challenged Shakespeare's hegemony in the English educational system, New Historicism remained comparatively apolitical. Its practitioners seldom related their historical inquiries to contemporary social and political problems. They were also criticized by leading feminists for indifference to women's roles in early modern England and to women's contemporary issues. In the second decade of the twenty-first century, New Historicism is no longer new; its emphasis on the multiplicity of cultural forces shaping—and disseminated by—early modern texts is now commonly combined with other theoretical approaches.

One such approach is a renewed consideration of Shakespeare's plays as performance texts. Some scholars mine the archives for information about the size and structure of London's early theaters, others examine the various acting companies' personnel, and still others examine clues in the text, particularly staging, that suggest how a particular scene might have been performed.[23] Interest in original staging practices has also been stimulated by the founding of London's Globe Theatre, and more recently by the Blackfriars Theatre in Staunton, Virginia, where actors have tried to replicate early modern staging practices. Hoping to provide a similar visual experience to the spectators' at the original Blackfriars (the King's Company's indoor theater), Staunton's American Shakespeare Center uses lighting comparable to the candlelight in Jacobean England (Fig. 5.3). The Center also hosts biennial conferences where theater practitioners and scholars share ideas about how the plays were performed in Shakespeare's day. Another mode of performance criticism, best epitomized in the United States by Charles M. Shattuck's two-volume survey of Shakespeare on the American stage, focuses on the ways Shakespeare has been performed from the seventeenth century to the present. More recently, the study of Shakespeare's

Figure 5.3. The stage of the Blackfriars Theatre as seen from the upper gallery. Courtesy of the American Shakespeare Center in Staunton, Virginia.

plays as adapted for film and in other new media has become a burgeoning subfield. Interest in performance has also affected the teaching of Shakespeare. Since the 1980s, the National Endowment for the Humanities has sponsored summer workshops for secondary and college teachers that focus on performance as a mode of instruction. Across America, Shakespeare is no longer taught simply for his rhetorical excellence, moral wisdom, or poetic language; in the twenty-first-century classroom, the play is the thing.

While character criticism dominated during the nineteenth century, New Criticism took over in the mid-twentieth-century, and feminism and New Historicism gained ascendancy in the 1980s, professional approaches to Shakespeare in the early twenty-first century are eclectic and pluralistic, with no one school of thought in charge. It is increasingly difficult to characterize contemporary American scholarship because interactions between American Shakespeare scholars and their counterparts elsewhere in the world are now so frequent and collaborative. If anything is distinctly American about the way Shakespeare is currently taught, it reflects the pluralism of America's educational system. Unlike British secondary schools, America's schools do not have set texts for standardized exams. Whether private or public, America's many schools, colleges, and universities have no centralized curricula and, as a result, they offer Shakespeare courses taught from various approaches to diverse populations who, in turn, bring their own experiences to the texts. As the growing number of academics who share seminar presentations at the Shakespeare Association of America's annual meetings attests, such diversity ensures that in America professional Shakespeare is alive and well.

* * *

While American scholars are quick to discuss Shakespeare's poems and plays, most of them have given relatively little attention to the author. During the final quarter of the twentieth century, it seemed as if Samuel Schoenbaum (1927–96) had cornered the American market on that subject. Born and educated in New York City, Schoenbaum began his teaching career at Northwestern University, later moved to the City University of New York, and spent his final years as Director of the Center for Renaissance and Baroque studies at the University of Maryland. As his *New York Times* obituary explains, he "regarded himself as an archival sleuth. He managed to uncover previously unrecorded manuscripts and biographical records pertaining not only to Shakespeare, but also to other writers."[24] His lifelong ambition was to write the definitive Shakespeare biography, a project he never finished, but his preliminary work was prodigious. In 1970 Schoenbaum published *Shakespeare's Lives*, a 768-page study of the details of Shakespeare's life complemented by a survey of what biographers have said about him ever since.[25] *Shakespeare's Lives* was followed in 1975 by *William Shakespeare: A Documentary Life*, which reproduced in facsimile all the extant documents that relate to Shakespeare's life, including real estate transactions, law suits, and wills.[26] Shakespeare's many subsequent biographers—from America or elsewhere—owe Schoenbaum a lasting debt, whether they are summarizing the life in a few pages or several hundred.

Following Schoenbaum's death, a new wave of Shakespeare biographies by American authors has appeared, with contributions of varying magnitude. At the short end of the spectrum is the novelist and travel writer Bill Bryson's summary for the Eminent Lives series, *Shakespeare: The World as Stage*;[27] among the full-length biographies,

Will in the World: How Shakespeare Became Shakespeare,[28] the hefty volume by Harvard professor and chief editor of W.W. Norton's edition of the complete works, Stephen Greenblatt, is more thorough in its use of the surviving evidence but also relies heavily on his speculations about the dramatist's religion and emotional life as reflected in the plays' plots, characters, and language.

Greenblatt is not alone in his desire to understand Shakespeare through his writings. As James Shapiro of Columbia University has demonstrated, although it may seem like gospel today, not until the eighteenth century did a widespread conviction take hold that an author's life was reflected in his work. The modern imperative to find links between the man and the writings has also encouraged those who find the details of Shakespeare's business dealings—chronicled so well by Schoenbaum—to be inconsistent with the dramatist's lofty language and ideas. The belief that no son of a glover from Stratford could possibly have understood the law, codes of chivalry, courtly love, court life, and so much more, was a matter of faith for Delia Bacon, who believed that a coterie led by Sir Francis Bacon was the real author of Shakespeare's plays (see Chapter 2, pp. 63–7). In the twentieth century and since, the perceived disconnect between the details of Shakespeare's business transactions and the poetry he wrote has energized advocates for Edward de Vere as the true author of Shakespeare's works.

The campaign for Oxford began in England in 1920 when J. Thomas Looney published *"Shakespeare" Identified in Edward de Vere, the Seventeenth Earl of Oxford*, a lengthy exposition of deficiencies in the man from Stratford's claim.[29] Influenced by the teachings of the positivist philosopher August Comte, Looney found incredible the proposition that the author of *The Merchant of Venice* could have himself loaned money at interest. Looney argued more broadly that the plays highlight the value of England's medieval feudal order and the importance of the monarch; surely the man who wrote them had to share that noble heritage. Looney's ideas attracted many followers, including Sigmund Freud, who admired and devoured Shakespeare as a child, later rejected the Baconian argument but agreed with many anti-Stratfordians that multiple minds must have created such a prodigious corpus, and finally, after reading Looney, converted to Oxfordianism. Freud's protracted anguish over the authorship question puzzled his first and most intimate biographer, Ernest Jones—a confirmed Stratfordian—and subsequent writers on Freud.

In 1922 the Shakespeare Fellowship, a new organization devoted to proving the Earl of Oxford's authorship, had more than forty members by the end of the year, almost entirely British. The organization's mission was invigorated substantially in 1928 with the publication of Bernard M. Ward's sympathetic biography of Oxford, and gradually Looney's Oxfordian fervor worked its way to the United States. In 1937 Louis P. Bénézet, later a professor at Dartmouth College, published *Shakspere, Shakespeare and de Vere*, outlining de Vere's claims; in the same year Charles Wisner Barrell explained Looney's theories to a popular audience in the *Saturday Review of Literature*, and two years later Eva Turner Clark organized an American branch of the Shakespeare Fellowship. It nonetheless took several more decades for the Oxfordian theory to catch fire with Americans.[30]

The chief invigorator was Charlton Ogburn, Jr. (1911–98), a Harvard-educated journalist who served in military intelligence during World War II and afterward in the State Department until 1957, when he retired to become a full-time writer. Ogburn absorbed his Oxfordian convictions from his parents, who wrote several books on the subject, including *This Star of England: "William Shake-speare," Man of the Renaissance*.[31] The younger Ogburn continued their work with an article in *Harvard Magazine* (1974), in which he contended that the works of all creative writers reflect their life experiences, and that "nothing in the Stratford man's life illuminates the poems and plays of Shakespeare." Shakespeare's "abiding preoccupation was evidently with money," Ogburn insisted, because what documentary evidence we have is about his business dealings and real estate transactions. Yet when we turn to the plays, he argued, we find that "no writer ever wrote more consistently from the point of view of a nobleman than Shakespeare."[32] In 1976 Ogburn was elected president of the Shakespeare Oxford Society, where he expanded his argument in an attack on academic Shakespearians: "English faculties, abetted by a generally subservient press, show how far entrenched authority can outlaw and silence dissent in a supposedly free society.... We are dealing here with an intellectual Watergate, and it greatly behooves us to expose it."[33] Tapping into Americans' post-Watergate obsession with government conspiracies, Ogburn continued the campaign in

1984 with the voluminous *The Mysterious William Shakespeare: The Myth and the Reality.*[34]

In 1987 the Oxfordians attracted public attention when three justices of the United States Supreme Court—William Brennan, Harry Blackmun, and John Paul Stevens—served as judges in a moot trial on the authorship question in Washington, DC, before 1,000 spectators. Although the judges ruled for Shakespeare (Stevens later changed his mind), the issue resurfaced in 1989 when PBS's *Frontline*, a television program devoted to journalistic exposés, aired "The Shakespeare Mystery" (co-produced in 1987 by Yorkshire Television and Boston's WGBH). Here Ogburn's campaign was more successful: before three and a half million viewers the spokesmen for Shakespeare—Samuel Schoenbaum and the British scholar A. L. Rowse—seemed like stuffy academics, while the Oxfordians offered an exciting new theory.

Since that trial, a handful of American proponents of the Earl of Oxford as the author of Shakespeare's plays have received Ph.D.s in English literature—a very few specializing in the Early Modern period—and joined American English Departments. The Shakespeare Fellowship now boasts a growing international membership, and after many years of circulating its arguments through newsletters and websites, the organization has since 2009 sponsored its own printed journal, *Brief Chronicles: An Interdisciplinary Journal of Authorship Studies*. Yet while the authorship question has great appeal to those Americans outside of academia who love conspiracy theories or have only passing familiarity with Shakespeare and the literary and social contexts of his times, the vast majority of academic Shakespearians in the United States remain unconvinced by anti-Stratfordian arguments.

* * *

If he were alive today, Horace Howard Furness would surely be gratified that the New Variorum project he began continues under the auspices of America's Modern Language Association, the largest and most influential professional organization for academics who teach in English and foreign language departments. He might be even more pleased at the diversity, scope, and intensity of the work of America's academic Shakespearians. Furness could become a professional Shakespearian when his wife's inheritance allowed him the leisure to pursue his scholarly interests, yet with his work as a trustee at the University of Pennsylvania, he maintained an abiding interest in education. Unlike Furness, today's professional Shakespearians generally have one firm foot in the classroom, the other in the archive. In contrast to their nineteenth- and early-twentieth-century predecessors, they no longer seek to deliver Shakespeare's exact meaning but, instead, pose innumerable unanswered questions about Shakespeare the man, his works, and the context of his times. Furness would probably like that too.

Notes

1. James M. Gibson, *The Philadelphia Story: Horace Howard Furness and the New Variorum Shakespeare* (New York: AMS Press, 1990), esp. 57–77.
2. Anonymous, "Why We Have No Shakespearean Scholars," *Round Table* 4 (1866), repr. in Peter Rawlings (ed.), *Americans on Shakespeare 1776–1914* (Aldershot: Ashgate, 1999), 245–6 (quotation from 246).
3. George B. Churchill, "Shakespeare in America," *Jahrbuch der Deutschen Shakespeare-Gesellschaft* 42 (1908), xiii–xlv (quotation from xliv).
4. Michael D. Bristol concludes in *Shakespeare's America: America's Shakespeare* (London: Routledge, 1990), 64, that "Furness helped to create the idea of Shakespeare scholarship as a profession."
5. Georgianna Ziegler provides an overview of Folger's extensive reading in "Duty and Enjoyment: The Folgers as Shakespeare Collectors in the Gilded Age," in Virginia Mason Vaughan and Alden T. Vaughan (eds.), *Shakespeare in American Life* (Washington, DC: Folger Shakespeare Library, 2007), 101–11.
6. Quoted from ibid. 104.
7. Horace Howard Furness to Emily Folger, Wallingford, Pennsylvania, July 25, 1894, quoted in ibid. 102.
8. John Bartlett, *A Collection of Familiar Quotations: With Complete Indices of Authors and Subjects* (Cambridge, MA: John Bartlett, 1855); John Bartlett, *Bartlett's Familiar Quotations: A Collection of Passages, Phrases, and Proverbs Traced to Their Sources in Ancient and Modern Literature*, 17th edn, ed. Justin Kaplan (Boston: Little, Brown, 2002); John Bartlett, *Bartlett's Shakespeare Quotations*, foreword by Justin Kaplan (Boston: Little, Brown, 2005); Helen M. Whall, "Bartlett's Evolving Shakespeare," in Richard Burt (ed.), *Shakespeare after Mass Media* (New York: Palgrave, 2002), 287–94.

9. [John Bartlett,] *Choice Thoughts from Shakspere, by the Author of "The Book of Familiar Quotations"* (London: Whitaker, 1861), quotation from the Preface; John Bartlett, *The Shakespeare Phrase Book* (Boston: Little, Brown, 1881).
10. John Bartlett, *A New and Complete Concordance or Verbal Index to Words, Phrases, & Passages in the Dramatic Works of Shakespeare* (London and New York: Macmillan, 1894). This work was reissued at least six times between the first and the most recent printing (2010).
11. For a full account, see Mary C. Hyde, "The Shakespeare Association to the Folger Shakespeare Library on its 40th Anniversary, April 21, 1972," *Shakespeare Quarterly* 23 (1972), 219–25.
12. Bristol, *Shakespeare's America*, 108.
13. Harry Levin, *Shakespeare and the Revolution of the Times* (New York: Oxford University Press, 1976), 19.
14. This discussion draws on, among others, Gary Taylor, *Reinventing Shakespeare: A Cultural History from the Restoration to the Present* (New York: Weidenfeld & Nicolson, 1989), 285–94.
15. Carolyn Ruth Swift Lenz, Gayle Greene, and Carol Thomas Neely (eds.), *The Woman's Part: Feminist Criticism of Shakespeare* (Urbana: University of Illinois Press, 1980).
16. See Irene G. Dash, *Wooing, Wedding and Power: Women in Shakespeare's Plays* (New York: Columbia University Press, 1981); Carol Thomas Neely, *Broken Nuptials in Shakespeare's Plays* (New Haven, CT: Yale University Press, 1985); and Marianne Novy, *Love's Argument: Gender Relations in Shakespeare* (Chapel Hill: University of North Carolina Press, 1984).
17. Stephen Greenblatt, "Learning to Curse: Aspects of Linguistic Colonialism in the Sixteenth Century," in *Learning to Curse: Essays in Early Modern Culture* (New York: Routledge, 1990), 16–39.
18. Kim F. Hall, *Things of Darkness: Economies of Race and Gender in Early Modern England* (Ithaca, NY: Cornell University Press, 1995).
19. Mary Floyd-Wilson, *English Ethnicity and Race in Early Modern Drama* (Cambridge: Cambridge University Press, 2003).
20. Lara Bovilsky, *Barbarous Play: Race on the English Renaissance Stage* (Minneapolis: University of Minnesota Press, 2008); and Ian Smith, *Race and Rhetoric in Renaissance England: Barbarian Errors* (New York: Palgrave, 2009).
21. Daniel Vitkus, *Turning Turk: English Theater and the Multicultural Mediterranean, 1570–1630* (New York: Palgrave, 2003); Linda McJannet, *The Sultan Speaks: Dialogue in English Plays and Histories About the Ottoman Turks* (New York: Palgrave, 2006); and Benedict S. Robinson, *Islam and Early Modern English Literature* (New York: Palgrave, 2007).

22. Stephen Greenblatt, *Renaissance Self-Fashioning from More to Marlowe* (Chicago: University of Chicago Press, 1980).
23. For two examples, see Roslyn Lander Knutson, *Playing Companies and Commerce in Shakespeare's Time* (Cambridge: Cambridge University Press, 2001); and Alan C. Dessen and Leslie Thomson, *A Dictionary of Stage Directions in English Drama, 1580–1642* (Cambridge: Cambridge University Press, 1999).
24. www.nytimes.com/1996/03/30/arts/samuel-schoenbaum-69-expert-on-shakespeare.html (accessed July 9, 2010).
25. Samuel Schoenbaum, *Shakespeare's Lives* (Oxford: Clarendon Press, 1991).
26. Samuel Schoenbaum, *William Shakespeare: A Documentary Life* (New York: Oxford University Press, 1975).
27. Bill Bryson, *Shakespeare: The World as Stage* (New York: Atlas Books, 2007).
28. Stephen Greenblatt, *Will in the World: How Shakespeare Became Shakespeare* (New York: Norton, 2004).
29. J. Thomas Looney, *"Shakespeare" Identified in Edward de Vere, the Seventeenth Earl of Oxford* (London: C. Palmer, 1920).
30. James Shapiro, *Contested Will: Who Wrote Shakespeare?* (New York: Simon & Schuster, 2010), 192–3; Bernard M. Ward, *The Seventeenth Earl of Oxford, 1550–1604* (London: J. Murray, 1928). Louis P. Bénézet, *Shakspere, Shakespeare and de Vere* (Manchester, NH: Granite State Press, 1937). Charles Wisner Barrell, "Elizabethan Mystery Man," *Saturday Review of Literature*, May 1, 1937.
31. Dorothy and Charlton Ogburn, *This Star of England: "William Shake-speare," Man of the Renaissance* (New York: Coward-McCann, 1952; rev. edn. 1955).
32. www.pbs.org/wgbh/pages/frontline/shakespeare/debates/ogburnarticle.html (accessed July 2, 2010).
33. Quoted in Shapiro, *Contested Will*, 204.
34. Charlton Ogburn, Jr., *The Mysterious William Shakespeare: The Myth and the Reality*, 2nd edn. (McLean, VA: EPM Publications, 1992).

6

Popular Shakespeare

On November 12, 1993, a Public Broadcasting Service TV *Frontline* program on "The Shakespeare Mystery" featured Louis Marder, a professor of English literature who spent most of his career at the University of Illinois, Chicago Circle. The professor was asked about his participation in the Boston Bar Association's Mock Trial on the authorship of Shakespeare's plays, where Marder had been an expert witness for the Stratfordians, arguing that the evidence proved beyond a doubt that William Shakespeare was indeed the author of the plays attributed to him. Marder was a logical choice to speak on the controversial issue at both the Mock Trial and on PBS. As the founder in 1951 and editor (until 1991) of the widely circulated *Shakespeare Newsletter*, he had sought subscribers outside the academic community, and in the pages of his quarterly publication he frequently included trivia, jokes, and cartoons, all related to Shakespeare. Despite his Stratfordian position, he even-handedly published essays and advertisements for Oxfordian proponents of Edward de Vere, although most were not professional Shakespearians. Marder's involvement with this intense ongoing debate in public arenas was typical of a man who tried to bridge the gap between the academic Shakespeare taught in schools and colleges and the popular Shakespeare disseminated through mass media. In the Fall 2009 issue of *Shakespeare Newsletter* which announced Marder's death, the current editors, Tom Pendleton and John Mahon, sought a venue to house Marder's collection of Shakespeare memorabilia. Like Marder's newsletter, his 20,000-item legacy combined the scholarly (books and manuscripts) with the popular (engravings, statues, toys, and other ephemera).

Marder's crossover between the professional and popular is not as unusual as it might seem to people outside the Shakespeare industry. Indeed, many academics take pride in their Shakespeare kitsch, whether the artifact is a rubber duck, bobble head, action hero, or beanie baby. Such whimsical items inevitably draw a chuckle from students and colleagues because of the striking juxtaposition of high culture's most famous poet with a child's toy or advertising gimmick; at the same time, these objects are a comforting proof that Shakespeare still sells and, in that sense, somehow still matters. In the world beyond the walls of academe, such material artifacts demonstrate the entrepreneur's drive to capitalize on the American citizens' desire to play with Shakespeare.

By the beginning of the twentieth century, when Shakespeare was taught in every public school across the United States, Americans were deeply invested in Shakespeare's cultural capital. Adding a Shakespeare tag to a political cartoon or advertisement signaled an in-joke—that the text's author and the text's reader shared knowledge of Shakespeare that marked him or her as educated and culturally aware. Merchants exploited Shakespeare's image or language to assure buyers of the item's quality; political cartoonists used it to underscore the wit and wisdom of their position. One could rephrase "To be or not to be" in any form or fashion, knowing that the vast majority of Americans would recognize the line as Shakespeare's and take pleasure at the writer's cleverness (Fig. 6.1). Despite being taken out of context and without regard to historical accuracy, a Shakespearian tag simultaneously provided cultural authority and lighthearted pleasure.

What is true of kitsch, advertising, and politics applies even more profoundly to the realm of popular entertainment. When Hollywood wanted to prove that movie-making was an art form as well as a business, it turned to Shakespeare's plays. Looking for compelling storylines, the makers of Broadway musical comedies also appropriated Shakespeare. Beginning in the 1950s, television brought Shakespeare into America's living rooms. The hybrid—Shakespeare and the new media—had to be entertaining and accessible to a wide cross-section of Americans; often Shakespeare's language was abandoned in favor of colloquial American English. Nevertheless, in the words of cultural critic Marjorie Garber, "Shakespeare makes modern

3RD
1ST
2ND
TO BEE OR NOT TO BEE; THAT, MY FRIENDS, IS THE QUESTION!

Figure 6.1. Clifford Berryman's cartoon of President Franklin Delano Roosevelt as Hamlet, pondering the possibility of running for a third term (1940).

culture and modern culture makes Shakespeare."[1] Put another way, while a Shakespearian appropriation often shapes an audience's response, the appropriation itself—whether a film, Broadway musical, or television show—also shapes an audience's understanding of Shakespeare. This chapter explores that symbiotic process in American popular entertainment venues from the dawn of the twentieth century and into the twenty-first.

* * *

Perhaps no American embodied the twin drives of innovation and entrepreneurship more than Thomas Edison, inventor of the first moving picture machine. Not surprisingly, the English were the first to bring the new American technology to Shakespeare when in 1899 the English actor and impresario Herbert Beerbohm Tree shot a scene from his stage production of *King John* on London's Embankment. The extant print, featuring Tree's flamboyant stage rendition of

John's deathbed anguish, reveals the challenge posed by silent moving pictures. Nearly two decades would pass before Shakespeare on film became more than a visual archive of stage practices.

The earliest experiments in film technology had taken place in England and France, but America soon followed suit. As the twentieth century began, J. Stuart Blackton's Vitagraph Company, hoping to make the new media attractive to middle-class Americans, adapted several of Shakespeare's plays to short, one-reel silent movies.[2] Presenting an entire Shakespeare play in fifteen minutes required a kind of filmic synecdoche, in which a brief tableau could stand for several scenes in the original. Vitagraph selected plays that were well known to American audiences so that viewers could draw from their own knowledge to fill the gaps. In *Julius Caesar*, for example, a simple shot of the assassination could replace pages of dialogue. Blackton shot some scenes on location in Manhattan, including a lake in Central Park, but his assembly-line productions were mostly filmed at Vitagraph's studio in the Flatbush section of Brooklyn. Underemployed stage actors commuted from New York City to Flatbush for filming, and costumes were sometimes borrowed from Broadway shows. Despite the flimsy sets, primitive lighting, and static camera angles, Vitagraph's films aspired to respectability. Narrators were hired to read the intertitles, screenings were sometimes accompanied by lectures, and live music enhanced screen images. Between 1908 and 1912, Vitagraph brought eleven of Shakespeare's most popular plays to New York's teeming populace, many of whom might not have been able to afford a ticket to a stage performance.

In the years before World War I a burgeoning movie industry disseminated nineteenth-century stage Shakespeare to small town nickelodeons across the United States. The forty-minute *Richard III*, directed by James Keane, is a case in point. Its star, tragedian Frederick B. Warde, presented the same villainous Richard he had performed on stage. Born in England, in 1874 Warde had migrated to the United States, where he began his American career at Booth's Theatre in New York and subsequently joined Edwin Booth on tour. From 1909 to his death in 1935 Warde supplemented his income as a touring actor by lecturing on Shakespeare. Warde considered film a handy way to supplement his presentations and attract a wider audience. But even as early as 1913, film could offer effects more marvelous than his melodramatic King Richard. Director Keane added battle scenes populated by extras clothed as knights, some mounted on horses, and instead of Shakespeare's report of Henry Tudor's arrival at Milford Haven, Henry emerged from a genuine three-masted warship. The Shakespeare Film Company's *Richard III* consists of 77 separate scenes, some of them interpolated. Following the nineteenth-century stage tradition of using introductory material from Colley Cibber, the film begins with scenes from *3 Henry VI* and displays Richard's murder of Prince Edward and King Henry VI. Other scenes were added to clarify the plot for an audience unfamiliar with Shakespeare's text; one shows Edward signing his brother George's death warrant, another portrays Queen Anne drinking poison, and in a third Richard woos Princess Elizabeth to be his wife. Another innovation was a final frame of the film's star, Frederick B. Warde, in a tweed jacket similar to the one he wore on the lecture circuit.

Warde's second Shakespeare film, produced by the Thanhouser Film Corporation of New Rochelle, New York, and released in 1916, uses a similar frame. In the opening shot Warde the lecturer/actor pores over an edition of Shakespeare's plays, while the image of Warde dissolves into an aged King Lear. Warde brought to this role the full arsenal of nineteenth-century acting techniques, including "semaphore-like arm waving, much stalking about, considerable writhing, shaking of the head, finger wagging, and grimacing at the camera."[3] These histrionics were supplemented with impressive battle scenes of cavalry charges and foot soldiers in lethal combat.

After World War I, America's movie industry—unlike Britain's, in which a vibrant stage tradition lessened the demand for Shakespearian movies—continued to mine Shakespeare's plays.[4] Thanhouser, for example, produced several other silent Shakespeare films, including *Cymbeline* and *The Winter's Tale.* Studio moguls soon migrated to Hollywood, and by 1929 the medium was being revolutionized by the advent of talking pictures. A Shakespeare film was one of the first: in that year, Columbia Pictures featured silent film's favorite sweethearts, Douglas Fairbanks and Mary Pickford, in a feature-length *Taming of the Shrew.* Because few movie venues across the United States had facilities for talking pictures, Columbia filmed the *Shrew* in two versions, one silent and one with sound. Legend has it that director Sam Taylor doomed the film for many viewers by inserting this credit line: "By William Shakespeare with additional dialogue by Sam Taylor."[5] In reality, credits for both films indicated that this *Shrew* was an adaptation of Shakespeare's original. The film's lack of box office success was more likely caused by the lead actors' difficulty in adjusting to talking pictures. The soft-spoken Fairbanks had built his career on the visual impact of his manly poses, not his speech, while Pickford's voice was raspy.

Although Taylor's drastically cut *Shrew* failed to attract large audiences when it first appeared in 1929, the film (reissued in 1966) has much to recommend it. Taylor's *Shrew* initiated the American practice of featuring well-known screen stars in Shakespearian adaptations, whether they had stage training or not. William Cameron Menzie's Italian street scenes, populated with extras and strolling magicians, created a convincing *mise en scène.* Most important, the film gave Pickford the opportunity to play against her image as "America's sweetheart," Fairbanks to play with his swashbuckling persona. Fairbanks and Pickford, married to each other at the time, energetically portrayed the battle of the sexes as Petruchio and Kate, exploiting slapstick comedy whenever they met. Like the Petruchio of stage tradition, Fairbanks appears with whip in hand, but in this film Kate has a whip of her own, albeit shorter (Fig. 6.2). The film underscores Kate's subversion of traditional patriarchy in other ways as well. In an interpolated scene she overhears Petruchio's plan to tame her, reacting with a smile that implies, "We'll see about that." Act IV's stage business on the road to Padua is transposed to the bedroom, where the couple argue about what they see from the window, sun or moon. After accidentally hitting Petruchio's head with a stool, a maternal Kate comforts him with, "There, there." In the film's final banquet scene, after Kate proclaims the wife's duties to her husband, Pickford winks at Bianca, suggesting the sisters' subversive recognition of what every woman knows—just tell the men what they want to hear and do what you want. The film concludes on a note of social harmony when Petruchio pulls Kate to his lap for a proper kiss and the wedding party joins in song.[6]

Box office receipts were far greater for Hollywood's second feature-length talking Shakespeare film, Max Reinhardt's *A Midsummer Night's Dream* (1935). Born in Austria to Jewish parents, Reinhardt

Figure 6.2. Katherine (Mary Pickford) and Petruchio (Douglas Fairbanks) in Sam Taylor's 1929 film adaptation, *The Taming of the Shrew*. Courtesy of the Mary Pickford Institute for Film Education.

abandoned his successful career in Germany after the Nazi rise to power in 1933 and emigrated to the United States. In 1934 he mounted a spectacular production of *Dream* at the Hollywood Bowl, and not long after, Warner Brothers Studio asked him to direct a film version with William Dieterle. Using a bilingual German-English screenplay,[7] Reinhardt oversaw the production's details, including the construction of palatial sets. In hopes of attracting a mass audience, Warner Brothers filled the cast with familiar faces: Mickey Rooney as Puck, Dick Powell as Lysander, Joe E. Brown as Flute, James Cagney as Bottom, Anita Louise as Titania, and Victor Jory as Oberon; the future star Olivia de Havilland played Hermia. The soundtrack echoed Mendelssohn's familiar wedding march. Special effects allowed Rooney's Puck to fly through the air and prima ballerina Nini Theilade to float aloft. Reinhardt also exploited stunning lighting effects to contrast the wood's mysterious darkness to Theseus' incandescent art deco palace. But for many, the rude mechanicals—particularly Cagney's indefatigable Bottom and Brown's mugging Flute—stole the show. Although some Shakespeare purists were dissatisfied when the movie was first shown in 1935, Reinhardt's *Midsummer Night's Dream* remains an American film classic.[8]

Not so, however, for Irving Thalberg and George Cukor's *Romeo and Juliet*, which Metro Goldwyn Mayer released the following year. In an attempt to attract a more sophisticated audience, Thalberg cast British actor Leslie Howard as Romeo, John Barrymore as Mercutio, and film star Norma Shearer as Juliet. While Reinhardt had borrowed elements of popular 1930s musicals for his *Dream*, Cukor turned to opera and ballet, using Tchaikovsky's *Romeo and Juliet* for his sound track. He also spared no expense on costumes and scenic design. To this high-class mix he added some down-to-earth comic byplay from Andy Devine's thumb-biting Peter, a Capulet servant. But Howard and Shearer, then in their 40s, were too mature to represent realistically Romeo and Juliet's impetuous passion, and too much reverence for Shakespeare's original slowed the film's pace. Despite Cukor's best efforts, the 1936 *Romeo and Juliet* bombed, and for many years thereafter Hollywood assumed that Shakespeare was box office poison.

That assumption proved false in 1953 when MGM released its second filmic adaptation of a major Shakespearian play. Directed by Joseph L. Mankiewicz (well known for bringing British classics to American film), *Julius Caesar* featured a mixed cast of American film and British stage actors. In the age of McCarthyism *Julius Caesar* was standard fare in America's secondary schools, its plot interpreted to support conservative values and its famous funeral orations endorsed as rhetorical models. John Gielgud, Britain's most celebrated speaker of Shakespearian verse, played the lean and hungry Cassius. Another experienced British Shakespearian, James Mason, took Brutus' part, while seasoned American film actors Louis Calhern (Julius Caesar) and Edmond O' Brien (Casca) added solidity. Both female leads were performed by British actors who had moved to Hollywood: Greer Garson as Calpurnia and Deborah Kerr as Portia. Set against this

Figure 6.3. Mark Antony (Marlon Brando) delivers his funeral oration over Caesar's body in Joseph Mankiewicz's 1953 film adaptation of *Julius Caesar*. Photo: akg-images.

stellar cast was the young Marlon Brando as Antony. Known as "the Mumbler" for his understated performance as Stanley Kowalski in *A Streetcar Named Desire*, Brando was a confirmed method actor, and although many wondered whether he could handle Shakespeare's formal speeches, he won an Oscar nomination for Best Actor in a Leading Role for his seething Mark Antony (Fig. 6.3).

Unlike Hollywood's previous feature-length Shakespeare films, *Julius Caesar* was presented without substantial cuts in the text. Filmed in black and white, the actors wore Roman costumes on a mammoth set that included "crowded streets, steep staircases, elevated pulpits, pillars, balconies, statuary, and 1200 toga-clad extras milling before a painted backdrop of the entire ancient city."[9] Indeed, the film won the Academy Award for Best Art Direction and was nominated in several other categories. Produced with the same attention to concept and detail as Reinhardt's *Dream*, Joseph Mankiewicz's *Julius Caesar* demonstrated that Shakespeare could draw a mass audience if it were done well.

* * *

While Hollywood was figuring out how to put Shakespeare on screen, New York's Broadway decided to brush up its Shakespeare by transforming his plays into musical comedies. Unlike Hollywood's efforts to present the original text, albeit with cuts, the Broadway musical modified Shakespeare in hopes that even if audiences were largely unfamiliar with his work they would enjoy the fun. The new genre abandoned Shakespeare's language but kept many of his situations and characters, fleshing out story lines with songs and dances. Some adaptations relied more heavily on Shakespeare's original than others, but all sought to adjust the characters and story to American audiences' tastes and values.

Prominent songsmiths Lorenz Hart and Richard Rodgers were the first to imagine a Shakespeare-based musical. Hoping to capitalize on the uncanny resemblance between Hart's brother, comedian Teddy Hart, and another well-known comic, Jimmy Savo, they seized upon *The Comedy of Errors* to cast the pair as Shakespeare's identical Dromio twins.[10] Although Lorenz and Hart abandoned all but a couple of lines from Shakespeare's text and substituted songs for much of the dialogue, they kept the characters' names and setting. With a book by George Abbott and choreography by George Balanchine, *The Boys from Syracuse* opened in November 1938 at New York's Alvin Theatre and ran for 235 performances to rave reviews. Audiences enjoyed the original plot's uproarious confusion between the other identical twins, Antipholus of Syracuse and Antipholus of Ephesus, but they were also titillated by the Dromios' comic by-play and bawdy jokes. The role of Luce, a kitchen maid, was expanded so that she could swap sexual badinage with both Dromios. The Courtesan, too, had more to say than she did in Shakespeare, and joined Luce in a comic song about the challenges of finding an honest man. Combining thinly veiled sexual humor with Balanchine's energetic choreography and Rodgers and Hart's brilliant score, *The Boys from Syracuse* also pleasured its audience with anachronistic Shakespearian allusions, such as the Merchant's advice that, "If anyone asks you any questions, say you don't know the language . . . it's all Greek to you."[11] Who said Shakespeare couldn't be fun?

In contrast to *The Boys from Syracuse*'s popular success, *Swingin' the Dream* opened November 29, 1939 at New York's Center Theatre, which held as many as 4,000 people, and closed less than two weeks later. No script survives, but this adaptation of *A Midsummer Night's Dream* was a crossover hybrid between the white ethnic majority's stage Shakespeare and African American swing music. *Swingin' the Dream* featured several popular African American performers; Louis Armstrong, for example, portrayed Bottom and Butterfly McQueen was Puck, while Pearl Bailey's brother Bill and the Lindy Hoppers performed dances choreographed by Agnes de Mille. Interspersed with Shakespeare's text were swing numbers from Benny Goodman and songs by composer Jimmy Van Heusen. With so many talented participants, it is difficult to understand why *Swingin' the Dream* failed. Perhaps the combination of the African American community's swing music and high culture's Shakespeare was too innovative for contemporary audiences; perhaps, too, four years before Paul Robeson's appearance on Broadway as Othello, white Americans were not quite ready to see African Americans performing Shakespeare in a mainstream theater.

Yet African Americans were integrated into the first musical to win a Tony award for Broadway's best play: *Kiss Me Kate*. With songs by Cole Porter, a book by Bella Spewak, and choreography by Hanya Holm, *Kiss Me Kate* was loosely based on Shakespeare's *The Taming of the Shrew*. Beginning with "Another Op'nin, Another Show," sung by Hattie (a black maid), and including a dance number, "Too Darn Hot," that featured several African American dancers, *Kiss Me Kate* provided minor roles for black actors but reserved the production's Shakespearian scenes for whites. *Kiss Me Kate* opened on December 30, 1948, in New York, where it ran for 1,077 performances, and its 1999 Broadway revival won twelve Tony awards. *Kiss Me Kate* was also made into a feature film in 1953, starring Katherine Grayson and Howard Keel, but modified to give "Too Darn Hot" to dancer Ann Miller and eliminate the black performers.

Like Shakespeare, Porter and Spewak set Petruchio's tempestuous wooing of Kate within a frame. Instead of Christopher Sly's encounter with a noble Lord, the musical showcases a group of contemporary actors as they prepare to mount a musical version of Shakespeare's comedy. Lilli Vanessi and Fred Graham, who are to play Kate and Petruchio in the show, were once married but are now divorced, and their bitter quarrels threaten the production's success. Despite Fred's flirtation with hoofer Lois Lane and Lilli's engagement to the wealthy but strait-laced Hamilton Howell, in typical musical comedy fashion the divorced pair rediscover their love for each other and reconcile at the end, underscoring the sacredness of heterosexual marriage. *Kiss Me Kate* also intersperses some brief, but mostly authentic, scenes from *The Taming of the Shrew* with the comic gags, songs, and dances typical of a Broadway musical.

Just as the Dromios interpolated entertaining comic routines in *The Boys from Syracuse*, two gangsters who are pressuring Fred (Petruchio) for payment of a gambling debt capitalize on Shakespeare's cultural status. Confessing that they learned their Shakespeare during an eight-year stint in prison, they recognize the poet's value, especially when a fellow wants to impress a girl. Each line of their soft shoe number, "Brush Up Your Shakespeare," concludes with a witty Cole Porter pun on a Shakespearian play. Examples: "If your blonde don't respond when you flatter'er,/Tell her what Tony told Cleopatterer," and "With the wife of the British Embessida/Try a crack out of *Troilus and Cressida*." When this ditty turned out to be a showstopper, Porter added progressively bawdier encore verses. Composed by the classically educated Cole Porter and sung by actors playing self-educated underworld thugs, "Brush Up Your Shakespeare" complicates the traditional binary between highbrow and lowbrow. Playing with Shakespeare's titles—and his language—is for everyone.

Kiss Me Kate remains one of the most successful musical comedies ever produced on Broadway, but could a Shakespearian *tragedy* be similarly adapted? As early as 1949, while *Kiss Me Kate* was still riding high, composer Leonard Bernstein brainstormed with choreographer Jerome Robbins as to whether some version of *Romeo and Juliet*, set in New York's slums and titled *East Side Story*, could be a suitable musical. The entry for January 6, 1949, that he later wrote for his "West Side Log" reads: "Feelings running high between Jews and Catholics. Former: Capulets, latter: Montagues. Juliet is Jewish. Friar Lawrence is a neighborhood druggist. Street brawls, double death—it all fits." Arthur Laurents, who eventually wrote the "book," joined the discussions, but it wasn't until 1955 that the trio abandoned their original Jewish–Catholic scheme and decided that the Capulets and Montagues would be two warring teenage gangs (Sharks and Jets), "one of them newly-arrived Puerto Ricans, the other self-styled

'Americans'." Shakespeare's tragedy, originally set in Verona, was thus made distinctly American in its representation of the problems of minority assimilation into American culture. Stephen Sondheim joined the collaboration to write the lyrics, and in the summer of 1957, *West Side Story* opened in Washington, DC. On his personal copy of *Romeo and Juliet* Bernstein had earlier penciled in the margin, "an out and out plea for tolerance," a sentiment he repeated upon *West Side Story*'s successful opening: "there stands that tragic story, with a theme as profound as love versus hate."[12]

Laurents decided not to keep any of Shakespeare's language. In "a translation of adolescent street talk into theater" he instead used rapid-fire colloquial slang,[13] but he borrowed Shakespeare's fast-moving scenic design, leading the young lovers inexorably to death. Laurents's scheme is even more compressed than Shakespeare's, with the entire action taking a mere forty-eight hours. In juxtaposition to each of the young lovers Shakespeare had set an older mentor whose experience and cynicism provided leavening for the lovers' idealism; Laurents substituted the Jets' leader, Riff, for Mercutio (who pales by comparison with Shakespeare's mercurial original), and for Juliet's nurse he added Anita, a girl who knows the ropes. Robbins's brilliant choreography stylized the feud's violence, but as in Shakespeare, essential to the fighting was the male adolescent's compulsion to prove his masculinity and attain an identity through violence. While Shakespeare provides no explanation for the longstanding feud between two families of similar status within the community, the collaborators' decision to change *East Side Story* to *West Side Story* shifted the conflict from a religious contest of Jew versus Catholic and rooted it in America's most problematic conflict, race, signified in *West Side Story* by the ethnic differences between Puerto Rican and Anglo street gangs. Through Bernstein's romanticized music, adolescents throughout the United States could see themselves in the Romeo and Juliet figures (Tony and Maria) trapped in a world of violence they did not make, hoping that "There's a place for us, somewhere."

West Side Story has been revived several times since 1957, and with minor modifications it was made into a motion picture in 1961 that won ten Oscars, including Best Picture. It remains the only Broadway rendition of a Shakespearean tragedy, and no subsequent Shakespearian musical has achieved its iconic status. Although no one has replicated Bernstein's symphonic brilliance or Robbins's athletic choreography, a handful of Shakespearian rock musicals have successfully entertained New York audiences. *Your Own Thing*, a rock version of *Twelfth Night*, with a book by Donald Driver and songs by Hal Hester and Danny Apolinar, opened in 1968 at the off-Broadway Orpheum Theater and ran for 933 performances. Like *West Side Story*, *Your Own Thing* avoided any direct use of Shakespeare's language, but its exploration of gender ambiguity through impossibly identical male and female twins mirrored *Twelfth Night* and moved *West Side Story*'s plea for racial tolerance to another kind of minority: people discriminated against because of their sexual orientation. As was the fashion in the swinging sixties, when Orson, the Orsino figure and owner of a nightclub, realizes that Charlie, the boy he loves, is really the female Viola, he breezily switches from homoeroticism to heterosexuality—it doesn't matter because you should always do your own thing.

Another musical Shakespearian comedy followed in 1971 under the auspices of Joseph Papp's New York Shakespeare Festival when John Guare and Mel Shapiro adapted *Two Gentlemen of Verona*. Like all Papp productions, the cast was multiracial, with actors of color in lead roles, most notably Puerto Rican Raul Juliá as Proteus, and African American actors Clifton David as Valentine, Diane Davila as Julia, and Jonelle Allen as Sylvia. Following Shakespeare's original more closely than any previous musical comedy, Guare and Shapiro interspersed this *Two Gentlemen of Verona* with additional, colloquial dialogue and energetic rock numbers that highlight the speaker's or singer's ethnicity. After an eighteen-month run, first at the Delacorte Theatre and later on Broadway, the production succeeded critically and financially, and in 2005 it was revived as part of the Public Theatre's fiftieth anniversary celebration.

Shakespeare-as-musical did not disappear in the 1990s, though it has not achieved the success it enjoyed with *Kiss Me Kate* and *West Side Story*. Bob Carlton's *Return to the Forbidden Planet*, loosely based on a 1956 science-fiction filmic adaptation of *The Tempest*, originated in England, but it enjoyed a good run in New York in 1989, and its reliance on 1960s and 70s rock and roll lends it an American flavor. *Play On!*, first performed at San Diego's Old Globe in 1997, moves Shakespeare's *Twelfth Night* to New York during the Harlem

Renaissance, with Duke Ellington's swing music punctuating the plot. *Bomb-itty of Errors*, a hip-hop version of *The Comedy of Errors* crafted by four white students at New York University, was performed off-Broadway in 1999. Like *Return to the Forbidden Planet*, *Fools of Love*, an adaptation of *A Midsummer Night's Dream*, also incorporates popular music from the 1950s and 60s in a hybrid intended for schoolchildren. These later musicals appropriate Shakespeare's cultural authority much as creators of Shakespeare kitsch do—by merging his image or aspects of his plots and characters with rock-and-roll classics in the hope that nostalgic baby boomers will enjoy the combination.

* * *

Two years before *Kiss Me Kate* opened on Broadway, producer Michael Todd brought a Shakespearian performance to New York City that had already shaped many Americans' perceptions of Shakespeare on stage. On December 13, 1945, Maurice Evans' *G.I. Hamlet* opened at the Columbus Circle Theatre, where it ran for 147 performances. A classically trained British actor who moved to the United States in the 1930s, Evans had served as a US army major in the Central Pacific during World War II, leading a company of sixty soldiers whose assignment was to entertain the bored and tired troops. Evans, committed to Shakespeare's "universal truth," added some of his plays to the usual USO fare, beginning with *Macbeth* in 1943. Encouraged by its success, Evans staged *Hamlet* the following year, but in order to make the production fit within the two hours and forty-five minutes of off-duty time the soldiers were granted before Lights Out, he had to cut the text drastically. Working with Sgt. George Schaefer, who would later become an important television director, Evans sought a *Hamlet* that would entertain—and inspire—the troops. Not surprisingly, they cut the Fortinbras material, but more controversially they also eliminated the gravediggers' scene and much of the Players' dialogue. As Evans reflects in his Preface to the published acting text, most of the soldiers had no preconceived notions about what should or shouldn't be included. The men in the audience would soon be in battle or "staggering with fatigue and confusion after their first encounter with the enemy," Evans observed; indeed, each GI was "in his own way a Hamlet, bewildered by his uninvited circumstances... and groping for the moral justification and the physical courage demanded of him."[14] Evans didn't want a wishy-washy, mentally unbalanced protagonist but rather a man of action caught in unusual dilemmas who, like his viewers, was "compelled to champion his conception of right in a world threatened by the domination of evil" (p. 16).

Evans used military costumes to encourage the GIs' identification with Hamlet. The Danish prince wore the formal evening attire of an Edwardian gentleman, Gertrude (Mary Adams) and Ophelia (Janet Slauson) appeared in long dresses, and the rest of the cast had uniforms appropriate to their character's rank. The goal was to "suggest visually the imminence of war... and emphasize for our soldier audience the immediacy of the happenings" (p. 21). With music composed by Pfc. Roger Adams and sets designed by Sgt. Frederick Stover, the *G. I. Hamlet* was performed before thousands of young American men, many of whom had never seen a Shakespeare play. Evans recalled that "our audience reacted with the kind of rapt attention which is every actor's dream," and it seemed the connection he desired between Hamlet and World War II's soldiers was attained one night when Hamlet concluded the "To be or not to be" soliloquy with "Thus conscience doth make cowards of us all," and a voice from the audience cried out, "'Boy, you ain't kiddin!'" (p. 23).

A result of the *G.I. Hamlet* was that a wide swath of American veterans considered Maurice Evans the premier Shakespearian actor. After the war, when a burgeoning television industry sought to gain cultural cachet by performing the classics, Evans was the obvious choice to bring Shakespeare into America's living rooms. Beginning in 1953 with *Hamlet*, Evans was a regular in the *Hallmark Hall of Fame*'s live, feature-length Shakespeare presentations, watched by millions of Americans. Directed by his former sergeant, George Schaefer, Evans spoke Shakespeare's verse with what seemed an appropriate British accent in scripts forced into the ninety-minute format. For the 1954 season, he portrayed Richard II; the following year Judith Anderson joined him in a color transmission of *Macbeth*; in 1956 he played a somewhat aged Petruchio to Lilli Palmer's Katherine in *The Taming of the Shrew*; in 1957 he was Malvolio in *Twelfth Night*; and in 1960 he performed for the last time in the series with a reprise of his Macbeth opposite Judith Anderson and as

Prospero in *The Tempest.* Thus for good or for ill, the middle-aged Maurice Evans defined for an entire generation of Americans what Shakespeare was; "[t]housands of school children exposed to the 16mm rental version grew up thinking of the Macbeths as looking like Maurice Evans and Judith Anderson."[15]

Hallmark Hall of Fame was not the only game in town. Between 1949 and 1979 nearly fifty major Shakespeare productions were televised in the United States. Charlton Heston—recognized for his roles as Moses and Ben-Hur and his advocacy for the National Rifle Association—was a major Shakespearian player, appearing as Cinna in CBS's *Julius Caesar* in 1949, as Petruchio in a modern-dress *Taming of the Shrew* in 1950, and as Macbeth in 1951. Richard Chamberlain, known for his portrayal of Dr. Kildare in a popular television series, performed *Hamlet* in 1970, again for *Hallmark.* But eventually imports from Britain drove American television Shakespearians out of business, especially after 1979 when public television stations began regular screenings of The Shakespeare Plays, sponsored in the United States by Time-Life, and produced in England by the BBC. More often than not, when a Shakespeare production was presented on public television, it originated in England. Notable exceptions are James Earl Jones's *King Lear* (broadcast in 1977), a *Much Ado About Nothing* set in the United States in the era of Teddy Roosevelt's rough riders (1973), and Kevin Kline's modern-dress *Hamlet* (1990), which were originally performed as part of New York's Shakespeare Festival/Public Theater. All three productions eschewed Maurice Evans's kind of British verse-speaking for American colloquial speech and were in a variety of other ways recognizably American. *King Lear,* for example, brought to the screen a classically trained African American actor in the title role, while Kevin Kline's casually dressed, understated Hamlet knocked the Prince off his British pedestal. Joseph Papp's *Much Ado About Nothing* was perhaps the most Americanized interpretation, with Dogberry and company recast as Keystone Cops with bells and whistles, Beatrice (Kathleen Widdoes) smoking in the gazebo, and Benedick (Sam Waterston) drifting down stream in a canoe.

* * *

Lacking Papp's irreverence, many American television producers of Shakespeare took their mission to bring high culture to the masses too seriously, often leading to deadly dull productions. But in the last half of the twentieth century Americans could find entertaining and innovative live Shakespeare performances in their own or nearby communities, often in an outdoor venue, in what has come to be known as "Festival Shakespeare." Many communities, especially smaller cities in rural areas, have embraced this popular summer activity, and the number has grown appreciably in the late twentieth century and early twenty-first. A 1995 survey identified as many as 100 from every region of the country and almost every state.[16] Many belong to the Shakespeare Theatre Association of America, founded in 1991 as a forum for Shakespearian acting companies in North America to share best practices and "promote better teaching of Shakespeare in the schools."[17] Most festivals feature small-scale community-sponsored productions mounted in a park, but a handful are full-fledged repertory companies that offer audiences, in addition to Shakespearian and other classical plays, new works by contemporary dramatists. Like baseball games and Fourth of July parades, Shakespeare in the park has become an American summer ritual.

Whether on a large or small scale, Festival Shakespeare customarily shares several characteristics. Because such productions are aimed at a broad cross-section of the population, they stress interaction with the audience, often using theater-in-the-round staging, broad acting styles, and fast pacing. Shakespeare's text is usually cut to a two- to three- hour format. It is seldom otherwise altered, but sometimes scenes are rearranged and in-jokes appropriate to a particular community are interjected. Sometimes the performances are free, but in all cases the goal is to make Shakespeare accessible to nearly everyone. Set in picturesque outdoor venues, festivals often evoke a bucolic image of merry olde England, with music and comestibles similar to the offerings at a Renaissance fair. On a more serious note, many festivals supplement their performances with educational programs for local school children or lectures open to the public. Often a local college or university provides rehearsal space as well as young actors to supplement equity performers. Festival Shakespeare has consequently been a major player in American education's shift from teaching Shakespeare as a great poet to be read in class or a library to a performance-based curriculum. Many of America's classically trained actors began their careers with Festival Shakespeare.

The Oregon Shakespeare Festival (OSF), the oldest and most influential Shakespeare festival in the United States, was founded in 1935 by Angus L. Bowmer, a faculty member at Southern Oregon Normal (now Southern Oregon University) in Ashland, a small town at the foot of the Siskiyou Mountains near the Oregon–California border. In 1893 Ashland had built an amphitheater sufficiently large to accommodate up to 1,500 people who traveled from surrounding communities for the summer Chautauqua festival. This structure was replaced in 1917 with a larger, dome-covered building, but it fell into disuse after the Chautauqua movement waned, and in 1933 WPA workers tore down the dome, leaving only the cement walls. While Bowmer was pursuing a master's degree in theater arts at the University of Washington, he had met the British actor B. Iden Payne, a proponent of William Poel's movement to return the staging of Shakespeare's plays to their Elizabethan roots. The Chautauqua's open-air cement frame, Bowmer decided, was akin to an Elizabethan theater: "The dome had just been taken off and it gave me the impression of a 16th century sketch of the Globe theater. I began to do some research and got excited about the possibility of producing a Shakespearean work there." In anticipation of what is now called "original staging practices," Bowmer eschewed elaborate scenery in favor of rapid movement from one scene to another, making use of the upper and lower stages without pause. The actors were clad in elaborate costumes based on Elizabethan designs, crafted largely by his wife, Lois. Bowmer made few cuts in Shakespeare's text, but he insisted that the performance would become a stultified museum piece if it did not entertain: "To an audience who pays admission to be entertained, the scholar should be as unobtrusive as the electrician."[18]

Bowmer recruited students and faculty colleagues to mount performances of *The Merchant of Venice* and *Twelfth Night* within the old Chautauqua's walls as part of Ashland's July Fourth celebration in 1935. Charging $1 for reserved seats, the Festival surprised its organizers when it covered expenses, and as the program expanded over the years, the Oregon Shakespeare Festival grew into a tourist destination for Americans living up and down the west coast (Fig. 6.4). The Elizabethan Theatre was rebuilt in 1959 and in the early twenty-first century holds 1,200 spectators; in 1970 a capacious indoor theater, named for Bowmer, enabled OSF to accommodate even more

Figure 6.4. The Oregon Shakespeare Festival's Elizabethan Theatre in 1947. Courtesy of the Oregon Shakespeare Festival.

visitors, and in 2001 OSF added an experimental "black box" theater. In the summer months, when OSF is running plays in repertory at all three theaters, Ashland's winter population of 20,000 more than doubles.

Inspired by the Oregon Shakespeare Festival's success, the number of Shakespeare Festivals that serve as tourist destinations has expanded exponentially. Located in scenic Balboa Park, San Diego's Old Globe Theatre, which began in 1935 as an exhibit for the California Pacific International Exposition, hosts up to 250,000 people a year. The Utah Shakespeare Festival in Cedar City, founded by Fred C. Adams in 1961, began with a replica of London's Globe, supplemented in 1989 by the Randall L. Jones indoor theater; in 2003 the Festival lured 150,000 patrons to its performances, and it has burgeoned into a year-round operation. In addition to its lively performances, Utah Shakespeare attracts summer travelers with its proximity to Bryce Canyon and other national parks. Meanwhile, east coast residents have succumbed to the winning mix of staged Shakespeare and bucolic environment. In 1978 Tina Packer, who learned her trade in England with the Royal Shakespeare Company, founded Shakespeare and Company in Lenox, Massachusetts, at the foot of the Berkshire Mountains not far from Tanglewood's renowned summer music festival. Destination festivals like those in Utah and Massachusetts, supported by local governments and business organizations, have an economic as well as an aesthetic focus, aiming, in Bowmer's words, to "draw people to stay for a time, and to spend money in the community."[19]

In some respects, Shakespeare in the park simply continues a longstanding American tradition of locally based programming, whether lyceums, Chautauquas, or reading clubs, designed to provide audiences with pleasurable opportunities for cultural enrichment and education. The festivals, like their forerunners, are decentralized; their quality and scope vary greatly depending on a community's resources and commitment. Because the expenses of travel and lodging at "destination" festivals can mount to hundreds of dollars, audiences at San Diego's Old Globe or the Oregon Shakespeare Festival tend to be middle-class. In contrast, locally produced Shakespeare in the park, especially in metropolises like Oklahoma City, St Louis, or Minneapolis, is geared to the local community. Shakespeare in the Park is more likely to keep ticket prices low and therefore accessible to everyone, regardless of age, class, or economic status.

Following Joseph Papp's lead, companies large (OSF, for example) and small (Oklahoma City) commit to multiracial casts that reflect the diversity of twenty-first-century America. The African American Shakespere [*sic*] Company, founded in San Francisco in 1994 to "unlock the realm of classic theatre to a diverse audience... in a style that reaches, speaks, and embraces their cultural aesthetic," sports the motto, "Envisioning the classics with color."[20] Whatever tensions remain between Shakespeare's perceived elite cultural status and democratic ideals, in America's Festival Shakespeare, the plays are for everybody.

* * *

Like their nineteenth-century predecessors, twentieth-century Shakespearian burlesques often provide social and political commentary, especially in times of national crisis. Barbara Garson's skewering of Lyndon Johnson in *MacBird*, which debuted in early 1967, is a good example.[21] It begins with the designation of "MacBird" (Senator Johnson of Texas) to be "Ken O'Dunc's (John Kennedy's) running mate in 1960, prompting the witches to chant: "All hail MacBird! All hail the Senate's leader! All hail MacBird, Vice President thou art! All hail MacBird, that shall be President!" (p. 5). MacBird and Lady MacBird plot how to hasten the predicted presidency, which they accomplish at Dallas when O'Dunc comes to visit the MacBird ranch. After MacBird slays the president's reputed assassin ("Who could refrain when Ken O'Dunc lies dead?" [p. 20]), "Robert" and "Teddy" suspect a conspiracy and await a better time to challenge MacBird. Later, with the new president entangled in the war in "Viet Land," Robert tells his friends that

> I'm now prepared for exile in the East,
> But there I mean to organize my troops,
> And with my force of liberals from New York,
> I shall return to make that fat bird squawk. (p. 37)

MacBird consults the witches again, who assure him that "MacBird shall never, never be undone/Till burning wood doth come to Washington" (p. 43)—which it does when rioting black Americans torch the city's cherry trees. In the showdown at the Democratic convention of 1968, MacBird, seeing the witches' prophecy come true, dies of a heart attack and Robert assumes the mantle of power. The conclusion of this script is obviously ahistorical; it was written before Johnson abjured renomination and Robert Kennedy was assassinated. Both events undermined a clever political parody that played well on stage and reads well in print but survives only as a poignant souvenir of the 1960s.

Charles S. Preston's *T'e Tragedy of King Rich'rd T'e T'ird* (1972) bears some resemblance to *MacBird*.[22] Both plays lampooned sitting presidents, both barely disguised the leading political figures of the day (Sir George O'Govern, Sir Thomas Eagle, Sir Kid Tennedy in Preston's play), and both collapsed when fact failed to mirror fiction. Preston acknowledged his indebtedness to his distant and immediate predecessors ("with apologies to William Shakespeare and Barbara Garson" [p.1]) and the unpredictability of events ("due to circumstances beyond our control," readers of the Errata are asked to substitute "Sgt. Striver" for "Sir Thomas Eagle" throughout the script). In the climax of this stridently anti-war skit, Richard tells his second in command,

> Spiro, I'd bet my life upon this play
> In which the end runs straight, then cuts away;
> But I must have a bomb to make the pass,
> Without one I am like to lose my ass;
> Still, e'en if I am stricken to the ground,
> No more will they have Dick to kick around.
> A bomb! A bomb! my kingdom for a bomb! (p. 11)

O'Govern wins the ensuing fight. Peace and prosperity return. But, of course, it didn't turn out that way.

Parodists had better luck with Nixon's second term. David Edgar's *Dick Deterred* (1974) ridiculed the Watergate scandal and the President's attempts at cover-up. Although the author is British, the subject and setting are quintessentially American; audiences and reviewers praised it on both sides of the Atlantic. Employing a variety of verse forms, the script follows Nixon's career from his candidacy for president in 1968 to his resignation from office in 1974. In the concluding battle against his enemies, led by the Earl of Richmond (Sen. Sam Ervin of North Carolina, chief investigator of the Watergate episode), King Richard pleads vainly for "A goat, A goat, My kingdom for another Scapegoat!" (p. 109). Senator Ervin starred again in 1974 in Jeremy Geidt and Jonathon Marks's "The Tragical History of Samlet, Prince of Denmark," which featured the senator as Samlet, Claudius as President Nixon, Felonius as Attorney General John Mitchell, Horatio as Senator Hubert Horatio Humphrey, with Ehrlicrantz and Haldenstern in the roles of presidential advisors John Ehrlichman and Bob Haldeman.[23] While Richard Nixon leads all American presidents as the butt of Shakespearian travesties, few recent chief executives have been immune. The last year of the twentieth century saw publication of *MacClintonlet: William Shakespeare Covers the Clinton, Lewinsky, Starr Scandal*—a title that loosely summarizes the story.

Although most of the extant Shakespeare burlesques appear to have been written primarily for performance, many texts must have amused readers who never saw them enacted, and some were never meant for production. A prime example of the latter is Richard

Armour's *Twisted Tales from Shakespeare, in which Shakespeare's best-known plays are presented in a new light, the old having blown a fuse; . . . intended to contribute to a clearer misunderstanding of the subject* (1957). In barely 150 pages, Armour presents a condensed version of Shakespeare's complete works: introductory essays on Shakespeare's life, the Elizabethan theater, and Shakespeare's writings; droll summaries (with footnotes, as befit a former student of George Lyman Kittredge) of *Hamlet*, *Macbeth*, *A Midsummer Night's Dream*, *Romeo and Juliet*, *The Merchant of Venice*, and *Othello*; and appendices on the sonnets and the authorship controversy.[24] Like many of Armour's numerous parodies of serious topics, *Twisted Tales* earned an enthusiastic following, especially among schoolteachers who used it to enliven their classes on "the Beard of Avon" (p. 3).

The American penchant for Shakespearian burlesque—which depends on a rudimentary knowledge of his plots and characters—is perhaps best exemplified by the United States' own RSC, the Reduced Shakespeare Company. This take-off on Britain's Royal Shakespeare Company began as a pass-the-hat enterprise in 1981 when Daniel Singer, Jess Borgeson, Michael Flemming, and Adam Long put together a twenty-five-minute spoof of *Hamlet* for the Renaissance Pleasure Faire in Novato, California. Two years later, Singer and Long created a twenty-minute version of *Romeo and Juliet*, which they performed at Renaissance fairs and street festivals. In 1987, with Borgeson back in the group, they assembled an hour-long show—a comic abridgement of thirty-five of Shakespeare's plays—for the Edinburgh Fringe Festival in Scotland. Eventually that script, *The Complete Works*, became a staple in theaters and festivals around the world. Expanded to ninety-seven minutes, the RSC's *Complete Works of William Shakespeare (Abridged)* ran for nine years in London's West End, and a video version was released in 2001. The RSC's success stems from its zany use of comic gags as a substitute for Shakespeare's plots and characters. As its official website notes, "The Reduced Shakespeare Company is a three-man comedy troupe that takes long, serious subjects and reduces them to short, sharp comedies."[25] For *The Complete Works*, one member of the company generally narrates a play's basic plot, interrupted with comic by-play, often bawdy, performed energetically by the other actors; they expedite matters by treating ten different comedies as one basic plot: boy wants girl, there is an obstacle, it is overcome. The actors speak Shakespeare's most famous lines, but for the most part the plays are reduced to farcical gags. The feud that opens *Romeo and Juliet*, for example, is rendered as a Three Stooges punching routine, while *Titus Andronicus* is a two-minute cooking show and *Othello* an extended rap. After its phenomenal success with Shakespeare, the RSC has moved on to the Bible, the *Complete History of America*, and many other topics with which American audiences have a basic familiarity. The RSC has become something of a franchise. It often has more than one active troupe; its scripts have been translated into over a dozen languages; and like much of American pop culture, it has been performed to wild enthusiasm all over the world. All because four young men took delight in burlesquing Shakespeare!

Today Shakespeare's major plays can also be enjoyed in extended comic book form (including Japanese mangas), produced across the globe in many languages and graphic styles. But this was not always the case. Like the Reduced Shakespeare Company, comic-book Shakespeare originated in America. In 1941 Albert L. Kantner founded *Classic Comics*, with the goal of tapping into a growing education market. The name was changed to *Classics Illustrated* in 1947, and to this day *CI* comics are cherished collectibles. Kantner sold his comics to individuals on newsstands and in batches to schools. Shakespeare's plots were often cut to fit the comic book form, "the most common cuts being the comedy scenes, and often sex and violence."[26] His first attempt at Shakespeare, *Julius Caesar* (1951), was so successful that it spawned imitators, including a *Famous Authors* series by Dana E. Dutch that abandoned Shakespeare's language and made the plays into illustrated stories. Kantor eventually bought out *Famous Authors*, and during the 1950s he increased his offerings to include *A Midsummer Night's Dream*, *Hamlet*, *Macbeth*, and *Romeo and Juliet*—plays that were commonly taught in American secondary schools. While *Classics Illustrated* replicated Shakespeare's language in a somewhat staid format, its successors in the United States and abroad currently rely less on language, more on the quality of their graphics. In this popular art form, Shakespeare's plots and characters, if not his poetry, remain accessible to a mass audience.

* * *

As the Reduced Shakespeare Company's success demonstrates, the easiest way to bring Shakespeare to everyone regardless of age or ethnicity is to change his language or omit it altogether. Not surprisingly then, after World War II the film and television industries recontextualized Shakespeare, changed his language, and adapted his plots in accord with recognizable film genres. *Forbidden Planet* (1956), one of the earliest science fiction films ever made, moved *The Tempest* to a distant time and place: planet Altair IV in the year 2257. Loosely based on Shakespeare's plot, *Forbidden Planet* tapped into contemporary American anxieties about ethical issues surrounding the use of nuclear weapons. Its hero, Dr. Morbius (Walter Pidgeon), played Prospero as a scientist who had traveled from Earth to Altair IV twenty years earlier, only to have his wife and shipmates mysteriously die, torn apart by "some terrible incomprehensible force," leaving behind only Dr. Morbius and his daughter, Altaira (Anne Francis). Morbius spends his time studying the archaeological remains of an ancient civilization, the Krell, who had prospered on Altair IV thousands of years earlier before they became extinct. The key to their success and their extinction, he discovers, is a huge thermonuclear generating plant so powerful that the Krell no longer needed any kind of instrumentation. Morbius tries to appropriate this force for himself, but when confronted by a party of visitors from planet Earth, he realizes its true danger. Emanating from Morbius's subconscious desire to destroy the newcomers, a mysterious force seeks and kills members of Commander Adams's (Leslie Nielsen's) visiting crew. Once Morbius realizes this power's danger, he sends his daughter with Commander Adams back to earth and then obliterates himself along with the nuclear capability he has mastered. If one looks carefully, *Forbidden Planet* has several parallels to Shakespeare's *Tempest*: Robby the Robot who does Morbius's bidding is the Ariel figure; Cookie (Earl Holliman) is the drunken Stephano's counterpart; while Commander Adams, like Ferdinand, falls in love with Altaira, the Miranda figure. The transformation in Caliban is most striking, however, for he truly is the "thing of darkness" Morbius must acknowledge. *Forbidden Planet* figures Shakespeare's "savage and deformed slave" as a mysterious electromagnetic force unleashed by Morbius's secret will to destruction.

In hopes of presenting characters a mass audience can relate to, other filmic recontextualizations have exploited recognizable movie conventions, sometimes transforming Shakespeare's kings and queens into everyday Americans. *Macbeth*, for example, spawned two gangster films. British director Ken Hughes's *Joe MacBeth* (1955) featured American actors Paul Douglas in the Macbeth role and Ruth Roman as his wife, but British actors in most of the minor roles. The film combines Shakespeare's Macduff and Fleance into one character, Lennie, who is shot dead by the police after he accomplishes his revenge. The gangster motif is also palpable in William Reilly's *Men of Respect*, which was released in the United States in 1991 during the "Godfather" craze. The hero, Mike Battaglia (John Turturro), is discontented with his lowly position in one of New York's mob families; spurred by his ambitious wife (Katherine Borowitz), he shoots the godfather, Charlie D'Amico (Rod Steiger), and assumes control of the organization. Battaglia also murders the wife and children of his chief rival, Matt Duffy (Peter Boyle), who allies himself with D'Amico's son Mal (Stanley Tucci) to take revenge. Using dialogue typical of an American gangster movie, *Men of Respect* is slavishly faithful to Shakespeare's plot. In order to fulfill the witches' prophecies, delivered by three homeless mystics, for example, Matt Duffy explains that he was delivered by caesarian section. A later, less conventional appropriation of *Macbeth* moved the action to a fast-food restaurant in rural Pennsylvania. *Scotland, PA* (2001) made Shakespeare's tragedy into a black comedy with Christopher Walken playing Lt. Ernie McDuff, the persistent cop who uncovers Joe and Pat McBeth's murder of Norm Duncan, the restaurant's owner.

Turner Network television drew upon another characteristically American film genre—the western—when it set *King Lear* on a Texas ranch in 2002's *King of Texas*. Speaking with an American accent, British actor Patrick Stewart plays John Lear, a cattle baron whose brutal treatment of his ranch hands incenses his daughters to rebellion. More innovative is Paul Mazursky's 1982 *Tempest*, where Phillip (John Cassavetes) is a New York architect; disaffected from his life and his wife, Antonia (Gena Rowlands), he escapes with his daughter, Miranda (Molly Ringwald), to a Greek island. Phillip attacks the island's only native, Kalibanos (Raul Juliá), when he tries to kiss Miranda. Using iconic plays whose characters and plots are well known to many Americans, these films are accessible to a mass audience, many of whom take additional pleasure in identifying the Shakespearian resonances.

Films crafted for America's adolescents are even more bankable because teenagers consume more mass media than any other segment of the population and, also more than other segments, are made aware—at school if not at home—of Shakespeare's iconic position in the national culture. Australian director Baz Luhrmann's *Romeo + Juliet* transformed Shakespeare's tragedy for the MTV generation in 1996 by casting Leonardo DiCaprio and Claire Danes as the star-crossed lovers, larding the pulsating soundtrack with pop music, and setting the action in an American city rife with corruption, drug trafficking, and gang violence. Despite making drastic cuts, Luhrmann kept the original words, and the resulting disconnect between images of contemporary American life at its most tawdry (the use of "Sword 9mm series S" guns for the duel, for example) and Shakespeare's poetry jarred many viewers. Still, Luhrmann's inventive *Romeo + Juliet* was widely embraced, even in America's public schools, as Shakespeare for a new generation. Even more intriguing, the Australian director's exploitation of American pop culture suggests its international appeal.

Michael Almereyda's 2000 *Hamlet*, set in contemporary New York City, also kept Shakespeare's language but substituted visual images of laptops, camcorders, and cell phones for huge cuts in the text. The ghost of Hamlet Sr. appears out of a vending machine, Claudius's spy network includes CCTV cameras, and the Mousetrap is Hamlet's homemade video. With a young Hamlet (Ethan Hawke, almost comatose with ennui) and a rebellious Ophelia (Julia Stiles), this truncated *Hamlet* resonated with many younger audiences.

By the end of the twentieth century, Shakespearian adaptations transferred Luhrmann and Almereyda's explorations of contemporary mass culture to a high school setting and abandoned Shakespeare's language altogether. *10 Things I Hate About You* (1999) moved *The Taming of the Shrew* from Renaissance Italy to an American high school where a surly Kat (Julia Stiles) rebels against her classmates' conformity. After her father forbids Kat's younger sister Bianca (Larisa Oleynik) to go out with boys until the boy-hating Kat accepts a date, Bianca's anxious friend Cameron (Joseph Gordon-Levitt) hires a newcomer, bad boy Patrick Verona (Heath Ledger), to court the elder sister. The wooing games of Shakespeare's *Twelfth Night* were also replicated in *She's the Man* (2006) when Viola Hastings (Amanda Bynes) masquerades as her twin brother so that she can realize her dream of playing on the varsity soccer team. Such appropriations downplay Shakespeare's complexities to reinforce majority ideals of heterosexual, romantic love, but they were welcomed by high school teachers as a bridge to Shakespeare's original texts.

The transition from play to an adolescent flick is more problematic in Tim Nelson Blake's *O*, a teenage version of *Othello* (2001) set in a southern prep school, which uses Shakespeare's plot to probe America's perennial obsession with race and violence. The film transforms Othello, a respected Venetian military leader, into Odin "O" James (Mekhi Phifer), an athletic African American who has been recruited for the basketball team. Lacking Iago's famed "motiveless malignity," the teenage villain Hugo (Josh Hartnett) seethes with jealousy because his father, the basketball coach played by Martin Sheen, pays so much attention to Odin, the captain and star player. Hugo retaliates by convincing Odin that his girlfriend, Desi (Julia Stiles), has had sex with another student, and Odin predictably strangles her in a confused and violent frenzy. Much is lost in this transition, particularly when Othello's eloquent speeches become Odin's and Desi's teen-speak, and the effort to be true to Shakespeare's plot—as in the inclusion of the handkerchief—makes no sense in the context of an American secondary school.

While filmic appropriations of Shakespeare's plays have gained an ambivalent public attention in recent decades, American novelists have also, with varied success, recast the Bard. Like many film directors, contemporary authors will often bring Shakespeare into a conventional plot with a recognizable format. In Simon Hawke's *A Mystery of Errors* (2000), young Shakespeare teams up with Symington Smyth to solve a mysterious murder; Tad Williams's *Caliban's Hour* (1994) makes Shakespeare's monster a sympathetic hero with Gothic overtones; and Jennifer Lee Carrell's best-selling thriller, *Interred with Their Bones* (2007), sets the quest for Shakespeare's lost play *Cardenio* into a convoluted plot strikingly similar to Dan Brown's *The Da Vinci Code*.

Other writers appropriate Shakespeare's dramas not simply to capitalize on his name recognition but to interrogate his cultural authority. Jane Smiley's Pulitzer prize-winning *A Thousand Acres*

(1991) reframes Shakespeare's *King Lear* from a feminist perspective. Moving the plot to Nebraska's farmland where Larry (Lear) decides to retire and turn his thousand acres over to his three daughters, Smiley narrates the story from Ginny's (Goneril's) viewpoint as an abused daughter. *A Thousand Acres* (made into a feature film in 1997) sometimes makes the Lear sisters act out of character, as when Ginny tries to poison Ruth (Regan) with canned sausages. Still, Smiley's explanation of Lear's relationship with his daughters answers some of the questions feminist critics have posed about Cordelia's relationship with her sisters and Goneril and Regan's behavior in acts II–V. In addition, Smiley's exploration of environmental issues puts *King Lear*'s insights into man's troubled relationship with nature into a twentieth-century framework.

* * *

In the twenty-first century, American popular Shakespeare—or Pop Shxx, as it is sometimes called—is everywhere. Its primary purpose is entertainment—Americans love to have irreverent fun with the famous author. But it is also symptomatic of the democratization of American mass culture. Although the goal of Shakespeare for everybody is sometimes honored in the breach, the promoters of films and festivals universally proclaim a desire to make Shakespeare accessible to all. In addition to the media discussed here, countless other facets of America's pop culture use and abuse Shakespeare: music, graphic arts, cartoons, toys, games—you name it. Whether on television, in film, or on the festival stage, Shakespeare plays to a broad cross-section of the American public. Even when his language is altered, his work provokes continuing discussion and new interpretations. If in 1929 American audiences supposedly frowned on Sam Taylor's putative admission that he had added dialogue to Shakespeare's *Taming of the Shrew*, today few viewers would care.

Notes

1. Marjorie Garber, *Shakespeare and Modern Culture* (New York: Anchor Books, 2009), xiii.
2. See Kenneth Rothwell, *Shakespeare on Screen* (Cambridge: Cambridge University Press, 1999), 6–13, for discussion of the Vitagraph Company,

and William Uricchio and Roberta E. Pearson, *Reframing Culture: The Case of the Vitagraph Quality Films* (Princeton, NJ: Princeton University Press, 1993), esp. ch. 3.

3. Rothwell, *Shakespeare on Screen*, 23.
4. See Michael T. Gilmore, *Differences in the Dark: American Movies and English Theater* (New York: Columbia University Press, 1998).
5. Hugh Munro Neely, Director of the Archive at the Mary Pickford Institute for Film Education, claims never to have seen the oft-discussed credit line, "Additional Dialogue by Sam Taylor."
6. Barbara Hodgdon analyzes this scene in *The Shakespeare Trade: Performances and Appropriations* (Philadelphia: University of Pennsylvania Press, 1998), 14–15; Rothwell, *Shakespeare on Screen*, 28–34.
7. Now in the Folger Ball Collection at the Folger Shakespeare Library.
8. See Rothwell, *Shakespeare on Screen*, 39.
9. Ibid. 44–8.
10. Frances Teague, *Shakespeare and the Popular American Stage* (Cambridge: Cambridge University Press, 2006), 111.
11. Quoted from ibid. 115.
12. Bernstein's log quotes are taken from http://www.westsidestory.com/archives_excerpts.php (accessed June 25, 2010).
13. http://www.westsidestory.com/archives_factsheet.php (accessed June 25, 2010).
14. Maurice Evans, "Preface," *Maurice Evans' G. I. Production of Hamlet* (New York: Doubleday, 1947), 15–16.
15. Rothwell, *Shakespeare on Screen*, 103.
16. Ron Engle, Felicia Hardison Londrés, and Daniel J. Watermeier, *Shakespeare Companies and Festivals* (Westport, CT: Greenwood, 1995).
17. http://www.staaonline.org (accessed June 30, 2010).
18. http://www.osfashland.org/about/archive/angus_quotes.aspx (accessed June 24, 2010).
19. Ibid.
20. http://www.african-americanshakes.org (accessed June 30, 2010).
21. Barbara Garson, *MacBird* (Berkeley, CA, and New York: Grassy Knoll Press, 1967).
22. Charles S. Preston, *T'e Tragedy of King Rich'rd T'e T'ird, "My Kingdom for A Bomb"* (York, PA: Sammy's Dot Press, 1972).
23. David Edgar, *Dick Deterred: A Play in Two Acts* (New York: Monthly Review Press, [1974]); Jeremy Geidt and Jonathan Marks, "The Tragical History of Samlet, Prince of Denmark," in *Watergate Classics*, *Yale/theatre* 5 (special issue 1974), 24–51; Henry E. Jacobs and Claudia D. Johnson, *An Annotated Bibliography of Shakespearean Burlesques, Parodies, and Travesties*

(New York: Garland, 1976), #31; R. Louis Oueinaught [pseudo.], *MacClintonlet*..., 2nd edn (n.p.: Washington Oaks Publishing, 1999).

24. Richard Armour, *Twisted Tales from Shakespeare* (New York: McGraw-Hill, 1957).
25. http://www.reducedshakespeare.com/aboutus (accessed December 16, 2011).
26. Quote from Mike Jensen, "Shakespeare Comic Books, Part II," *Shakespeare Newsletter* 56.4 (2006). Jensen presented his analysis of Shakespearian comic books in three parts; part I appeared in *SN* 56.3 (2006), Part III in *SN* 57.1 (2007).

7

American Shakespeare Today

In 1988 historian Lawrence Levine caused a substantial tremor in Shakespearian circles by proposing that late nineteenth- and early twentieth-century America witnessed a profound split between "highbrow" and "lowbrow" Shakespeare. Levine argued that in the early nineteenth century Shakespeare's plays were integral to all segments of American culture, regardless of socio-economic class or geography; "Shakespeare," he contended, "*was* popular entertainment in nineteenth-century America." By the middle of the twentieth century, however, Shakespeare's status within American culture had shifted. He "had become the possession of the educated portions of society who disseminated his plays for the enlightenment of the average folk who were to swallow them not for their entertainment but for their education."[1] The separation of "legitimate theater" from burlesque, vaudeville, and other forms of popular entertainment during the last half of the nineteenth century is a major thread in Levine's argument and carries some weight, but, as many critics have noted, it distorts Shakespeare's role in American culture. Although we have found it convenient to consider Shakespeare as taught in schools and colleges—academic Shakespeare—as separate from the circulation of his plays in popular mass media—popular Shakespeare—we believe that Levine's emphatic binary between highbrow and lowbrow overlooks the myriad ways Shakespeare has influenced the lives of everyday Americans from the late nineteenth century to the present.

The Shakespeare clubs founded in the 1880s and 90s across the country in communities large and small are a case in point. Such clubs numbered in the hundreds and could be found in forty-six states;

American women (and sometimes men) met there regularly to read and discuss Shakespeare. Levine is certainly right that by the 1880s Shakespeare was perceived as a literary classic, and for many women Shakespeare clubs provided a welcome educational outlet. But at the same time the clubs had fun with Shakespeare: mounting skits and burlesques, keeping scrapbooks, and sharing food, drink, and conversation. If some of that socializing drifted away from Shakespeare, he was still the magnet that drew club members together. To borrow Levine's terms, Shakespeare clubs were a hybrid of highbrow reverence and lowbrow fun.

Levine makes the case that early nineteenth-century audiences who flocked to Shakespeare's plays were heterogeneous, much like the crowd at a modern sporting event (p. 24). The "legitimate" theaters founded later in the century, such as Augustin Daly's upscale theater in New York City, sought an elite clientele and presented Shakespeare's plays as classic, almost sacred, works. But as previous chapters have shown, since the middle of the eighteenth century, Shakespeare, whether adapted or straight, has remained a staple in America's cultural diet. Like its early nineteenth-century forebears, Festival Shakespeare, especially "Shakespeare in the Park," attracts heterogeneous audiences who expect to find both enlightenment and entertainment in the experience. Even as some festivals are disbanded because of organizational or budgetary problems, new ones are founded; by 2007 there were at least 200 Shakespeare festivals in the United States, and in 2010 the Shakespeare Theatre Association of America's web site listed 123 member organizations from all parts of the United States and Canada.[2]

Levine's analysis was crafted before the internet and other new media revolutionized the ways Americans seek and receive both information and entertainment. Even if Shakespeare was divorced from everyday culture between the 1890s and 1980s, post-modern pastiche has brought him back. Baz Luhrmann's *Romeo + Juliet*, which (as noted in Chapter 6) ushered in a series of Shakespeare adaptations set in teenage culture, is a good example. Luhrman's setting of Shakespeare's tragedy in a contemporary American "Verona Beach" conveyed the young lovers' urgent passion in a pop context that young audiences can understand. So do graphic editions of Shakespeare's texts that illustrate each scene, using a comic book format to integrate visual images with Shakespeare's language. Amateur thespians—mostly in jest but sometimes quite seriously—put their performances of Shakespearian scenes on YouTube for all to see. To raise money, the Washington (DC) Shakespeare Company presented a performance of *Hamlet* in Klingon, the language used by the inhabitants of Kronos on television's *Star Trek*. In popular media of all sorts Shakespeare continues to appeal to a broad swath of the American populace.

To be sure, a split sometimes emerges between "academic" Shakespeare and such popular pastimes. Al Pacino's 1996 documentary, *Looking for Richard*, sets up the binary by juxtaposing the comments of erudite British Shakespearians like Emrys Jones with remarks from people on the streets of New York City. Pacino's companion in this endeavor, Frederic Kimball, concludes that American actors don't need any "f—ing academics" (particularly British academics) to tell them about Shakespeare. But this binary, too, is overblown; academic pronouncements are the straw man for Pacino to work against. As we noted in an earlier chapter, contemporary American academics, educated in the age of new media, are more likely to integrate popular Shakespeare into their courses than to declaim against it.

Rather than relying on Levine's opposition between highbrow and lowbrow, our survey of Shakespeare's role in American culture identifies several recurring themes, expanded below, that remain pertinent in the twenty-first century. At the same time, some new trends are likely to reshape Americans' relationship with Shakespeare. It is understandably more difficult to analyze the present than the past, but this chapter focuses on where Shakespeare is now and makes a few tentative suggestions as to what his future may hold.

* * *

The introduction to this book proposes that from the outset Americans took a utilitarian and often moralistic approach to Shakespeare. Reading and understanding Shakespeare was "good for you." That conviction, somewhat modified, still holds. In the 1994 film *Renaissance Man*, for example, Danny DeVito played an advertising executive who takes a job at Fort McClary teaching English language skills to the company's least competent soldiers. After several comic false starts, he finally succeeds by reading Shakespeare out loud to them; in particular, he relates *Henry V* to their own experiences and aspirations as soldiers. However sentimental this film may have seemed to reviewers at the time, *Renaissance Man* underscored the American conviction that mastering a Shakespeare text is empowering, partly for the satisfaction of meeting a difficult challenge, partly for the insight into humanity that his words provide, and, in the case of *Renaissance Man*, for the light that it shines on particular lives at particular times.

What was fictionalized in *Renaissance Man* became reality at the Luther Luckett Correctional Center, a medium-security prison in La Grange, Kentucky. Over a period of eight years, Curt Tofteland, a theater practitioner at the Kentucky Shakespeare Festival, provided coaching in performing Shakespeare to male prisoners who had been incarcerated for serious crimes. Tofteland's production of *The Tempest* was featured in the 2005 film documentary, *Shakespeare Behind Bars*, directed by Hank Rogerson. With its emphasis on forgiveness and restoration, *The Tempest* provided hardened criminals with the opportunity to reassess themselves and their lives. In a book with the same main title, *Shakespeare Behind Bars: The Power of Drama in a Women's Prison*, Jean Trounstine chronicles her work with women prisoners at Massachusetts' Framingham Women's Prison, including her class's performance of *The Merchant of Venice.* Caught up in the criminal justice system themselves, Trounstine's students found Shakespeare's exploration of the counterclaims of law and mercy pertinent to their own lives.[3]

While the LaGrange, Kentucky, and Framingham, Massachusetts, programs were designed for men and women who were already serving prison sentences, an innovative program in western Massachusetts substitutes Shakespeare for prison time. Over the last ten years the Berkshire County Juvenile Court's Judge Judith Locke has participated in "Shakespeare in the Courts": adolescent offenders are sentenced to a five-week intensive course that culminates in a performance of one of Shakespeare's plays. Like the fictional characters in *Renaissance Man*, participating teenagers are reluctant, even truculent, at the beginning, but the acting exercises teach them to work together and to overcome the challenge of Shakespeare's language. With help from Shakespeare and Company in Lenox, Massachusetts, the offenders complete their sentence by presenting a play for their friends and relatives at the end of the course. In 2010, for example, when they presented *Henry V* at Lenox's Founders' Theatre, probation officer Nancy Macauley observed that the experience had altered the "kids' self-esteem and willingness to embrace something new."[4]

Such prison programs reinforce the persistent American conviction that studying Shakespeare will make you a better person, but with a difference. The reading clubs founded in the late nineteenth century embraced Shakespeare for his moral wisdom and insights into the human experience. The programs described above focus instead on the social process of performing Shakespeare, which is believed to build confidence and foster teamwork. But the selected texts—*Henry V*, *The Tempest*, and *The Merchant of Venice*—suggest that the desire to relate Shakespeare's characters and themes to the participants' lives remains almost the same as it did for previous generations.

Decentralization is a second continuing theme in American Shakespeare. Despite the federal government's twentieth-first century initiatives to enact national educational standards for America's schools, there is still no set Shakespeare text that secondary students must master, nor is there any standardized teaching method. While *A Midsummer Night's Dream*, *Romeo and Juliet*, *Julius Caesar*, *Macbeth*, and *Hamlet* remain favored high school texts, teachers are now nearly as likely to introduce their students to *The Tempest* or *King Lear*. America's Shakespeare theaters, too, are diverse and decentralized. Washington, DC, for example, boasts two: The Shakespeare Company of Washington performs in an intimate space in Arlington, Virginia, offering experimental performances, while the Shakespeare Theatre in downtown DC presents upscale, standardized productions in repertory at the Harman Center for the Arts and the Lansburgh Theatre. Some Shakespeare companies focus on summer performances in the park, while others—like the Oregon Shakespeare Festival and Chicago's Shakespeare Theatre—offer a year-long repertoire of Shakespeare and other classic plays. With no national curriculum and no national theater, the United States' approach to Shakespeare is as varied as its terrain and its people.

The history of Shakespeare in America, as the previous chapters demonstrate, is in many respects the history of individuals for whom Shakespeare was not simply a pastime, but a calling. Horace Howard Furness's Variorum Shakespeare editions, Henry Clay Folger's library,

Augustin Daly's theater, Joseph Papp's Shakespeare Festival—all were the product of American artistry, ingenuity, and entrepreneurship. And that has not changed. Major Shakespeare venues in Washington, DC, Chicago, and Lenox, Massachusetts, would not exist were it not for the efforts of directors Michael Kahn, Barbara Gaines, and Tina Packer. Without the visionary zeal of Ralph Alan Cohen, the small town of Staunton, Virginia, snug in the Shenandoah Valley, would never have boasted a replica of Jacobean London's Blackfriars Playhouse and become home to the American Shakespeare Center. Just when it seemed Britain's Kenneth Branagh had taken charge of Shakespeare on film, America's Julie Taymor adapted Shakespeare's most violent tragedy, *Titus Andronicus*, in an excitingly eclectic *Titus* (1999), followed a decade later by a gender-bending *Tempest*, starring Helen Mirren as Prospera, Duchess of Milan.

On a much more mundane level, marketers of kitsch like the Beanie Babies know that Shakespeare has widespread commercial as well as cultural value, whatever his physical form. Shakespeare, in fact, is America's favorite kitsch—although manufactured almost invariably in Asia. It sells in Britain, too, of course, most notably in Stratford-upon-Avon and London (though the buyers, in all likelihood, are disproportionately American), but in the United States a selection of Shakespeare kitsch can be found at most Shakespeare Festival theaters, at novelty shops and mainstream bookstores, and in mail order catalogues. It comes in clothing (teeshirts, sweatshirts, baseball caps, neckties, scarves), pottery (plates, pitchers, mugs, figurines), paper products (calendars, stationery, note pads, posters), puppets (finger-size to life-size), games (playing cards, jigsaw puzzles, board games), jewelry (earrings, pendants, pins), as well as pillows, lamps, wall hangings, doorknockers, nutcrackers, wristwatches, thimbles, and statuettes in countless sizes and shapes. And that list is far from exhaustive. Although there is no feasible way to quantify the total number of such items and the sales they generate, anecdotal evidence suggests that Shakespeare has few serious competitors in this multimillion dollar enterprise. In certain regions of the United States, Elvis Presley (Nashville and vicinity) and George Washington (Mount Vernon and the District of Columbia) may give the Bard some serious competition, but nationwide and over the long haul, William Shakespeare appears to be the memorabilia champion.

To acquire a Shakespeare souvenir in the eighteenth century, one had to cut a chip from his chair or buy a carving from his mulberry tree; in the twenty-first century, one only need spend a few dollars—or many dollars—at any of a thousand or more venues from coast to coast. Mementoes of the Bard are everywhere. That doesn't mean that his plays are more often read or watched or are better understood now than they were before the present commercial craze, but it does suggest that most Americans know, at least superficially, who he was (and is) and that he carries universal cultural cachet.

The popularity of Shakespeare kitsch implies a fourth theme running through America's relationship with the poet: having fun (Fig. 7.1). From the nineteenth century's burlesques to twentieth-century Broadway musicals, American audiences have enjoyed

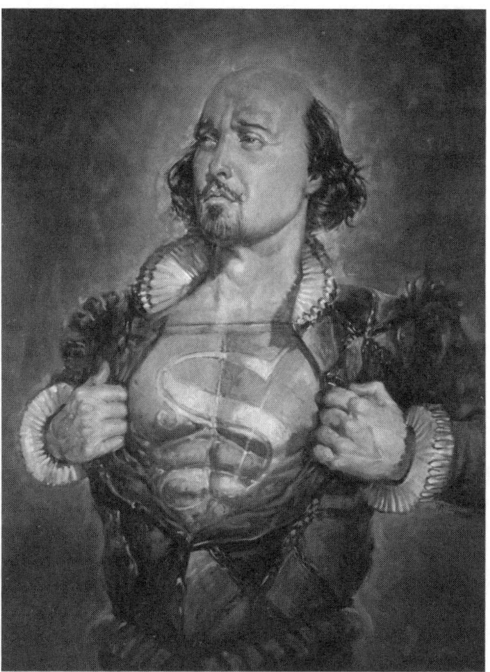

Figure 7.1. William Shakespeare as Superman. From a painting by Mathew McFarren.

appropriations of Shakespeare's best-known plays. In the twenty-first century, new Shakespeare musicals borrow plots, characters, and motives to attract younger and more diverse audiences. In its 2009–10 "Shakespeare Exploded" program, under the leadership of artistic director Diane Paulus, the American Repertory Theatre in Cambridge, Massachusetts, featured two home-bred adaptations and one British import. *Best of Both Worlds* transformed *The Winter's Tale* into a rhythm and blues musical. Joined by local gospel choirs, the African American cast sang their way through Shakespeare's plot, with Ezekiel, a leading entertainer, substituting for Leontes and his friend Maurice taking the Polixenes role. With book and lyrics by Randy Weiner and music by Diedre Murray, Leontes' jealousy, Hermione's determination, Paulina's outrage, and Florizel and Perdita's young love were rendered through soulful music instead of Shakespeare's language. The resulting hybrid brought a different sort of audience to the ART than have its more traditional Shakespearian productions. Even more radical was *The Donkey Show*, loosely based on *A Midsummer Night's Dream*, but spiced with a Dionysian emphasis on Bottom's priapic powers. Set to 1970s disco music, *The Donkey Show* was more of a rock concert than a theatrical performance, especially when members of the audience were invited to join the dancing.

The ART's irreverent treatment of Shakespearian motifs was criticized by many of Boston's Shakespeare purists, but Paulus argued that "Shakespeare Exploded" had succeeded by attracting a more diverse and youthful audience. Immersed in a world of postmodern pastiche, the millennial generation still loves the idea of Shakespeare. References to Shakespeare's most memorable characters and phrases run through America's popular culture just as they did 150 years ago, but, as Levine noted of Shakespeare in early nineteenth-century America, he has to be integrated into contemporary culture, often through bits and snatches. The newspaper comic *Pearls Before Swine* showed postmodern pastiche at work when it created a pun on the much-abused phrase, "To be or not to be" by reference to Bea Arthur, the star of the 1990s situation comedy *Maude*. The punch line, "To Bea or not to Bea," depends on an unlikely tie between Shakespeare's most famous words and a contemporary television icon; however lame the pun may seem, it forges a link that readers of the Sunday comics can readily grasp.

The ongoing appropriation of Shakespeare's plots, characters, and language in popular media—musicals, comics, advertising, political cartoons—suggests that in the twenty-first century he is not simply a literary classic to be suffered through in high school and soon forgotten. Whether at traditional venues like repertory theater companies, college classes, or reading groups, or in newer electronic media, Shakespeare permeates American culture today much as he did 200 years ago. He has even found a place on America's social media. Sarah Schmelling's "Hamlet (Facebook New Feed Edition)" playfully transforms Hamlet's complicated plot and characters into Facebook comments, such as "Hamlet's father is now a zombie"; "Rosencrantz, Guildenstern, and Hamlet are now friends"; "Hamlet posted an event: A Play That's Totally Fictional and in No Way About my Family"; and, finally, "Denmark is now Norwegian."[5]

Another twenty-first-century development is American fascination with Shakespeare the man. While, as Chapter 5 explains, questions about the authorship of his plays continue to be raised by a vocal minority, even those who accept the man from Stratford as the genuine poet share the desire to know more about him. During the last decade, novels, plays, and films have catered to this longing by concocting fictional accounts of Shakespeare's life and activities. Tom Stoppard's *Shakespeare in Love* (1998), for which American actor Gwyneth Paltrow won an Academy Award, is perhaps best known, but other, lesser-known fictional accounts of Shakespeare the man have recently garnered attention. In 2009 the Oregon Shakespeare Festival premiered *Equivocation*, a play by director Bill Cain that moved to New York's City Center in 2010. *Equivocation* opens a fictional window into Shakespeare's activities shortly after the Gunpowder Plot of 1605. When Robert Cecil asks Will Shagspeare (known as Shag) to write a new play following the official governmental narrative of the plot, the dramatist struggles with the fine lines between truth and fiction—equivocation. On a less serious note, Matt Saldarelli's *Getting Even with Shakespeare*, a satiric comedy performed in 2010 at Manhattan Repertory Theatre's Winterfest, brings five Shakespearian tragic heroes together in a New York City bar, where they spend the evening bitching about the way Shakespeare scripted their deaths and plotting revenge against him. Perhaps more than ever, Shakespeare himself is a subject of serious and not-so-serious study and endless speculation.

In the twenty-first century, two serious Shakespearian appropriations hark back to the work of previous generations even as they seek a contemporary audience. Recalling Jacob Adler's performances in the vibrant Yiddish theater, director Eve Annenberg's *Romeo and Juliet in Yiddish*, screened at Lincoln Center in 2011 as part of New York's Jewish film festival, features first-time actors who grew up in Brooklyn's Chasidic community. Instead of Montagues and Capulets, the warring families come from Salmar and Lubavitch Chasidic sects, while Friar Lawrence is a rabbi. In the same year trombonist Delfeayo Marsalis conducted a thirty-six-city tour of his own reworking of Duke Ellington and Billy Strayhorn's "Such Sweet Thunder" that maintains the original's Shakespearian characters and themes, but expands the songs with additional jazz interludes.[6] By building upon twentieth-century appropriations, contemporary artists pay homage both to Shakespeare and to the work of their twentieth-century predecessors.

* * *

The clearest contemporary trend is that it is increasingly difficult to identify a characteristically "American" Shakespeare. The Shakespeare Theatre Association of America held its 2010 conference in London at the International Globe Centre; Royal Shakespeare Company productions tour to American venues, appearing in Ann Arbor, Michigan one year, at New York's Lincoln Center another year. Americans act in British films. Kenneth Branagh, for example, featured Denzel Washington as Don Pedro in *Much Ado About Nothing* and Charlton Heston as the Player King in *Hamlet*. When a film such as Julie Taymor's 2010 *The Tempest* is directed by an American, features noted British actors, was rehearsed in England, and was filmed mostly in Hawaii, is it British or American? British director Sam Mendes' "Bridge" Company deliberately courts such hybridity. In each of its three seasons, Mendes has cast both British and American actors; plays are staged in repertory at New York's Brooklyn Academy of Music and move to London's Old Vic. The seeming interchangeability of British and American actors suggests that the distinction between film and stage acting is the pertinent category, not the actor's country of origin.

The new media have also made non-Anglophone Shakespearian adaptations readily available. Akiro Kurasawa's Japanese versions of *Macbeth* (*Throne of Blood*), *Hamlet* (*The Bad Sleep Well*), and *King Lear* (*Ran*) are incorporated into American and British "Shakespeare on film" courses. The internet provides information about Shakespeare productions staged around the world, with the result that performances are increasingly eclectic. A production of *The Tempest*, for example, might combine the commedia dell'arte techniques developed by Italy's Giorgio Strehler for the Caliban/Stephano/Trinculo comic scenes with a Japanese bunraku Ariel.[7] On stage and in film, Shakespeare is increasingly cosmopolitan.

* * *

The clues to Shakespeare's future in America remain mixed. Some suggest a diminution of public interest. Many "festival Shakespeare" venues, for example, have expanded their repertoires to include other classical dramatists, new work by contemporary playwrights, and the occasional musical comedy, all on the grounds that Shakespeare alone is no longer a sufficient drawing card. The Great Lakes Shakespeare Festival, founded in 1961, recently signaled this shift by changing its name to "Great Lakes Theater Festival," although Shakespeare's major plays continue to be featured in its repertory. Every summer, hundreds of "Shakespeare in the Park" productions still offer performances at reasonable prices to a broad swath of Americans.

Reports of Shakespeare's disappearance from America's academic curricula also seem exaggerated. Although Shakespeare is less likely to be a required author, his plays are regularly taught in required courses in America's secondary schools and elective courses in liberal arts colleges. Graduate students in early modern English literature continue to specialize in Shakespeare. The more significant academic change may be pedagogical. Teaching methods, by and large, are livelier than they were a hundred years ago. Students frequently participate in scene work, and many instructors use video clips to illustrate how particular scenes can be performed. And although there is now more emphasis on contemporary writers, including writers of color, in English literature curricula, and therefore less room for early modern writers like Sidney, Spenser, and Donne, Shakespeare is still taught—even if he is sometimes the only early modern writer the students encounter. While that is not an ideal situation, it seems clear that Shakespeare will remain a crucial building block in America's literature courses for the foreseeable future.

Shakespeare is also still alive in American film-making. In 1999 Michael Hoffman, who co-founded the Idaho Shakespeare Festival, produced and directed a screen version of *A Midsummer Night's Dream* set in nineteenth-century Monte Athena, Italy, and featured American actors Kevin Kline (Bottom), Michelle Pfeiffer (Titania), Stanley Tucci (Puck), and Calista Flockhart (Helena). Al Pacino took Shylock's role in Michael Radford's 2004 *Merchant of Venice*; Julie Taymor's *Titus Andronicus* and *The Tempest* have already been mentioned. Filmic Shakespeare is not likely to disappear, though it more often brings together actors and directors from Britain, America, and elsewhere in the Anglophone world.

It is too soon to tell what impact the internet and other electronic resources will have on the dissemination of Shakespeare's plays throughout the dynamic cultural shifts. On the one hand, they may reduce the market for print editions of Shakespeare's texts; on the other hand, the Complete Works can be downloaded as an application for BlackBerries and iPhones. Is the corpus of any other writer available as a telephone application? If any American (or anyone else) can gain access to all of Shakespeare all of the time by pushing a few buttons, his continuing role in American culture seems assured. As James Russell Lowell observed nearly a century and a half ago, "Life is short and Shakespeare is long."[8]

Notes

1. Lawrence Levine, *Highbrow/Lowbrow: The Emergence of Cultural Hierarchy in America* (Cambridge, MA: Harvard University Press, 1988), quotations from 21, 31.
2. Yu Jin Ko, "Shakespeare Festivals," in Virginia Mason Vaughan and Alden T. Vaughan (eds.), *Shakespeare in American Life* (Washington, DC: Folger Shakespeare Library, 2007), 89–99; http://www.staaonline.org (accessed June 30, 2010).
3. Jean Trounstine, *Shakespeare Behind Bars: The Power of Drama in a Women's Prison* (New York: St. Martin's Press, 2001).
4. http://news.change.org/stories/judge-sentences-kids-to-shakespeare-instead-of-jail (accessed December 16, 2011).
5. http://www.npr.org/templates/story/story.php?storyId=130265532 (accessed October 4, 2010).

6. *Worcester [MA] Telegram and Gazette*, January 20, 2011.
7. See e.g. Julie Taymor's 1986 *Tempest*, staged at New York's Theatre for a New Audience.
8. James Russell Lowell, "White's Shakspeare," *Atlantic Monthy* 3 (1859), 259.

Further Reading

Overviews

Many books and essays with titles identical or very similar to this book's have agendas different from our volume and from each other. The most notable include the earliest, Frank M. Bristol, *Shakespeare and America* (Chicago: Hollister, 1898), a short survey of Shakespeare's role in America since the seventeenth century that laments the paucity of quality performances and scholarship in the late nineteenth century; and George B. Churchill, "Shakespeare in America" (see Ch. 5), an address to the German Shakespeare Society on the poet's birthday in 1906 and subsequently printed in *Jahrbuch der Deutschen Shakespeare-Gesellschaft*, covers much the same ground more concisely but shares Bristol's pessimism. Two decades later, Ashley H. Thorndike was relatively optimistic in his address to the British Academy, published as *Shakespeare in America* (see Ch. 3), a sympathetic review of the long history of Shakespeare on stage and in print through the early twentieth century. Similarly, Dunn, *Shakespeare in America* (see Chs. 2 and 3), covers almost the same time period but much more thoroughly. Despite its lack of documentation, Dunn's book was the most comprehensive and scholarly overview at the time of publication, though it does not, of course, address post-World War II stage productions, musical adaptations, films, and other forms of popular culture. Robert Falk, "Shakespeare in America: A Survey to 1900," *Shakespeare Survey* 18 (1965), 102–18, is concerned primarily with nineteenth-century American criticism, especially by non-specialists such as Emerson, Melville, Whitman, and Lowell, but also discusses American trends in acting and editing. Louis Marder, *His Exits and Entrances* (see Ch. 3) includes a wide-ranging chapter on "Shakespeare in the United States" and in other chapters touches on Shakespeare in the American experience. Michael D. Bristol, *Shakespeare's America, America's Shakespeare* (London: Routledge, 1990) is a lengthy, sophisticated analysis of the complex interaction between Shakespeare and American society. Peter Rawlings, "Shakespeare Migrates to America," the introduction to *Americans on Shakespeare, 1776–1914* (see Chs. 2 and 5), 1–28, provides contexts for the anthology's sixty extracts from professional and amateur critics. Kim C. Sturgess, *Shakespeare and the American Nation* (see Ch. 2) tries to explain how and why nineteenth-century Americans adopted Shakespeare so avidly. *Shakespeare in American Life*, ed. Virginia Vaughan and Alden Vaughan (cited in several chapters), an exhibition catalogue, contains—in addition to descriptions and photographs of numerous exhibit items—nine original essays by Shakespeare specialists on topics such as musicals, films, jazz, and festivals.

Shakespeare on stage

Early American stage history has been closely studied despite a paucity of theatrical records from the seventeenth and eighteenth centuries. Especially valuable are four older works cited in Chs. 1 or 2: Rankin, *The Theater in Colonial America*; Shattuck, *Shakespeare on the American Stage: From the Hallams to Edwin Booth*; Pollock, *Philadelphia Theatre in the Eighteenth Century*; and the first volume of George Odell, *Annals of the New York Stage*. A major supplement to those volumes is the relatively recent Johnson and Burling, *Colonial American Stage, 1665–1774* (also cited in Ch. 1). Among many useful monographs on the colonial and Revolutionary eras are Paul Leicester Ford, *Washington and the Theatre* (New York: Dunlap Society, 1899); Brooks McNamara, *The American Playhouse in the Eighteenth Century* (Cambridge, MA: Harvard University Press, 1969); Odai Johnson, *Absence and Memory in Colonial American Theatre: Fiorelli's Plaster* (New York: Palgrave Macmillan, 2006), and Meredith H. Lair, "Redcoat Theater: Negotiating Identity in Occupied Philadelphia," in William Pencak (ed.), *Pennsylvania's Revolution* (University Park: Pennsylvania State University Press, 2010), 192–210.

The pervasiveness of Shakespeare in western migration is documented in Ralph Leslie Rusk, *The Literature of the Middle Western Frontier* (2 vols, New York: Columbia University Press, 1925); Helene Wickham Koon, *How Shakespeare Won the West: Players and Performances in America's Gold Rush, 1849–1865* (see Ch. 3); George R. MacMinn, *The Theatre of the Golden Age in California* (Caldwell, ID: Caxton Printers, 1941); and Susan Lee Johnson, *Roaring Camp: The Social World of the California Gold Rush* (New York: W.W. Norton, 2000), which is almost wholly limited to the Sierra Nevada region and ignores theater, yet is a corrective to the standard view of the gold rush's ethnic and cultural consistency. Philip C. Kolin (ed.), *Shakespeare in the South: Essays on Performance* (Jackson: University Press of Mississippi, 1983) addresses a section of the country too often slighted. More geographically comprehensive is David Grimsted, *Melodrama Unveiled: American Theater and Culture, 1800–1850* (Chicago: University of Chicago Press, 1968); the insightful Heather S. Nathans, *Early American Theatre from the Revolution to Thomas Jefferson: Into the Hands of the People* (Cambridge: Cambridge University Press, 2003); and Bruce A. McConachie, *Melodramatic*

Formations: American Theatre and Society, 1820–1870 (Iowa City: University of Iowa Press, 1992).

A reliable starting point for American theater history since the third quarter of the nineteenth century is the second volume of Charles Shattuck, *Shakespeare on the American Stage: From Booth and Barrett to Sothern and Marlowe* (Washington, DC: Folger Shakespeare Library, 1987). This volume covers the period from about 1870 to 1910, with an epilogue on the tercentenary of Shakespeare's death in 1916, but, as Shattuck acknowledges, the second volume (unlike the first) is largely limited to the eastern United States. Although Shattuck did not live to complete a projected third volume, which would have carried the story through the twentieth century, those years are partly covered by a variety of more specialized works, while vols 2–15 of Odell, *Annals of the New York Stage* extend the narrative and documentary coverage of its geographic area from the late 1790s to the mid-1940s.

Several American and visiting British actors are discussed in depth—especially Edmund Kean, William Charles Macready, and Edwin Forrest—in Cliff, *The Shakespeare Riots* (cited in Ch. 2), which, as the title implies, includes an extensive discussion of the Astor Place riot of 1849. The standard earlier work on that event, Richard Moody, *The Astor Place Riot* (Bloomington: Indiana University Press, 1958) remains useful. Book-length biographies of actors and impresarios of the nineteenth and twentieth centuries include Alan S. Downer, *The Eminent Tragedian: William Charles Macready* (Cambridge, MA: Harvard University Press, 1966), which examines Macready's rivalry with Edwin Forrest from the British star's perspective. Fanny Kemble, Charlotte Cushman, and Laura Keene are prominent in Faye E. Dudden, *Women in the American Theatre: Actresses & Audiences, 1790–1870* (New Haven, CT: Yale University Press, 1994). An engaging account of post-World War II American theatre is Kenneth Turan and Joseph Papp, *Free for All: Joe Papp, The Public, and the Greatest Theater Story Ever Told* (New York: Doubleday, 2009).

On Abraham Lincoln, *Macbeth*, and John Wilkes Booth, see in addition to the works cited in Chs. 2 and 3 the major biographies of Lincoln, as well as David Grimsted, *American Mobbing, 1828–1861: Toward Civil War* (New York: Oxford University Press, 1998); Nora Titone, "*My Thoughts Be Bloody": The Bitter Rivalry between Edwin and John Wilkes Booth that Led to an American Tragedy* (New York: Simon and Schuster, 2010); and Alexander Nemerov, *Acting in the Night: Macbeth and the Places of the Civil War* (Berkeley: University of California Press, 2010).

Shakespeare in print

On the editing and printing of Shakespeare's works in Britain and America, the essential volume is Andrew Murphy's comprehensive narrative and catalogue, *Shakespeare in Print* (see Chs. 1 and 3), but see also Paul Werstine, "Shakespeare," in D. C. Greetham (ed.), *Scholarly Editing: A Guide to Research* (New York: Modern Language Association, 1995), which discusses trends in editing Shakespeare's works from the late sixteenth century until the late twentieth. Studies of the book trade in early America include Paul Leicester Ford (ed.), *The Journals of Hugh Gaine, Printer* (2 vols, New York: Dodd, Mead, 1902; repr. 1970), which has a biography of Gaine that has been supplanted by Alfred Lawrence Lorenz, *Hugh Gaine: A Colonial Printer-Editor's Odyssey to Loyalism* (Carbondale: Southern Illinois University Press, 1972). Many of the versions of Shakespeare's plays witnessed by early American audiences are described in George Curtis Branam, *Eighteenth-Century Adaptations of Shakespearean Tragedy* (Berkeley: University of California Press, 1956); Dobson, *Making of the National Poet* (see Ch. 1); Jean I. Marsden, *Re-Imaged Text: Shakespeare, Adaptations and Eighteenth-Century Literary Theory* (Lexington: University of Kentucky Press, 1995); and other monographs, collections of essays, and anthologies of texts too numerous to mention here. Adaptations of individual plays are often best examined in the appropriate volumes of the "Shakespeare in Performance Series," gen. eds. James C. Bulman and Carol C. Rutter (Manchester: Manchester University Press, 1982–), or in scholarly articles like Nancy Klein Maguire, "Nahum Tate's *King Lear*: 'the king's blest restoration,'" in Jean I. Marsden (ed.), *The Appropriation of Shakespeare: Post-Renaissance Reconstructions of the Works and the Myth* (New York: Harvester Wheatsheaf, 1991), 29–42.

Early American attention to Shakespeare outside the theatre is addressed in Louis B. Wright, "The Purposeful Reading of Our Colonial Ancestors," *ELH: A Journal of English Literary History* 4 (1937), 85–111; Westfall, *American Shakespearean Criticism, 1607–1865* (cited in Ch. 2); and especially Barbara Mowat's refreshing look at "The Founders and the Bard," from which we quote in Ch. 1. Richard Beale Davis, *Intellectual Life in the Colonial South, 1585–1763* (3 vols, Knoxville: University of Tennessee Press, 1978) assesses early stage history, but more valuable, because harder to find, is the wealth of information Davis has uncovered about Shakespeare's works in southern libraries, private collections, estate inventories, and bookshops.

Nineteenth-century writers' fascination with Shakespeare is examined in a variety of books and essays, including Richard Clarence Harrison, "Walt Whitman and Shakespeare," *PMLA* 44 (1929), 1201–38; Floyd Stovall, "Whitman's Knowledge of Shakespeare," *Studies in Philology* 49 (1952), 643–69; F. O. Matthiessen, *The American Renaissance: Art and Expression in the Age of Emerson and Whitman* (New York: Oxford University

Press, 1941), on Melville; and E. H. Rosenberry, *Melville and the Comic Spirit* (Cambridge, MA: Harvard University Press, 1955).

Shakespeare in American education is the subject of numerous older works and a few of recent vintage. Marder's chapter on "Un-Willingly to School" in *Exits and Entrances* briefly surveys Shakespeare in British and American educational institutions between the seventeenth century and the middle of the twentieth. The role of William Holmes McGuffey in introducing generations of American youths to Shakespeare is examined (in addition to the works cited in Ch. 3) in Richard D. Mosier, *Making the American Mind: Social and Moral Ideas in the McGuffey Readers* (New York: King's Crown Press, 1947); and Dolores P. Sullivan, *William Holmes McGuffey, Schoolmaster to the Nation* (Rutherford, NJ: Fairleigh Dickinson University Press, 1999). On twentieth-century trends in American education, see Charles Frey, "Teaching Shakespeare in America," *Shakespeare Quarterly* 35.5 (special issue on "Teaching Shakespeare," 1984), 541–59; and the anthology by Kahn, Nathans, and Godfrey, *Shakespearean Educations* (cited in Ch. 3). The wider educational context of American education in which McGuffey's *Readers* should be understood can be approached through Lawrence A. Cremin, *American Education: The National Experience, 1783–1876* (New York: Harper and Row, 1980); Frederick Rudolph, *The American College and University: A History* (New York: Knopf, 1962); and Mark Sullivan, *Our Times: The United States, 1900–1925* (6 vols, New York: Scribner's, 1926–35), 2:7–48 ("The American Mind: Education"). A good introduction to the lyceum movement is Carl Bode, *The American Lyceum: Town Meeting of the Mind* (New York: Oxford University Press, 1956), while Angela G. Ray, *The Lyceum and Public Culture in the Nineteenth-Century United States* (East Lansing: Michigan State University Press, 2005) is more analytical. Chautauqua forums are briefly described in Joseph Edward Gould, *The Chautauqua Movement: A Episode in the Continuing American Revolution* (Albany: State University of New York, 1961), and more extensively and personally in Harry P. Harrison, as told to Karl Detzer, *Culture under Canvas: The Story of Tent Chautauqua* (New York: Hastings House, 1958). J[ane] C[unningham] Croly, *The History of the Woman's Club Movement in America* (New York: H. G. Allen, 1898) is an early attempt to describe a phenomenon that was still in progress.

Popular culture

Lawrence Levine's thesis on the bifurcation in nineteenth-century America into highbrow and lowbrow cultural polarities is most concisely set forth in his essay "William Shakespeare and the American People: A Study in Cultural Transformation," *American Historical Review* 89 (1984), 34–66;

Levine's fuller explanation, *Highbrow/Lowbrow,* is cited in Ch. 7. For the English context of America's fascination with Shakespearian relics and sites such as the Stratford birthplace, an entertaining survey is Ivor Brown and George Fearon, *Amazing Monument: A Short History of the Shakespeare Industry* (London: William Heinemann, 1939). From a different and more recent perspective, see Hodgdon, *The Shakespeare Trade* (see Ch. 6). Shakespeare in modern American popular culture is thoughtfully reviewed in Douglas Lanier, *Shakespeare and Modern Popular Culture* (New York: Oxford University Press, 2002); Teague, *Shakespeare and the American Popular Stage* (cited in Ch. 6); and Irene Dash's comprehensive *Shakespeare and the American Musical* (Bloomington: Indiana University Press, 2010). Robert Shaughnessy (ed.), *Shakespeare and Popular Culture* (Cambridge: Cambridge University Press, 2007) says much about popular culture in the United States, although its principal focus is on Britain.

Cultural and ethnic diversity

Performances of Shakespeare's plays by American minorities have generated a diffuse literature. On Yiddish theatre, in addition to the works cited in Ch. 4, see Iska Alter, "Jacob Gordin's *Mirele Efros*: King Lear as Jewish Mother," *Shakespeare Survey* 55 (2002), 114–27. On the beginnings of African American theatre see Marvin McAllister, *White People Do Not Know How to Behave at Entertainments Designed for Ladies & Gentlemen of Colour: William Brown's African & American Theater* (Chapel Hill: University of North Carolina Press, 2003). On Ira Aldridge see Herbert Marshall, *Further Research on Ira Aldridge, The Negro Tragedian* (Carbondale: Southern Illinois University Press, 1970), and Bernth Lindfors (ed.), *Ira Aldridge, the African Roscius* (Rochester, NY: University of Rochester Press, 2007). Handy guides to black theatrical personnel are Bernard Peterson (ed.), *Profiles of African American Stage Performers and Theatre People, 1816–1960* (Westport, CT: Greenwood Press, 2001) and Anthony D. Hill and Douglas Q. Barnett, *Historical Dictionary of African American Theater* (Lanham, MD: Scarecrow Press, 2009).

The rise and demise of blackface performances has attracted much recent scholarly attention. Although many of the best works perforce give little space to Shakespeare in light of the relative paucity of Shakespeare spoofs among the thousands of minstrel shows and other blackface entertainments, modern writings establish a necessary context for understanding the genre and Shakespeare's place in it. Toll, *Blacking Up: The Minstrel Show in Nineteenth-Century America* (see Ch. 3) is a solid introduction, but some of his conclusions are questioned in Eric Lott, *Love and Theft: Blackface Minstrelsy and the American Working Class* (New York: Oxford University Press, 1995); Dale Cockrell, *Demons of Disorder: Early Blackface Minstrels and their World* (Cambridge and New York: Cambridge University Press, 1997); David Krasner, *Resistance, Parody and Double-Consciousness in African American Theatre, 1895–1915* (New York: Palgrave, 1997); and William J. Mahar, *Behind the Burnt Cork Mask: Early Blackface Minstrelsy and Antebellum American Popular Culture* (Urbana: University of Illinois Press, 1999). An earlier but still relevant work is Hans Nathan, *Dan Emmett and the Rise of Early Negro Minstrelsy* (Norman: University of Oklahoma Press, 1962). Important essays are Ray B. Browne, "Shakespeare in American Vaudeville and Negro Minstrelsy," *American Quarterly* 12 (1960), 374–91, which emphasizes songs and jests on the popular stage, and Francesca T. Royster, "Playing with (a) Difference: Early Black Shakespearean Actors, Blackface and Whiteface," in Vaughan and Vaughan (eds.), *Shakespeare in American Life* 35–47. Reprints of many American burlesques are available in vol. 5 of Stanley Wells (ed.), *Nineteenth-Century Shakespeare Burlesques* (see Ch. 3) and Gary D. Engle, *This Grotesque Essence: Plays from the American Minstrel Stage* (Baton Rouge: Louisiana State University Press, 1978). The other side of the skin-color coin is examined in Glenda E. Gill, *White Greasepaint on Black Performers* (New York: Peter Lang, 1988).

Authorship

A lively and controversial literature addresses the challenges to William Shakespeare of Stratford-upon-Avon as the author of the canon. For well-informed brief versions of the ongoing controversy, see Bryson, *Shakespeare: The World as Stage* (cited in Ch. 5), 181–96; Lanier, *Shakespeare and Modern Popular Culture,* 132–42; and Jonathan Bate, *The Genius of Shakespeare* (London: Macmillan, 1997), 65–100. Longer treatments are three other works cited in Ch. 5: Schoenbaum, *Shakespeare's Lives*, rev. edn., for authoritative background; the second edition of Ogburn, *The Mysterious William Shakespeare,* for the fullest expression of the Oxfordian position; and Shapiro, *Contested Will*, for the most complete discussion of the continuing controversy. For collections of documents, in addition to the books by Schoenbaum cited in Ch. 5, see his *William Shakespeare: A Compact Documentary Life* (Oxford: Oxford University Press, 1977) and *William Shakespeare: Records and Images* (New York: Oxford University Press, 1981).

Reference books

Many of the topics and personalities discussed in this book are treated briefly but dependably in modern encyclopedias and handbooks. The careers of most British actors who performed in America before the second quarter of the nineteenth century are extensively reported in Philip H. Highfill, Jr, Kalman A. Burnim, and Edward A. Langhams (eds.), *A Biographical Dictionary of Actors, Actresses, Musicians, Dancers, Managers and Other Stage Personnel in London, 1660–1800* (16 vols, Carbondale: Southern Illinois University Press, 1973–1993); while most British itinerants of the early period as well as those who arrived later are sketched in H. G. C. Matthew and Brian Harrison (eds.), *Oxford Dictionary of National Biography* (60 vols, Oxford: Oxford University Press, 2004), or in the earlier *Dictionary of National Biography*, ed. Leslie Stephens and Sidney Lee (66 vols, London: Smith, Elder, & Co., 1885–1901). Valuable documentation for the London context of American productions can be found in William Van Lennep et al. (eds.), *The London Stage, 1600–1800: A Calendar of Plays... Compiled from the Playbills, Newspapers and Theatrical Diaries of the Period* (14 vols, Carbondale: Southern Illinois University Press, 1965–1979). Prominent American actors and other theater personnel are sketched in John A. Garraty and Mark C. Carnes (eds.), *American National Biography* (24 vols, New York, Oxford University Press, 1999), or the older *Dictionary of American Biography*, ed. Dumas Malone et al. (20 vols, New York: Scribner's, 1928–1936). Shorter sketches can also be found in the comprehensive Shakespeare compendia, which are especially useful for relatively minor actors and for specific topics. The ageing but still valuable *Reader's Encyclopedia of Shakespeare*, ed. Oscar James Campbell and Edward G. Quinn (New York: Crowell, 1966) until recently claimed to be "the only encyclopedia of Shakespeare and his works" but is now joined by a spate of similar books or sets of books. Especially useful on American topics is the *Cambridge Guide to American Theatre*, ed. Wilmeth and Miller (cited in Ch. 2). The most recent comprehensive set is *The Shakespeare Encyclopedia: Life, Works, and Legacy*, ed. Patricia Parker (5 vols, Santa Barbara, CA: Greenwood, forthcoming).

Important collections of essays include Don B. Wilmeth and Christopher Bigsby (eds.), *The Cambridge History of American Theatre* (3 vols, Cambridge: Cambridge University Press, 1998–2000); Weldon B. Durham (ed.), *American Theatre Companies* (3 vols, New York: Greenwood, 1986); and Engle and Miller (eds.), *The American Stage: Social and Economic Issues from the Colonial Period to the Present* (see Ch. 1). Useful documentary collections include Jürgen C. Wolter (ed.), *The Dawning of American Drama: American Dramatic Criticism* (Westport, CT: Greenwood, 1993) and Barry B. Witham (ed.), *Theatre in the United States: A Documentary History* (Cambridge: Cambridge University Press, 1996).

Index

Bold numbers denote references to illustrations